D0250959

I HAD IT ALL THE TIME

When Self-Improvement
Gives Way to Ecstasy

ALAN COHEN

I HAD IT ALL THE TIME
WHEN SELF-IMPROVEMENT GIVES WAY TO ECSTASY

©1995 by Alan Cohen   ISBN 0-910367-531

Alan Cohen Publications
455-A Kukuna Road
Haiku, Hawaii 96708

Cover Art by Ken Johnston
For information about Ken Johnston's visionary art, contact:
Heartworks, Post Office Box 4805, Tulsa, Oklahoma 74159-0805.

"The Answer Lies Within" by Michael B. Putman and Catherine Wilson, ©1989 Music From The Heart, Post Office Box 290307, Brooklyn Center, Minnesota 55429.
Used by permission. All rights reserved.

To order *I Had It All the Time:*

Bookstores contact:
            Bookpeople   New Leaf Distributing Co.
            DeVorss & Co.   Specialist

Personal Orders – Call **1-800-462-3013**

or write to: Hay House
                   Post Office Box 5100
                   Carlsbad, California 92018-5100

For a free catalog of Alan Cohen's books, tapes, and workshop schedule, call or write the above address or phone number.

Visit our website at www.alancohen.com

To Kelly

For lighting my life

By Alan Cohen

Books

Are You as Happy as Your Dog?
Dare to Be Yourself
A Deep Breath of Life
The Dragon Doesn't Live Here Anymore*
Handle With Prayer*
Happily Even After
Have You Hugged a Monster Today?
I Had It All The Time*
Joy Is My Compass
Lifestyles of the Rich in Spirit
My Father's Voice
The Peace That You Seek
Rising in Love
Setting the Seen

Also available as Book on Tape

Cassette Tapes

Deep Relaxation
Eden Morning
I Believe in You
Journey to the Center of the Heart *(also CD)*
Living From The Heart
Peace

Video

Wisdom Of The Spirit

The end of all our exploring
will be
to arrive where we started
and know the place
for the first time.
– T.S. Eliot

It is my joy to acknowledge the angels who have contributed in so many ways to the birth of this book.

My heart is deeply grateful to Kelly Kurz for her contin·ued belief in me and my work, her caring and encouragement to make the vision a reality.

Jade Sherer has worked by my side tirelessly to bring the richest service to those I touch through my programs and writing.

Spirit sent a quiet powerful light being, Karuna, who played a key role in readying the manuscript for production.

Several dedicated individuals offered their editorial support, which contributed significantly to the final product. Many thanks to Marla Pitt, Linda Johnson, Susan Vasbinder, and Batyah Elizabeth, and Ann Chores.

Ken Johnston's magnificent cover artwork is equalled only by his huge heart and commitment to visionary service.

The cover graphics bear the heartful and talented touches of Daya Ceglia and Lightbourne Images.

I also honor my friends who have been a constant source of inspiration and empowerment: Charley Thweatt, Barry and Joyce Vissell, Rev. Mary and Ed Morrissey, Carla Gordan and Mary Guide, Mark and Dean Tucker, Oceana McDermott, Living Enrichment Center, and all of my friends in Unity and Science of Mind.

A special note of gratitude to Kenny and Julia Loggins, who remind me that life is only as good as our heart is alive.

I further honor the readers who tell me of the blessings they have received through my books and seminars. I keep your letters and messages as reminders that our mighty purpose is a shared adventure.

There was a time long ago, or so it seems now
Before I became who I am
When I pictured myself as a small empty cup
And yearned to be filled to the brim

I've searched for the answers so much of my life
From teachers I placed high above me
Trying on wings that simply weren't mine
In hopes that the winds would come lift me

I've pored through the books, through new and old
The rituals came and they went
The talisman's power in time left me cold
And none of it seemed heaven sent

The answer lies within, my friend
The answer lies within
The mountain can't hold it
The teachers don't own it
The answer lies within

One morning, at odds with the world I had made
I stood at my mirror in tears
But I suddenly saw that the face that stared back
Held no trace of the hunger or fears

I saw at that moment, so brilliantly clear
All the wisdom my life had collected
The student was ready, the teacher was here
In a way I had never expected

We balance our lives between ignorance and bliss
With a prayer divine wisdom will find us
And yet our greatest sin is our fear to exist
In the knowledge that God lives within us

So I don't need the mountains, the books or wings
And I don't need somebody to save me
No, all I need is to claim all the answers within
And to follow them clearly and bravely

The answer lies within, my friend
The answer lies within

– Michael B. Putman and Catherine Wilson

Foreword

The story is told of the Persian rascal-sage Nasrudin, who found himself on the bow of a ferry boat with a pompous intellectual. Bloated with his own erudition, the scholar began to quiz and criticize Nasrudin's education.

"Have you ever studied astronomy?" asked the professor.

"I can't say that I have," answered the mystic.

"Then you have wasted much of your life. By knowing the constellations, a skilled captain can navigate a boat around the entire globe."

A few minutes later the learned one asked, "Have you ever studied meteorology?"

"No, I haven't."

"Well, then, you have wasted most of your life," the academician chided. "Methodically capturing the wind can propel a sailing ship at astounding speeds."

After a while the fellow inquired, "Have you ever studied oceanography?"

"Not at all."

"Ah! What a waste of your time! Awareness of the currents helped many ancient peoples find food and shelter."

A few minutes later Nasrudin began to make his way toward the stern of the ship. On his way he nonchalantly asked the fellow, "Have you ever studied swimming?"

"Haven't had the time," the professor haughtily responded.

"Then you have wasted all of your life – the boat is sinking."

Sooner or later we reach the point where living the truth becomes more important than seeking it. Knowledge, techniques, and experiences pale in the face of the riches of the heart. Learning must give way to being.

Recently I invited the members of a lecture audience to "bid" on the amount of money they have spent on fixing themselves. I asked the participants to estimate their investment in self-help books, self-improvement seminars, consciousness trainings, meditation techniques, counseling and therapy, vitamins and dietary supplements, health spa memberships, cosmetic surgeries, psychic consultations, sundry crystals and amulets, travel to exotic lands in search of truth, and any other quest proceeding from the thought, "This will really do the trick for me."

Responses ranged from "Every penny I have ever earned," to "more than my husband can afford" to over a hundred thousand dollars – the cost of a home in many parts of the U.S., or the gross national product of some South American nations.

Many of us have been amassing information, techniques, and personal growth programs for many years. Some of us have become so addicted to the process of seeking that we would not know what to do if we actually found what we were looking for. In the film *The Princess Bride* there is a character named Inigo Montoya who spends most of his life searching for the man who killed his father. When he finally finds the man and does him in, a friend asks Inigo, "So, now that you have avenged your father's assassin, what will you be doing?" Inigo stops in his tracks, a blank look washes over his face, and he admits, "I don't know – I have been in the revenge business for so long, I don't think I will know what to do without it!"

Like Inigo, many of us have built an identity around searching for the truth. We have become professional patients, clients, students, seekers, and disciples.

Two contemporary gurus, Calvin and Hobbes, sum up our situation:

Hobbes: Whatcha doin?

Calvin: Getting rich

Hobbes: Really?

Calvin: Yep. I'm writing a self-help book! There's a huge market for this stuff.
    First, you convince people there's something wrong

with them. That's easy, because advertising has already conditioned people to feel insecure about their weight, looks, social status, sex appeal, and so on.

Next, you convince them that the problem is not their fault and that they're victims of larger forces. That's easy, because it's what people believe anyway. Nobody wants to be responsible for his own situation.

Finally, you convince them that with your advice and encouragement, they can conquer their problem and be happy!

Hobbes: Ingenious. What problem will *you* help people solve?

Calvin: Their addiction to self-help books! My book is called, *"Shut Up and Stop Whining: How to Do Something with Your Life besides Think About Yourself."*

Hobbes: You should probably wait for the advance before you buy anything.

Calvin: The trouble is, if my program works, I won't be able to write a sequel.[1]

Like the reader for whom Calvin intends to write, many of us have been fixing ourselves for a long time. Every season there emerges a new and revolutionary volume or method that *really* gets to the core of why we are so screwed up. But how many of these books really do penetrate to the heart of our wholeness?

This could be the last self-help book you will ever read. If you grasp its principles, you will not need to fix yourself again. In contrast to many self-help techniques which play on the reader's sense of inadequacy, this volume makes a clear and uncompromising stand for your innate strength. I do not purport to add to the truth you know; everything you need to know is already within you. Instead I shall remind you that you have simply been looking for answers in the wrong place – out there instead of within you.

This book will not have a sequel; to the contrary, it heralds the end of a long and self-diminishing train of thought – the notion that you need to be something other than you are. It will not introduce you to a revolutionary technique; but it will introduce you to yourself. This book will not direct you to a mystical master or exotic gems – but it will assist you to unearth your own hidden treasures and awaken the master within you.

This book has one message which will be presented from many different angles, until you are so sure of its dynamic truth that you will swear you wrote it yourself. You are not a black hole that needs to be filled; you are a light that needs to be shined. The days of self-improvement are gone, and the era of self-affirmation is upon us. It is time to quit improving yourself and start living.

I Had It All the Time is a refresher course. It will refresh your memory of who you are and what you came here to do. It will awaken your heart with a new courage to follow your dreams and put your deepest intuitions and inclinations into action. And it will restore your soul as you remember that you are greater than any circumstances you may encounter. The Spirit within you is greater than anything in the outer world. The power of your life is now returned to your own hands, where it has always been. You had it all the time.

Alan Cohen

I HAD IT ALL THE TIME

WHEN SELF-IMPROVEMENT GIVES WAY TO ECSTASY

ALWAYS HAD IT, ALWAYS WILL 1
ORIGINAL INNOCENCE 17
YOU CAN'T PREPARE TO BE YOURSELF 31
LET IT BE EASY 45
FOLLOW YOUR SPIRIT 71
CARPE DIEM! 99
THERE AIN'T NO FUTURE IN THE PAST 111
A HEART ACT TO FOLLOW 125
THE BIG PICTURE 137
DOORS TO THE LIGHT 145
IF YOU CAN'T FIX IT, FEATURE IT 155
THE ATTITUDE OF GRATITUDE 167
GRACELAND 185
GOOD ENOUGH TO BE TRUE 203
SHAKE UP, WAKE UP 215
MIND MATTERS 227
LOOKING IN FOR NUMBER ONE 239
CREATE OR DIE 249
YOU CAN'T STEAL HOME WITH YOUR FOOT ON THIRD .. 259
FIRST CLASS FLYING 267
THE FUTURE ISN'T WHAT IT USED TO BE 283
BURN THIS BOOK 299
I'M OFF TO BE THE WIZARD 309

I HAD IT ALL THE TIME

*When Self-Improvement
Gives Way to Ecstasy*

ALWAYS HAD IT,
ALWAYS WILL

Not this crude leather; luminous beings are we!
– Yoda

What would you do if someone swore that you knew the secret of life and put you on a stage to tell it? The *Totally Hidden Video* television show set up a hysterical prank on precisely this theme. For the gag, a Federal Express driver was asked to deliver a package to a religious temple (fabricated by the television show). Unknown to the driver, the pranksters had taken a photo of him and replicated it as a painted portrait, depicting the young man dressed in the royal regalia of the fictitious sect.

When the delivery man arrived, the disciples (actors hired by the program) took one look at him and began buzzing excitedly. They ushered him to the front of the sanctuary and invited him to sit on a plush cushion of honor. Then they revealed to him that he was the chosen one, the long-awaited prophet foretold in their scriptures. To allay any doubts, a servant parted the altar curtain where, lo and behold, hung the majestic portrait of the deliverer, "painted by a visionary centuries ago."

"Please," begged a disciple, "give us some words of wisdom."

The driver surveyed the portrait and looked over the throng of expectant devotees. A hush fell over the assembly. He sat down on the pillow, took a deep breath, and spoke: "Life," the sage explained, "is like a river."

The disciples "oohed" and "aahed" on the heels of his utterance, hanging fervently on every sacred word.

"Sometimes life flows easily, and sometimes you encounter rocks and rapids," the guru illustrated, "but if you hang in there and have faith, you will arrive at the ocean of your dreams."

Again the students swooned with ecstasy. More "oohs" and "aahs." This was indeed the day they had been waiting for!

"Well, that's about it," Swami Fedex curtly concluded, "I have to go now and make some more deliveries."

Reluctantly the devotees rose, bowed reverently, and sheepishly cleared the way for the anointed one. Amid profuse veneration he made his way to the door.

Now here is the amazing postscript to the story: the program played the same trick on several Fedex drivers, each of whom found profound words the moment he sat on the cushion. The invitation to wax profound brought forth the inner wisdom in these unassuming fellows.

Deep within our heart, each of us knows the truth. The answers we seek, the power we strive for, and the acknowledgement we attempt to gain, abide inside us. Given the opportunity (being placed on the cushion) or the challenge (being pushed against a wall) we know what we need to know, to do what we need to do.

The Crucial Shift

Who are you?

Perhaps you have come to the point in your life where you are asking this all-important question. Be careful how you answer, for *in your response lies your destiny*. If you think you are small, oppressed, or worthless, your world will confirm your belief. If you see yourself as a whole, creative being, here to express joy, give and receive love, and make a contribution to life on the planet, so will your self-image be affirmed. As Henry Ford noted, "Think you can, or think you can't, and either way you'll be correct."

2

Master Key:

We Are Spiritual Beings
Going Through a Material Experience.

You and I are more than our bodies, emotions, thoughts, and experiences. We lived in spirit before we arrived on earth, and we will live in spirit after we depart this world. While we are here, we live in spirit, too – but if we believe we are limited, we will not enjoy our magnitude. *Our noblest purpose in life is to remember our spiritual nature in the face of suggestions and appearances that we are material only.*

Our spiritual nature is the only thing the world cannot tamper with or take from us. No matter what experiences we pass through, what we gain or lose in the drama of earth, and what people enter or leave our life, our true self remains whole, intact, and perfect. We always had it, and always will.

Oh, God

Let's handle the God thing right now. The word elicits all kinds of reactions. Like many people in our culture, you may be turned off to anything that has to do with God or religion. Many religions, especially in the Judeo-Christian tradition, have painted a picture of a fierce, angry, and vengeful God, an old man with a white beard sitting on a distant cloud, ready, willing, and able to mow down sinners who don't toe the line.

Sound familiar?

The God referred to in this book is not the one you most likely learned about in Sunday school or church. The God I name is a God of only love. He/She/It lives *inside* of you, expressing through you, as you. The God of only love abides within your own heart, speaking to you through your deepest inclinations, leading you to greater fulfillment. The Spirit I know is not a dealer of pain, but a remover of it.

If you don't like the word God, then skim right past it. I don't care if you do, and neither does God. If you would rather substitute "Love," "Spirit," or "Uncle Louie," please go right ahead. Fortunately, God is not as attached to that particular name as some of the religions that have grown up around it. Let's face it – misguided representatives of religions have given God a bad name. Now it's time to restore the beauty and dignity of the power of love, by whatever name you know it.

Let's also get clear on the relationship between spirituality and religion. All religions began with spirituality, an exuberance and enthusiasm for the wonder of life. At some point, however, many religions became bogged down with institutionalism, which put a serious damper on the spirit in which the organization was founded. (Most prophets and luminaries would be quite disappointed with the religions that grew in their wake.) In spite of this, most religions still harbor (relatively small) sects that maintain the original spirit of the religion.

The spiritual path is based on the spirit of an endeavor rather than its form, the essence more than the appearance, the heart before the dogma. While religion tends to be narrow and competitive, the spiritual path is all-embracing. It is said that religion teaches obedience, while spirituality teaches self-discipline. It is also said that religion is for those who are afraid of hell, and spirituality is for those who have already been there. Many on the spiritual path have gone through religion, and find themselves declaring, "There must be more to life than what I see practiced here." At that point the spiritual adventure begins.

The journey we take together does not exclude religion (indeed it embraces the highest that religion has to offer) but neither is it limited to any particular creed. Our odyssey will not bind us with more labels; it will free us from the limiting identities we have accepted. We seek not more self-recrimination, but self-discovery. We are not attempting to get rid of anything we are; we are learning to celebrate everything we are.

4

This journey invites you to look at who you are and how you are living your life. Such self-scrutiny may at first seem frightening, but don't stop here. To the contrary, if you fear to look within, this book was written for you; it will demonstrate to you that you are entirely lovable.

Now let's get on with our adventure. . .

Don't Shoot the Screen

When motion pictures first became popular, a group of cowboys went into a Montana town to watch their first movie. The film came to a scene in which a band of Indians was kidnapping a young pioneer woman and dragging her back to their camp. Upon viewing this abduction, a cowboy in the back of the theater stood up and furiously fired a barrel of bullets at the screen. The film stopped, the lights came on, and the audience laughed to behold but a blank screen with six bullet holes in it.

We are equally fooled if we use the movie of life (playing on the screen of our mind) to gauge our identity or measure our worth. If you believe that you are who your parents, teachers, minister, or Tylenol ads tell you that you are, you may shrink to feeling very small and helpless. If you fight, hurt, or retaliate against those who do not affirm your worth, you are wasting bullets. Your efforts to prove yourself to others are as useless as shooting the screen.

If you know your worth, you do not need anyone else to confirm it, and if you do not recognize your value, you will not gain it by getting others to approve. If you don't like the movie you are watching, don't bother shooting the screen; instead, change the movie – or better yet, turn on the light.

This world is like a tunnel of movies through which we pass. You have probably gone to a dramatic or frightening movie with which you became emotionally involved. You may have cried, screamed, laughed, white-knuckled your armrest, or even wet your pants. You might have felt excited, depressed, fearful, angry, romanced, or sexually stimulated by the images on the screen. Yet when the last credit rolled and the lights came on, you remembered that it was just a movie. Although you were temporarily immersed in the drama, the real you remained undaunted by the pictures before you.

While experiences seem real as we pass through them, we emerge with ourself intact. The proof of this is that *you are still here.* Consider all of the wild and crazy escapades you have had, the dangers you have overcome, and the fears you have surpassed. Still you sit reading this today. You are here. You have your self. You have always had it – your true self – and you always will. After all is said and done, there remains an "I am" that lives beyond the character portrayed on the screen. We are spiritual beings going through a material experience.

Ships Passing in the Night

In junior high school I developed an industrial-strength crush on a girl named Kathy MacKenzie. I was in seventh grade, Kathy was in eighth, and her locker was just down the hall from mine. From the moment I saw Kathy, I was a basket case. She was gorgeous, gleamed a sparkling Pepsodent Smile, and was a living incarnation of the All-American-Girl-Next-Door-Cheerleader-Miss-Popularity-Prom Queen-Barbie-Perfect Dream Girl. My days revolved around seeing Kathy in the hall and fantasizing that one day she might be mine. I wrote sonnets to her dancing eyes, drew sketches of her golden tresses, and walked past her house in the evenings to see if she was home. Cupid had me nailed, big time.

Unfortunately, I never read Kathy the poems, showed her my sketches, or knocked on her door. I never even talked to her. Every time I got near Kathy, you see, I became a quivering blob of knocking knees, throbbing heart, and knotted tongue. I became so self-conscious that I could not even approach Kathy. I held such severe self-doubts and fears that she would reject me, that it seemed a lot safer to love her from a distance. So seventh grade came and went and the girl of my dreams went on to high school without me. (Kathy, if you read this, give me a call.)

Looking back on this teen drama, I am reconsidering the idea of being "self-conscious." Now I realize that for all my anxious embarrassment, I was not self-conscious at all. I was conscious of my fears, my self-judgments, my fantasies of rejection, and a whole cobwebbed batcave of dark beliefs about who I was – none of which had anything to do with the self I have since discovered myself to be.

What we call self-consciousness is a terrible misnomer. To truly be Self-conscious is to be God-realized. For millennia, mystics have echoed, "I *am* being, awareness, and bliss." Jesus proclaimed, "I and the Father are one." Our real identity is founded in Spirit; everything else is a fleeting story. Our passage is like a great steamship moving through a foggy night at sea. Steadily the boat cuts through the mist, while all the boat's activities carry on unimpeded. Morning will come, and the fog will lift. Meanwhile, the boat moves on toward its chosen port.

Behind the Mask

Science fiction master Ray Bradbury made a tongue-in-cheek assessment of William Styron, a critic whom Bradbury felt was a little too full of himself. Bradbury noted, "His only problem is that he thinks he's William Styron."

My self-concept is not who I am. There is much more to me than my personality. The word "personality" comes from the Greek word *persona*, meaning "mask." I may present a mask to the world, and look upon the masks of others, but the actor is not the costume. I may fool others (and myself) into believing that I am the image I present, but that does not make the illusion a reality. We may develop intricate dances between our masks and external roles, but behind all the images and appearances our

7

inner self remains intact.

One of the ways we keep the illusion of smallness in force is to identify ourselves with limited commodities. Be careful who or what you refer to as "my self." We name all kinds of things our "self" that have nothing to do with who we really are. At an early age we were taught to equate our self with our body parts. During toilet training, after you got off the potty your parents may have asked you, "Did you wipe yourself?" If they saw you fondling your genitals you may have been reprimanded, "You mustn't touch yourself like that." If you skinned your knee, your mom anxiously asked, "Did you hurt yourself?"

Being constantly identified with our body (and subsequently our social characteristics), it was not long before we began to shift our perceived identity from our inner self as a spiritual being to our outer self in the form of body, emotions, and culturally assigned character. It is no accident that as older children and adults we developed insults that identify us with body parts. While anyone would be insulted to be called "you asshole" or "prick" or "butthead," as children we were taught in more subtle ways that this is who we are.

An important step to reclaiming our spiritual identity and power is *relanguaging* references to self. We tell a clearer truth when we refer to "my penis," "my knee" or "my profession" than "my self." Sexual organs, knees, and professions change, but Self does not.

Trade in that Clunker

Because we accepted limiting, illusory, and self-contradictory identities as children, many people are now going through major identity crises. Some are being forced to dig to the very foundation of their being to reassess who they are and what they are doing with their life. The search for the real "me" has been intensified by tremendous instability in the outer world. Marriages, families, careers, religions, political orders, economics, health care systems, and social mores no longer offer the security they once purported to provide. In the wake of tremendous societal upheaval, our deepened thirst for self-knowledge has brought us to the brink of breakdown and breakthrough.

Such psychic instability is not surprising. An identity crisis is the natural result of identifying ourselves with things that change. Because we have defined ourselves as the roles we play and the commodities we own, when the outer world shifts we become confused about who we are. We are not anything we can touch or name. We are spiritual beings going through a material experience. Nothing in form stays the same forever. Spirit is the only constant.

An identity crisis is a blessing. A false identity is a dangerous entity to maintain, as it distracts us from our true self and leads us to believe that we are less than we are. If you have an identity crisis, it is cause not for depression, but celebration. At first you may feel frightened and confused, but you are not being cast into darkness; you are being released from it. You are being put in a position to discover that you are more than you thought you were.

An identity crisis is a marvelous opportunity to trade in an old clunker of a self-image and step into one that suits you better. Do not, out of fear or desperation, grab at another small identity to substitute for the one that is falling away. This would be like exchanging a house you have outgrown for another of the same size. The entire purpose of your discomfort was to motivate you to search for larger quarters. Fear will try to persuade you that the loss of the old will leave you with nothing; but in truth it has cleared the way for something better, and you will gain.

Rather than fighting the change at hand, use it to practice living large. The Chinese language character for the word "crisis" is a combination of two other characters: "danger" plus "opportunity." You can set your sights on either road, and you will be shown more of that path. Walk toward the door that is opening rather than clawing at the one that is closing; only then will you cast off your self-concept in favor of your self.

The Myth of Self-Improvement

You could not improve your self if you tried. Your real self, Spirit, does not need improvement. The real you is stronger and deeper than any aspect of your life that could be corrected. If something about you can be improved, it is not the real you. You can perfect your backhand, get your teeth straightened, sharpen your public speaking skills, become more assertive, set goals more definitely, and trim inches from your hips – but these are all aspects of your persona, not the you that lives beyond appearances. There is nothing you can do to add to, or take away from your true self.

Many of us have been striving and sweating for years (perhaps lifetimes) to remedy our frailties. We see ourselves as broken, and then set out on a long and frustrating journey to fill our emptiness. But it is not fixing that we require; it is awakening. The more we try to repair ourselves, the more we find we need to fix. If you have ever owned a home (or British sports car) you probably found yourself on a never-ending treadmill of repairs and improvements; as soon as you completed one project, a new one called for your attention. Boat owners will tell you how much money and energy it takes to keep even a modest ship afloat. Trying to keep a self-image afloat is even harder. Like the Greek mythological figure Sisyphus, you feel as if you are rolling a huge boulder to the top of a hill, only to have it roll back on you as it nears the summit. You will not succeed at solving your life problems piecemeal; we cannot satisfy spiritual hunger with material solutions. It is our soul we need to nourish.

A country singer ruefully likens her lover's shallow attempts to improve himself, to "rearranging chairs on the deck of a sinking ship." While he makes cosmetic changes, his foundation is faulty. This is what many self-improvement regimes are about. They work with the outer presentation, but rarely get at the inner person, the core level from which lasting transformation proceeds. The successful weight-loss programs, for example, are those which deal with the client's self-image and the underlying emotional needs that cause overeating or poor dietary habits. Most overeating stems from a sense of feeling emotionally undernourished. Physical food is substituted for soul satisfaction, and weight is put on as a protection against feelings of insecurity. Considering the primacy of this factor, you can see how shallow and futile are attempts to permanently lose weight simply by changing one's diet or eating less. This is why most people who lose weight through self-denial end up gaining back the weight they lost (and sometimes more). They may have taken off the pounds, but they have not dealt with the mind-set that put the pounds on in the first place. The key to losing weight (or any other unwanted habit) is not self-denial, but *self-affirmation.* It is to rekindle our loving relationship with the self we valued before we turned to food to offset fear. If you can rediscover the inner beauty with which you were created, you will make a major stride toward successful weight loss or any other avenue of self-improvement. Ultimately, we heal only by getting to know and love the self we already are.

The way out is in. The path to freedom is to return to your source. At your center lives a being so radiant and magnificent that upon beholding it you will lovingly laugh at the notion of trying to improve what God made whole. Then are you free to enjoy what you are. Give up your efforts to become perfect by accepting the perfection in which you were created.

Greatness Unveiled

What, then, is the driving force behind the massive movement toward self-improvement? For what do we strive in reading self-help books, attending seminars, immersing ourselves in recovery programs, and undergoing therapies?

We are on a path of *self-discovery*. There is a fundamental difference between self-improvement and self-discovery. Self-improvement proceeds from the premise that you are incomplete and you need to fill in a gap in your character. Wholeness, from the perspective of self-improvement, is an ideal toward which we must continually strive, but never actually reach.

Self-discovery, on the other hand, assumes that you are already whole, and your purpose is to know and express more of who you are. The seeds of everything you can and will be, lie within you now. (A female fetus contains all the eggs she will ever produce as a woman.) To manifest your potential, shift your attention from fixing what is broken, to letting go of limiting beliefs that cloud your vision of your innate perfection. The path of self-actualization is an adventure from strength to greater strength, from good to better to best.

Swami Muktananda wrote a book called *Getting Rid of What You Haven't Got*. We spend a great deal of time trying to solve problems we do not really have. In her delightful poem, "If I Had my Life to Live Over," eighty-five-year-old Nadine Stair notes, "I would have a few more real problems, and a lot less imaginary ones." *A Course in Miracles* echoes that we do not have many little problems, as our split mind would have us believe. We have only one problem – the thought that we are separate from God and one another. Rectify that one error *in consciousness*, and everything we believed was wrong with us dissolves into the light like dew in the morning sun.

We are not here to trace our pathology back to its cause; we have undertaken that dark journey many times, and it is futile. We know our problems too well – we are experts on them, on intimate terms with our sicknesses. Instead we must become familiar with our divinity. We must take the golden thread of our magnificence and follow it home to the heaven within. The story of our life is not a fight against evil and misfortune; it is greatness unveiled.

Isness Is My Business

I had an Oriental friend named Chin Lee who held a revealing self-definition. Whenever I would ask him, "How are you doing?" he would answer, "Working on myself – like everyone!" Like Chin Lee, many of us have identified ourselves with *becoming* rather than *being*. The path of spiritual growth is the second highest game on the planet. The highest game is living from perfection. Eventually you must quit being a spiritual seeker to be a spiritual *finder*. You have likely come to the point where you are ready to live from overflow, not need.

One way we deny our power is to identify with the aspect of ourself that is evolving rather than the core that is whole. *The part of you that is becoming will never arrive.* When you identify with any trait that is less than whole, you step into a reality in which completion will never be attained. There is never a moment at which a piece of you will become all of you. Becoming is always becoming, and being is always being; the twain maintain parallel realities, but never meet.

When Moses discovered God in the burning bush on Mount Sinai, he asked, "What is your name?" God answered, *"I am."* Note that the Lord did not answer, "I am getting there," or "As soon as I graduate from therapy I will have my act together," or "When I reach the Diamond Level of my multi-level marketing distributorship, I will have it made." No, God made it very clear that Spirit is in a state of being, not becoming. *"I am."* Now.

As expressions of the same infinite being, we must refuse to identify ourselves with anything less. No excuses, delays, apologies, mitigating circumstances, requests for extensions, or dogs that ate the homework. Isness is our business.

In his book *The Quiet Mind,*[1] White Eagle advises, "Give up your lust for growth." When I read this suggestion, I was spending most of my time studying, getting counseling, attending workshops, and wondering how I could advance on the spiritual path. Then along comes a discarnate Indian telling me that my fervor for growth is a form of lust! How dare he insinuate that I *am* whole when I had a huge investment in *becoming* whole!

Growth is a marvelous path, but at a certain point it becomes a trap. We are human *beings*, not human *becomings*. We are not getting there; we are coming from there.

Our society is preoccupied with getting somewhere. We are obsessed with more, quicker, and cheaper. Our notion of "better" is usually tied to increase and acquisition. But more is not always better. Sometimes less is better. Sometimes enough is better. Our lust for acquisition has bled over to our spiritual process. More classes, more trainings, and more experiences do not necessarily mean more enlightenment. Sometimes they mean more confusion, distraction, and metaphysical indigestion. If you put new wine in an old wineskin, Jesus explained, the container will break and the wine will be lost. If we expect to upgrade our quality of life we are going to have to come to it from a different direction.

Enlightenment is not something out there we must acquire; it is something in here we are birthing. We will have what we are willing to find, but what we seek will elude us – not because it is unavailable, but because we proceed from the assumption that we do not already have it. Assume that you already have what you want (or at least the seeds of it within you) and the universe will manifest your dreams as you affirm, "I am."

The Light Within

A Course in Miracles reminds us, "I am as God created me." Jesus declared, "I am the way, the truth, and the life." You and I can – and must – claim the same identity with equal authority.

Every great prophet has echoed the same message: you *are* the light you seek. The knowledge of our wholeness is not gained through acquisition, but by discovery; nor is it achieved in steps, but through awakening. It is the result of a *quantum shift* in our identity and way of living. You cannot be the small person you thought you were, and know the magnificent one you are. You cannot identify yourself as empty and enjoy the riches of fullness. The time has come to cease looking and start finding; to quit growing and acknowledge knowing; to stop acting small and claim it all. We are ready to put aside the toys of childhood and walk in the majesty we were born to express.

14

ACTIVATION:

THE ROSE AND THE MIRROR

Imagine a circular room of mirrors, all spotlessly clean, perfectly reflecting everything in the room.

Picture at the center of the room a glass table with a crystal vase containing the most beautiful red roses you have ever seen. Notice the vibrant color of the roses, at the height of their bloom. Every rose is perfect in every way.

Notice how the roses are impeccably reflected by the mirror. Every image on the wall replicates the roses, from unique and fascinating perspectives. The reflection is so sharp, in fact, that you cannot tell the difference between the roses and their reflection.

The roses represent the attributes of God, and the reflection in the mirror represents our identity as an expression of God's qualities in this world. God is pure love, beauty, wisdom, harmony, and kindness. Like rays of light from the sun, we must, by virtue of our nature, be all that God is.

Say to yourself "God is love, therefore I am love". . . "God is peace, so I am peace". . ."God is wisdom, and I am wisdom." Add any other attributes of God that come to mind, and then identify yourself with them. Know the truth of your wholeness.

Behold, what manner of love the Father hath bestowed upon us that we should be called Children of God... Beloved, now are we the Children of God.

— 1 John 3: 1-2

ORIGINAL INNOCENCE

Open your eyes! The world is still intact;
it is as pristine as it was on the first day,
as fresh as milk!
                                    – Paul Claudel

I saw a twenty-year-old prostitute being interviewed on a talk show. When Candy was fourteen, her mother took her to a street corner in Los Angeles, gave her twenty dollars, and left her there. She hadn't had a home since that day.

I was struck by the hardness of this young woman's face. Though tender in years, she seemed old, tired, and heavily defended. She looked at least twice her age, and then some.

The show host announced that his staff had found Candy's father, whom she loved and had not seen for many years. Moments later he walked onstage and embraced his little girl, whose makeup was now streaming down her cheeks with her tears. I wish I had a picture of Candy's face when she saw her dad. In an instant those horribly painful years fell away, uncovering the tender child who had been cast unprotected into a cold world. Candy's innocence was not lost; it was just hidden.

Each of us, in our own way, has constructed a personal fortress to protect ourself from the harsh world into which we found ourselves thrown. To survive, we prostituted ourselves in some way. We sold out on who we are and denied what we are here to do. We made compromises with our integrity, said yes when we meant no, and gave ourselves away in ways that demeaned our sacred gifts. Some of us even came to believe that defense and denial were all that life was about, leaving us to wonder why we are even here.

Meanwhile the tender child within us lives. The innocent, trusting being has survived all of the holocausts, and rests secure in a harbor untouchable by the winds of outer change. The child did not die; she or he just took refuge until it was safe to come out again. Place that child in an environment of trust and love, and watch it come to life. There is no greater joy than to reclaim the tenderness of innocence.

Every soul on the planet has retained its divinity, whether the person knows it or not. The spiritual adventure is about regaining the vision of who we are, and living in the worthiness it reveals. The more we can remember our innate goodness, the quicker we can bring dad onstage to be reunited with the child he loves.

Like Father, Like Son

Scanning my car radio while driving along Route 101 near San Francisco, I was startled to hear a deep voice boom, "You are divine! You are a blessing to the world! You are a source of good to everyone you touch!"

"Dude!" I exclaimed aloud. "Someone on the radio is broadcasting the truth about who we are – what a phenomenal service!" The voice went on, "Your essence is love. Your being is eternal. Within you greatness resides."

With each pronouncement I felt brighter, lighter, and freer. (It is said that "the Spirit within us loves to hear the truth about itself.") Deep within me the words resonated like an ancient bell, and I turned the radio volume up. I was excited that these positive statements were being broadcast to thousands of people around the city; the voice of self-worth had found a place on commercial radio!

You can imagine my shock when the voice continued, "Yes, O God, you are all, and we are nothing." Bummer! "You are perfect and we are vile refuse beneath your holy feet. . .You are

18

divine, and we are contemptible. . .Save us from our wretchedness. . ."

Scan.................

I turned down the volume of the song on which the scan stopped, and had a good laugh. Here I was rejoicing in the affirmation of my divinity, while the speaker had divorced his own. He had correctly assessed the truth of God's perfection, but he stopped short when he failed to appreciate that the selfsame Spirit he adored, lived within him.

In 1536 French Protestant reformer John Calvin declared,

> God, who is perfect righteousness, cannot love the iniquity which He sees in all. All of us have that within us which deserves the hatred of God. . . and therefore the very infants themselves, since they bring with them their own damnation from their mother's womb, are born not by another's but by their own fault. For although they have not as yet brought forth the fruits of their own iniquity, they have the seed thereof inclosed within them; yea their whole nature is a certain seed of sin.[1]

I present this quote for your inspiration – but not for you to be persuaded by Calvin's words, which reveal a dreadfully darkened mind. We deserve a lot of credit for showing up on a planet steeped in such fanatical self-loathing. It took tremendous courage for us to walk into a belief system that defeats us the moment we adopt it.

Our position, however, is one with our purpose: we came to dismantle the notion of original sin and replace it with abiding innocence. Through holding our most hideous self-images up to the light, we expose them as flimsy facades. In confronting intensely dramatized self-hatred, we recognize that this is not who we are or how we would live. So hats off to Calvin for pumping up the shrieking voice of sin so we can realize its emptiness and dismiss it in the grace of a higher love.

Fine, Defined, Refined

Dr. Gerald Jampolsky, author of *Love is Letting Go of Fear*, offers this anecdote which sums up our longing to reclaim our original innocence:

A baby boy was born into a family which already had a four-year-old-son. As soon as the child arrived in their house, the elder son began to ask if he could be alone with his new brother. The parents, concerned that the older sibling might hurt the infant, were hesitant to allow the encounter. When the boy persisted, however, they agreed.

As a precaution, the parents switched on the audio intercom connected to the infant's quarters and monitored the interaction from another room. They heard the older boy approach the child's crib, lean over, and whisper to the baby, "Please tell me about God – I'm starting to forget."

We all know ourselves as spiritual beings, we have all forgotten it, and we are all in the process of remembering. The pundit Swami Satchidananda summarizes our personal evolution: "When we arrived here we were *fine*. . .Then we were *de-fined* . . .Now we must be *re-fined*." Here we have a clever depiction of our descent from heaven along with the prescription for our return. We started out fine, and we remain fine; the way to become re-fined is to recognize that the definitions laid over our divinity cannot change our true nature.

Rocks or Light?

On the island of Bali in Indonesia I discovered an entire culture of people still living in a state of original innocence. The Balinese are the happiest, most peaceful, and most loving people I have ever encountered. Their world is the closest I have seen to heaven on earth.

The Balinese have a custom which reflects their recognition

of original innocence. When a child is born in Bali, its feet are not allowed to touch the earth for the first hundred and fifty days of life. The Balinese regard their children as angels from heaven, and they do not want them to be shocked by contact with the heaviness of the world. Every Balinese child is constantly held until approximately five months of age. Then a colorful ceremony is held at which the child's feet are placed upon the earth, with prayers and blessings.

In Western culture we do not have such an understanding or respect for our original innocence. Most of us arrived not amidst reverence, but under bright lights, drugs, a slap on the behind, and immediate separation from our mother. As soon as we showed up, worldly identities were laid upon us. The first phrase you probably heard upon entering this world was a loud, "It's a girl!" or "It's a boy!" Immediately you were labeled with a self-concept that limited you to half of the population! In my seminars I ask participants, "How many of you, upon being born, heard your doctor exclaim, 'It's the light of the world!'?" Nary a hand is raised.

The Hawaiian spiritual tradition teaches that every child born into this world is like a "bowl of light," containing the beauty of heaven. What adult does not melt to gaze upon the angelic countenance of a sleeping infant? Even as they walk the earth, children remain largely in the kingdom of heaven and remind us of the home we miss and to which we long to return.

If rocks are placed into our bowl, the Hawaiian masters explain, the light of original innocence is hidden. Fear, anger, guilt, and unworthiness are some of the stones that mask our true brilliance. The more rocks in the bowl, the less light we shine. Eventually there remains but a tiny trickle of the essence with which we arrived. People bent with pain, shame, and depression, are like bowls whose light has been almost entirely displaced.

To restore our light to its original splendor, we do not have to go anywhere to get more light. *The light is already there*; it has just been obscured. Our need is to remove the rocks from the bowl and allow the light to shine.

The path of self-realization is founded on simply releasing that which is not us. We attain freedom as we let go of whatever does not reflect our magnificence. A bird cannot fly high or far with a stone tied to its back. But release the impediment, and we are free to soar to unprecedented heights.

Coming Home

One of Harrison Ford's most endearing roles is *Regarding Henry*, the story of a ruthless lawyer who loses his memory after an injury. The film marks the contrast between the conniving Henry whose twisted mind dominates his wretched life, and the gentle childlike being to which he reverts when his conditioned rational faculties are suspended.

The slick Henry we first meet is unscrupulous in business, heartless among his peers, adulterous behind his wife's back, and emotionally absent to his daughter. On a worldly level, Henry has everything going for him – money, status, and power. On a personal level, his life stinks. He has no idea how unhappy he is, nor does he realize the pain he daily inflicts on others.

After his injury, Henry becomes a new person – or more accurately, he becomes the innocent person he was before he learned to manipulate his world by power-tripping everyone he meets. The new (or original) Henry is wide-eyed, open-hearted, gentle of spirit, and lovably teachable. In light of Henry's refound childlike receptivity, his friends and family encourage his kindly nature, and he "grows up" again *sans* the guile he once wielded. Henry becomes the loving husband and father his family missed, undoes the messes he engendered as an unethical attorney, and has the chance to start all over. As Henry regains his original innocence, his world becomes new.

The key to Henry's transformation is that he becomes whole not by adding wisdom or skills to his repertoire, but by returning to his fundamental goodness – a monumental shift accomplished by removing the facade he had laid over his true self. Henry's tyrannically anguished life was not the result of what he was, but what he had become.

We can use Henry's rebirth as a dramatic model for our own healing. If we are in pain, it is because we have donned roles and values that do not truly befit us. In attempting to prove ourselves worthy and make ourselves beautiful, we obscure our inherent worth and beauty. The more we try to become what we think we should be, the farther we drift from what we are.

This self-effacing cycle ends only when we put aside what we have been taught, and return to what we know. Dr. Wayne Dyer distinguishes between knowledge and beliefs. Beliefs, Dr. Dyer explains, are notions we acquire from the outside world – the opinions, judgments, and world view of those who influence us. Knowledge, on the other hand, proceeds from within. We know what we know because we know it, and it has nothing to do with what anyone else tells us or does. The key to self-actualization is to proceed from knowledge rather than belief – to respect our innocent wisdom. We must forget what we have been taught so we can remember what we know.

Shoot Again

Many of us were taught that we entered this world with a legacy of evil, and so we must strive and suffer in this world to be redeemed from the iniquity we inherited just by being born. Our parents may have exacerbated our sense of unworthiness by telling us that we were a "mistake," and we weren't even supposed to be here in the first place.

But God doesn't make mistakes, and Her children are not born in sin. God is love, and whatever comes from God must also be love. As the offspring of a wise and caring Spirit, you cannot be an accident. There is no such thing as an "illegitimate" child. If you are alive, you are legitimate. Dark notions of illegitimacy proceed from the judgmental thoughts of a fearful mind, and have nothing to do with the laws of God, which are founded in affirmation and appreciation. There is a good reason for you (and your children) to be here, a noble purpose you are to fulfill. We live by divine appointment, and we must act with the confidence that this is so.

The belief in original sin is a rock in our bowl. To remove it, we must trace the word "sin" back to its original meaning, which has nothing to do with guilt, shame, or a call for punishment. The word "sin" derives from a Greek archery term meaning *"to miss the mark."* In archery, when you miss the bulls-eye you do not fall on your knees and beg for forgiveness. You do not take a whip and beat yourself. You do not run from the shooting range and find an authority to dole out penance. Any of these responses would only further delay your mastery of archery. Guilt and remorse do not facilitate your reaching the goal; they distract you from it. The wisest response to missing the mark is to note the error, assess what you need to do to be more accurate, and shoot again.

The mark we have missed is our innate splendor. We have identified ourselves with the rocks in our bowl instead of the light. We have seen ourselves as small, powerless, and abandoned by love – all cases of mistaken identity that betray our true self. To be released from the pain generated by thoughts of sin and evil, we must recognize that we are a part of God, spiritual in nature, ever bearing the seeds of a glorious destiny.

It is not God we are shooting toward; it is God we are shooting *from*. To shoot toward God is to believe that we are separate from God, which could not be farther from the truth. Rays of sunlight do not shoot for the sun; they *are* the sun extending itself to light and warm the universe. We are rays of God, extending blessing to everything we touch. We do not have to toil to attain God; we contain the riches we seek.

Into the Obvious

Actor Peter Sellers described his role in *Being There* as his most important characterization. (Ironically, it was Sellers' last part before his death.) In the film, Sellers portrays Chance, a simple-minded yet inherently wise gardener who grew up in such a sheltered environment that his mind never developed beyond that of a five-year-old. When he is suddenly cast into a cold and wily world, Chance retains his delightful innocence. Everyone who meets him doesn't quite know what to make of him, but they really like him!

Through a strange series of events, Chance meets the President of the United States, who is attracted to his earthy unpretentious wisdom. When the President asks Chance what he thinks about the current economic downturn, Chance tells the Chief Executive, "First there is the spring, when the plants bud; next comes summer, and the crops flourish; in the autumn we enjoy the harvest; and then in winter everything sleeps. Once again spring comes and the plants bud anew." The President equates Chance's imagery with financial cycles, and reformulates his economic program. Chance becomes a national hero and is named a presidential advisor. The humorous irony is that Chance knows nothing about economics; all he knows is gardening. The simplicity of his truth cut through the intellectual mire.

The final scene of *Being There* depicts a group of politicians speculating about Chance as the next president. As they are debating the merits of his nomination, Chance wanders off to a nearby park and walks over a pond – no one ever told him that he couldn't!

Imagine all that we, too, could do if we didn't know that we couldn't. Consider all that we would know if we didn't know so much! As we have made our world more and more complicated with convoluted concepts and mental machinations, we have obscured the truth. We have defined ourselves and our world so laboriously that we have lost sight of what is right before us.

A lecture promoter once introduced me to an audience as "a

man with a profound insight into the obvious." I took the introduction as a compliment. The truth is obvious. The truth is simple. We do not have to go far to find the answer. It is already within us, available if we are willing to see ourselves and our lives through innocent eyes.

The Sin that Never Happened

A Course in Miracles explains that real forgiveness is the recognition that, as divine beings, condemnation does not befit us. As forgiveness is commonly practiced in the world, we decide that an act is a sin, and then proclaim that we will overlook it. But as long as we believe that someone deserves to be hurt to offset iniquity, we but affirm the reality of the sin we purport to have pardoned. It is said that "we bury the hatchet, but then we remember where we buried it."

My friend Bob offers a striking metaphor for original innocence. When he was a senior in college, Bob saw a yearbook display in front of the university bookstore. As he very much wanted a copy of the yearbook, but had no money, Bob picked up a book when no one was looking, and took it.

Over the following days Bob began to feel guilty about stealing the yearbook. His shame became so overwhelming that he could think of hardly anything else. Finally Bob decided to confess his crime. He brought the yearbook to the bookstore manager and apologized for his misdeed. To Bob's surprise, the manager answered his confession not with reprimand, but laughter. "You didn't steal this yearbook, son," the manager told him. "It was free. We had an overstock, so we put the extras on the table with a sign offering the yearbook to anyone who wanted one, with our compliments. You just didn't see the sign."

You can imagine Bob's shock and relief in the light of the sin he never committed. In the same way, the sins we perceive ourselves to have committed are not sins at all, but simply errors in our consciousness. We didn't see the sign that forgave us.

26

Is Bob's story a blanket endorsement to go out and rape, pillage, and plunder? Hardly. It is a metaphor for the way we can release ourselves from the awful burden of guilt that so many of us carry. It offers a vision of innocence that takes us beyond our perception of evil. The lesson is not about behavior, but identity. If you believe you are guilty, you will find fault with everything you do. If you recognize your innocence, you will look with gentle grace upon every step you take. There is always a bigger picture than the one in which we believe ourselves to be damnable. The *Course* tells us, "I can be hurt by nothing but my thoughts." It is not what we do that hurts us; it is how we think about what we do. Healing is accomplished not by paying off our transgressions, but by learning to regard ourselves with the same appreciation in which God beholds us.

This aspect of an all-forgiving God is imbued in the hearts of loving parents. Mothers are prone to see their children's goodness. When I gave my mother the first copy of my book *The Dragon Doesn't Live Here Anymore*, she was shocked by the revelations I had recorded about my life. The next day she telephoned me and incredulously asked, "You didn't really do all those things you wrote about in the book, did you?"

"Yes, mom," I had to answer. "I did."

"You really went to California and walked around naked with people you had never seen before?"

"That's right."

"And you took LSD at the St. Louis Planetarium and went up onto the roof and scared a pack of cub scouts by looking into the telescope while they were looking out of it?"

"Yes mom, I did that, too."

"And you tried to get rid of your dormitory roommate by pouring a trail of cologne from his bed out under the door, and then going out into the hall and setting it on fire while he was sleeping?"

"Yes, I did all that and more. Do you still love me?"

Without a pause she returned, "Of course I still love you. What alternative do I have? I'm your mother."

God, being our Divine Mother, does not have an alternative either. If She could imbue my earthly mother with the propensity to find innocence in her child – no matter what – then certainly God can do the same. We do not need to bargain with God to forgive us, or suffer under self-prescribed penance to offset our sins; God has no consciousness of our sins whatsoever. Our innocence is a fact of life, in force before we even began our bartering or expiation. Our only need is to open to divine love so we may enjoy the state of grace in which we abide.

Out from Under the Basket

While advocates of our sinfulness are apt to quote biblical passages pointing to our unworthiness, many more scriptures affirm our magnificence.

Jesus said, "You are the light of the world; do not cover the light with a basket." He also taught, "Be ye perfect, even as your Father in heaven is perfect." He was not telling us to *become* perfect. He was telling us that our nature *is* perfect.

In the Book of Prophets we are told, "You are gods." We have not heard this declaration very often, as our culture maintains a huge taboo against claiming our spiritual identity. We live under a massive unspoken agreement to deny our divinity and define ourselves as "only human," in a million ways small. In his classic work, *The Book on the Taboo Against Knowing Who You Really Are*, Zen philosopher Alan Watts describes "our tacit complicity to ignore who, or what, we really are," complicated by "the prevalent hallucination that oneself is enclosed in a bag of skin."[2] We could no more be confined to a body than the ocean could be confined to a wave. Waves but skim the surface of a vast immeasurable realm which we may plumb if we wish to know the treasure beneath the obvious. *A Course in Miracles* tells us, "Salvation is a secret you have kept from yourself."

Many clairvoyants tell us that a large number of people on

the spiritual path retain subconscious past life memories of being burned at the stake by cultures that were so terrified of spiritual power that they had to get rid of anyone who began to tap into it. The most obvious casualty of the Taboo was Jesus, who so threatened the prevailing world with his declaration of perfection that his contemporaries crucified him to keep the light from disturbing the darkness.

To this day many of us live in denial or apology for our magnificence, fearing that claiming our divinity would be heresy. But it is not. Heresy is identifying with anything other than Spirit. We do not only carry the light – we *are* the light.

We need more biblical scholars who are willing to find evidence for our worth rather than our sinfulness. We do not have to look far for evangelists spouting arguments for our iniquities. Turn on the television or radio any Sunday morning, and you will find an army of preachers lobbying for our damnability. Many of them revert to base histrionics and emotional manipulation in attempts to nail fear-weary constituents to crosses of culpability. They play on already deep-seated feelings of unworthiness in an effort to win potential converts to the ranks of smallness. Rarely do they cite or become excited over the many biblical references, especially as lived and taught by Jesus, that underscore our magnificence. If such preachers argued as fiercely for our divinity as they do for our damnation, we would see rapid and amazing transformation on the planet. We would see people bent with lifetimes of shame, standing straight and tall to take their places as godly beings. Dark and sickened figures with sunken eyes and hearts would find their way out of bleak dungeons in which they have been shackled for years beyond measure. We would see a new religion on the planet, unpolluted with the oppression of guilt, powerful to lift its people on mighty wings to a heaven long denied.

Where will we find ministers to teach love over fear? Who will be the first to drop the cross of death and take refuge in original innocence? Who will loosen the iron fist clutching the reddened throats of downtrodden masses bowing at bloodied altars of self-abuse? Who will reinstate the name of God as a synonym for love?

I will give you a clue: Look at the hands that are holding this book. Trace the fingers back to the hands, and then to the arms that extend from your heart. These are the hands that hold the power to change the world. The same Spirit that guides these hands to write these words, speaks to the heart that reads them. The destiny of the world and all life – beginning with your world and your life – lies in the hands you behold.

Do not wait for preachers or teachers to release you. First they must release themselves by discovering their own worth. One who knows his own value draws no strength from condemnation; such a one recognizes that only love and forgiveness bestow true power. Look not to the darkness to find your way to the light; instead, find even a tiny ray of love and follow it home to its source.

Look again at your hands. *You* are to be a living expression of wholeness. It is not too much to ask; anything else is too little. Reclaim your original innocence. God requires not penance, only awakening. You will not storm heaven with dogma; the gates of paradise will open in your heart as you find within you the love you have sought through outer crusades.

Know where you come from: you come from Spirit. Know your true nature: you are born of the light. Know where you are going: you are destined to live in peace. Where is healing to be found? Only in the discovery that you belong to love. Look nowhere else.

*In kind forgiveness will the world sparkle and shine,
and everything you once thought sinful now
will be reinterpreted as part of Heaven.*
– A Course in Miracles

YOU CAN'T PREPARE
TO BE YOURSELF

There is nothing you need to do first to be enlightened.
— Thadeus Golas[1]

There is only one moment in which you can succeed at being who you are, and that is *now*. Authenticity is the single quality you cannot prearrange. When you rehearse who you will be, you lose who you are. Love, our true nature, expresses itself in the moment.

If you are thinking about what you are going to say, it is not the truth. Anxious preparation is an attempt to package an image in order to avoid judgment for perceived deficiencies. If you recognize that you already have within you all you need to handle any situation, you can show up any place at any time and proceed without rehearsal. Founded in the power of the moment, you can move beyond anxiety and call to yourself the success you desire.

The way to escape from worry about the future is to dive wholeheartedly into the present. If you can fully be here now, when "then" becomes "now," you will know exactly what to do and manifest results that work for everyone.

Now or Never

At a workshop I and several other participants were asked to stand before the group and answer an intimate question. As soon as the instruction was given, I began to formulate a response that would impress the audience. As those who preceded me were speaking, I heard hardly a word they said; I was too busy planning my "act." I was bent on manipulating people to approve of me – a vain pursuit at the dear price of the moments I missed as I rehearsed.

A Course in Miracles tells us, "The healed mind does not plan." This does not mean that we should not plan at all; indeed in this world there are things that call for preparation. A mind at peace does not plan *anxiously*. When we make a plan because we fear what will happen if we do not, we affirm that we live in an unsafe world, and reinforce our belief that we are in danger. Only a mind absorbed in frightful illusions stockpiles today to guard against tomorrow's lack, or builds a fortress to protect against future attack.

When led by anxiety, we can never fully protect ourself; there is never enough money, time, or support to make us feel safe. Our life is like a scene from the movie *Godzilla* in which we and millions of others are running madly through the streets, just inches ahead of a monstrous foot that will crush us if we do not run faster. But we will never outrun the devil we fear – because *the one we are running from is ourself.* Our need is not to run faster, but to confront the source of our terror. Rather then buying better running shoes, we need to shine more light on the perceived threat. The way to escape from what we fear is to recognize the truth about it. Nothing in the outer world is more powerful than we are. "Know the truth, and the truth shall set you free."

ACTIVATION:

NOW OR NEVER

Check what you believe you must do before you can be whole:

- ☐ Get my degree
- ☐ Find my soulmate
- ☐ Get rid of my soulmate
- ☐ Have a baby
- ☐ Get my parents to approve of me
- ☐ Make my first million
- ☐ Stop smoking
- ☐ Lose ten pounds
- ☐ Have larger breasts or _____
- ☐ Have smaller breasts or _____
- ☐ Get along with my ex-
- ☐ Own a Porsche
- ☐ Pay off the mortgage
- ☐ Write a bestseller
- ☐ Star in a movie
- ☐ Control my temper
- ☐ Heal my abuse trauma
- ☐ Overcome my sexual desires
- ☐ Live out my sexual fantasies
- ☐ Move to Hawaii
- ☐ See auras
- ☐ Wait for Mercury to get out of retrograde
- ☐ Become the head of the company
- ☐ Create world peace

Add your own requirements on a separate sheet of paper.

Read each item you checked, then affirm your wholeness now.

Write Now

The greatest creativity springs from the life in the current moment. When writing, I rarely feel that I am preparing for something else. I delight in bringing through ideas that illuminate and empower me; it just plain feels good to put my thoughts to paper. If no one else ever read my writing, it would still be entirely worthwhile to record it. I write because I love to write; the fact that you and others read it and may find value in it, is icing on the cake. The author of a famous Buddhist text noted in his introduction, "I have no pretense that I am writing for any purpose other than my own edification."

If I considered the prospect of writing an entire book, I don't know if I could or would do it. The idea of filling a volume with quality material seems overwhelming. Instead, I record one idea at a time – the one that excites me most – and somehow all the ideas add up to a book. I have written eight books in the last thirteen years. If at the outset someone had asked me to do that, I would have laughed and told them, "No way!" But there actually was a way – one insight at a time.

When I write, my attention is fully with the word and sentence at hand. The aliveness of each idea carries me to the next one. Each word is as meaningful as the final production of the book. *The journey is rewarding for its own sake.*

Readers and seminar participants often ask me how I can remember so many quotes and stories. The truth is, I don't remember them. They pop into my consciousness at precisely the moment they are to be written or spoken. My mind is one with the mind of God, and so is yours. We have direct access to all the wisdom of the universe. Our superconscious mind knows everything we need to know, when we need to know it.

Trying to remember things is a sure-fire way to keep your mind so cluttered and strained that you will be unable to access what you need to know in any given moment. When you give up trying to collect thoughts, however, you open your mind to God's infinite storehouse of knowledge. Collecting ideas is like walking around with a canned repertoire of jokes. I find spontaneous humor infinitely more alive and exciting than stock jokes. When people at a social gathering begin telling memorized jokes, I quickly find myself feeling bored and unfulfilled. I suspect that the joketellers are bored, and rather than confront their boredom, they fall back on "filler." Contrast this approach with the outrageous extemporaneous comedy of a comedian like Robin Williams, and you will recognize the qualitative difference between prepared presentation and real life. Much of Robin Williams' material is entirely unprepared, yet he is amply supplied by a bottomless reservoir of free-flowing zaniness. Williams' talent is a cogent demonstration that when we are receptive to the riches of the moment, we will never go hungry.

Accidentally on Purpose

Some of the world's greatest inventions and discoveries have emerged spontaneously. Radial keratonomy, the surgical process by which nearsightedness is corrected by making incisions in the eye, was discovered by "accident." A laborer in the Soviet Union was injured when a piece of shattered glass cut his eye. Instead of losing his eyesight, as he and his doctors expected, he gained it! The shard of glass had cut the eye in just the precise way so as to reshape his eyeball and relieve his lifelong myopia. In the wake of this "accident," researchers began to examine how they might recreate this process by design. Now many have had their eyesight restored as result of a "chance" event.

Inc. Magazine featured a fascinating cover story entitled, *"The Accidental Start-Up: Where Great Ideas for New Businesses Really Come From."* "Forget focus groups, market surveys, and business plans," touts the introduction. "What *really* counts in spotting great business opportunities are serendipity, ingenuity, street smarts, and fast footwork." *Inc.* recounts the stories of successful entrepreneurs who "stumbled" upon revolutionary ideas *in the process of spontaneous activities.* For example:

- A burr-covered hiker recognized that if nature's fuzz stuck to clothing so tenaciously, you could make artificial fuzz that would stick with equal tenacity. Thus: *Velcro*.

- A torsion spring fell off a workshop table and kept tumbling before a toolworker's astonished eyes. On the spot, it became *Slinky*.

- Dan Hoard and Tom Bunnell, founders of the three-million-dollar-a-year *Mambosok* company, unknowingly launched a mega-successful career when, *in fun*, Hoard lopped off a pants leg and put it on his head. "We would sit in front of the mirror and cry laughing," Bunnell recalls. "We said, 'We have to sell this. We have to at least try.'" The company moved $200,000 of Mambosoks in the first six months of operation.

Inc. offers some basic suggestions for creative endeavors:

- *Follow Your Bliss*. So what if your business idea is totally wacky? What amuses and impassions also motivates.

- *Focus, Schmocus*. Maybe you're better off without a clear vision. With no blinders to restrict your view on the marketplace, you have the eyes to see a hot opportunity when it comes your way.

- *Infidelity isn't Always a Sin*. That original Terrific Concept may not be the one that powers you to stardom. You're better off having the flexibility to change direction when a compelling but unrelated opportunity comes along.[2]

All of these discoveries point to the true creator's friendliest axiom: *Be in and open to the moment*. Stay present, and the answer you have been searching for may show up in the most unexpected way. Sometimes your answer is entirely unrelated to the one you were seeking – but what you discover will work a lot better than what you had planned.

Here's a delightful postscript to my discovery of the *Inc.* article: I found the magazine on my seat on an airplane. The issue was not part of the airline's inflight library; its cover label bore the name and address of a subscriber, who left it on his seat – by "accident."

Hold the Vision

A carpenter doing some work on my house was fretting over his arduous process of securing a loan to buy his first home. "These guys at the loan company are really putting me through the ringer," Curt complained; "I can't believe all the little financial details they want me to show them!"

Having gone through the same process several times, I told Curt, "Here's the key: Remember why you are doing it. You are going to have your own home. In a couple of years when you are sitting in your living room savoring the view of the valley, this process will seem trivial. Do the dance for a moment now, and you will reap a lifetime of value."

Holding the vision behind a project is the all-important key that makes the mundane steps bearable. If you feel bogged down or stymied by an aspect of a project, remember why you are doing it. Snags along the way seem formidable only when we forget the reason we began our adventure. Vision gives meaning to your process, as the big picture gobbles up the details as fuel for a higher purpose. No step is ever worth taking unless the vision behind it is more real and present than the difficulty the step may present. We are not proceeding *toward* the goal, but living *from* it. Instead of seeing ourselves in a state of lack which will be offset by the goal when it is achieved, we are bolstered by the energy we receive when we imagine that the goal is already a reality.

Consider the power of the vision that sustained Thomas Edison as he went through two thousand "failures" in his experiments that culminated in the invention of the incandescent light bulb! Or imagine the commitment that treasure hunter Mel Fisher must have held in his seventeen-year search for a sunken Spanish Galleon, which he eventually located along with millions of dollars worth of gold, gems, and artifacts. I know a woman who dove with Fisher's crew. She showed me a t-shirt worn by crew members, boldly displaying their motto for years: *Today's the Day!*

Stay on the Air

While being interviewed on a radio show, I made this analogy: "It would be a sorry event if this station went off the air for an hour in the middle of the broadcast day," I suggested. "In the course of our daily lives, however, we go 'off the air' for hours, days, and even years. We settle for careers, relationships, and activities that deaden us. Then we wonder why we feel we are missing something. It is crucially important that we stay on the air – fully present in life without interruption."

My friend Lili has a motto on her business card: *"Do it only if it's fun – and if you have to do it, find a way to make it fun."* If you are not enjoying what you are doing, stop and reevaluate why you are doing it. Are you allowing joy to guide you, or have you submitted to the tyranny of fear? *Enthusiasm gets results*; boredom undermines achievement. The word "enthusiasm" derives from the Greek *"en Theos,"* meaning "in God." When you are enthusiastic about anything – *no matter what it is* – you are expressing your godly nature.

If you feel that you are sacrificing your current happiness for a future reward, stop and consider the state of your heart. *Nothing is worth doing unless your heart is in it.* If your ultimate goal is real and alive to you, your current action will not feel like a sacrifice. Any sense of loss or depletion is a signal that you have veered from living your truth. Ask yourself what would have to be different for you to feel as if you are winning. Then ask the universe for it, and you may find that God has as much of an investment in your happiness as you do.

Master Key:

The Journey Is as Important as the Destination.

Beyond Planaholism

While most of us would not identify ourselves as addicts, *planaholism* is a debilitating addiction that can rob us of peace without our being aware of it. The hidden purpose behind a planaholic's feverish overscheduling is to avoid facing himself. He knows that if he gave himself even a small amount of space and time alone, he would have to feel the feelings he has repressed, face the relationships troubling him, and come to terms with the issues he has avoided. The planaholic sets up an endless array of jobs, appointments, and busyness to distract him from looking within.

If life become too peaceful, the planaholic will create new projects, dramas, crises, or emergencies. The planaholic's motto is, "Be sure there are always so many things going on that I will not have to face my pain." He may rationalize or even complain that he does not have enough time to be with himself or his loved ones, but the truth is that he has made himself so busy *for the very purpose* of not being with himself or his loved ones.

While it would appear that a planaholic is responding to the needs of his life, he is creating them. A planaholic is ruled by an internal adrenaline thermostat that initiates frenzy when drama falls below a specified threshold. Behind the frantic racing, there is a masterfully chosen purpose. The terminal scheduler is much more at choice than meets the eye.

The fearful part of the mind is correct in expecting that we will have to face our issues if we create more space in our life. But what that prickly ball of worries does not understand is that such a confrontation would bring only greater peace. *Self-awareness is always healing.* Just on the other side of the wall the planaholic has erected with his day-planner, awaits deep release, unprecedented freedom, and new avenues of creative self-expression. A moment of discomfort in confronting our shadow is a small price to pay for the realization that we are not the shadow at all. A few moments of feeling the pain is minuscule in light of the lifetime of aliveness available in its wake.

The turning point for a planaholic comes when he begins to value peace more than drama. His devotion to intensity has cost him the experience of his wholeness. When we shift our allegiance from chaos to clarity, outer circumstances rearrange themselves to reflect our intention. The universe is always willing to accommodate the purpose established in our heart.

Stand by Your Self

Early psychologist William James advised, "For God's sake, choose a self and stand by it!" Though he uttered this counsel two hundred years ago, we are still learning to master his advice. We gain more by taking a stand for something that turns out to be a mistake, than by making no choice at all. (*Moby Dick* author Herman Melville boldly advised, "Far better to fail at being yourself than to succeed at imitating another.") Even if your stand is in error, you will be led to the next level. If you take no stand or proceed in a wishy-washy manner, the universe can do nothing for you until you make some kind of statement. In college I had a lovable but noncommittal professor. One day in his office I noticed a sign posted by his secretary: *"Don – I would blow your mind if I could find it!"*

Folie de Doute ("the foolishness of doubt") is a pathological condition in which the sufferer obsessively doubts anything and everything he does. In *Anomalies and Curiosities of Medicine* (1896), G.M. Gould and W.L. Pyle recorded,

> *Gray mentions a patient who would go out of a door, close it, and then come back, uncertain as to whether he had closed it, close it again, go off a little way, again feel uncertain as to whether he closed it properly, go back again, and so on for many times. Hammond relates the history of an intelligent man who in undressing for bed would spend an hour or two determining whether he should first take off his coat or his shoes. In the morning he would sit for an hour with his stockings in his hand, unable to determine which he should put on first.*[3]

Humorous as these cases may strike us, they represent an absurd extreme of the kind of vacillation with which we have undermined our power. We go back and forth about what we want to do for so long that we end up doing nothing. In our fear of getting the wrong results, we get no results. Anxious hesitation represents a lack of faith in ourselves and the universe. It tells of our belief that we may make a choice that will put us outside of love's embrace. *This is impossible.* My teacher Hilda once asked a student who was anxious about making an important life decision, "Where could you fall but into the arms of God?" If mercy walks with us wherever we go – as it does – there is no place devoid of grace. Thus we can move forward and trust that even if we make an error, we will have the opportunity to choose again, and ultimately assume our right place. Sometimes the error is an integral part of the process of putting us where we were headed anyway. Consider the possibility that we are always in our right place, even if it does not seem so in the moment. If being in the "wrong" place contributes to getting us to where we want to be, it is our right place.

Master Key:

The Best Way to Get What You Want Is to Be What You Are.

I admire people who have the guts to be what they are. I respect those who act boldly from the highest truth they can see, without apology, compromise, or regret. It takes a lot of courage to be what you are in a world that has little value for authenticity. A friend of mine told me that sixty percent of her female friends have had breast enlargements. While such a procedure is valuable if it assists a woman to feel better about herself, the statistics tell me that there are a lot of people walking around who do not believe they are good enough as they are. People with cosmetic surgeries, fame, or money have a hard time distinguishing true friends from opportunists; they never really know if someone likes them for who they are, or for their breasts, prestige, or bank account. It's a terrible feeling to wonder if you are attractive for what you have, not what you are. Someone described the entertainment world as a "golden cage." While famous people live amidst great glamor and glitter, many are subconsciously imprisoned by the images they must uphold.

Maintaining a facade is a never-ending and all-consuming vicious cycle. Several years ago I considered undergoing a process of thickening my hair. As the hair on the back of my head was thinning, I feared going bald, and I projected that I might avoid embarrassment by having a surgical process done in which a matte of hair would be woven into my scalp. I went with my friend (for moral support) to a hair replacement center, where a technician gave me a consultation and offered me the opportunity to have the process done on the spot. While I was tempted to accept his invitation, I felt that I wanted to think about it.

Although the prospect of having a thick head of hair for life was attractive to me, I felt a certain uneasiness about living under a fake roof. There would be something about me that I would have to keep hidden. The driving motive behind most men's hair purchases is to be attractive to women. (Most hair replacement ads show the happy rug recipient sitting cozily next to a sexy blonde in a Victoria's Secret evening gown on a leather couch under indirect lighting, the babe voraciously running her slinky fingers through his irresistible mane.) I imagined meeting an attractive woman, inviting her onto my (non-leather/vegetarian) couch, and having her run her fingers though my hair, all the while worrying if she would discover that my hair was not my own. The feeling of deception and hiding became very uncomfortable.

Then I began to wonder if cosmetic procedures would end with hair replacement. Next might come nose sculpting, followed by a face lift, lyposuction, male pectoral implants, a penile implant, and then, and then, and then. I saw myself setting off on an endless wild goose chase of mask-making. I imagined waking up one morning and discovering a 60/40 poly/cotton tag on the back of my neck, certifying I had become a veritable walking implant! I thought of a country western singer I had seen on television who had obviously had so many face lifts that his belly button was up to his chin. He did not impress me as being a particularly happy or authentic fellow. On the other hand, I have seen people with no make-up, striking gray manes, and regal wrinkles, who are among the brightest lights I have seen in human bodies. The picture must outshine the frame.

So I made a decision not to go through with the procedure. That was a turning point for me – the road not taken. An amazing thing happened after that – I have hardly been concerned at all about my hair; I rarely think about it thinning, and hardly anyone ever comments on it. The issue is not in my consciousness, and has no power to run me.

If you have gotten, or are considering getting some kind of cosmetic surgery, please follow your heart about it. If such a procedure assists you to feel more comfortable and confident with yourself, and aids you to more fully bring forth your internal beauty, then I say, do it. In my process I had to dare to be myself, and in your process, so do you. Daring to be ourselves means something different for each of us. The point here is not to make a general rule about what one should or should not do; the point is to be true to our *heart's* intentions.

Living from Power

You do not need to prostitute yourself or create a false image to be successful. You are already created, as the Bible tells us, "in the image and likeness of God." Any attempts to improve on that image will only detract from your ability to manifest your chosen destiny. Instead of trying to import power through manufacturing a presentation, live *from* your power, and you will have all the power you ever need.

Self-appreciation is the greatest gift we can bring to others. When you love and honor what you are, you empower everyone you meet. In a world starving for authenticity, those who recognize their own value are the greatest change agents. It is not lazy or selfish to trust that what you already are, is good enough; it is the wisdom that will keep you on your right path. Yes, read, study, and practice to develop your skills; dress appropriately for your profession; plan what you need to, with integrity and efficiency; have your nose reshaped if you really want to. But do not do these things to become something that you are not; do them as an expression of what you are. Do them to draw forth the magnificent inner person yearning to be expressed. You will never succeed at becoming someone else, but you will always succeed at being what you are.

I do not seek good fortune – I am good fortune!
– Walt Whitman

LET IT BE EASY

Get off the cross – Somebody needs the wood.
– Dolly Parton, *Straight Talk*

Kneeling before the Toyota truck bumper in the oil-spotted parking lot of the NAPA auto parts store, I grunted my way through the simple task of replacing my pickup's directional light bulb. In the midst of my efforts, a woman walking by commented, "You sure look like you're struggling!"

I stood up, stunned. Even a passer-by detected my sense of strain! Stepping back, I observed myself holding my breath, clenching my jaw, and sweating – all over a couple of little screws! I had no idea I was laboring so profusely over such a menial project.

The voice that spoke to me was not just that of a passing stranger, but Truth. Not long before that day I had made a commitment to allow more ease in my life; here the universe was showing me that I still worshipped at the altar of travail.

Struggle is not an act; it is an *attitude*. If we believe that we must fight to get what we want, we will toil over everything we do. If we recognize, however, that the universe works more efficiently for us when we approach it with ease, life will serve us in miraculous ways.

Master Key:

Let it Be Easy. Struggle Is Not Required.

A friend of mine invited Arnold Patent, author of *You Can Have It All*,[1] to participate in a project she was sponsoring. After considering the invitation, Arnold told her, "I don't think I'll be a part of this venture. When I try the idea on for size, it feels like a struggle for me; my life is about ease."

My life is about ease. Now there is a powerful affirmation! Imagine how much more joyful and creative you would be if you refused to participate in anything that was a struggle, and relaxed into what you are doing so that it becomes a dance instead of a drudgery. You just might end up living heaven on earth!

Ease is more effective than struggle to obtain what you want. People with relaxed attitudes accomplish much more than those in a state of fearful stress or agitation. *Ease liberates energy for creative activity.* When I am immersed in worry or hurry, I make mistakes that cost me more time and energy than I would spend if I were in the flow of life. Strugglers make poor judgment calls, overlook important details, misplace items, and have to retrace their steps to correct errors. While fear and anxiety purport to protect us, they actually diminish our effectiveness and ultimately create even more work.

When I feel relaxed and refreshed, my mind is clear and alert, my intuition is keen, and I am aware of the right action to take. A knowing inner voice prompts me as to what to say and what to do in its right timing. I am aligned with the Force, and the power of creativity energizes me far more mightily than anxious manipulation. *Ease works.*

The Way Out of Struggle

Whenever you feel a sense of strain, ask yourself this question:

*How would I be doing this differently
if I were willing to let it be easy?*

One weekend I took a hike in the mountains with some friends. At the outset of our trek we descended into a valley amidst a shroud of heavy fog. After camping for several days we climbed out by way of the same trail in the sunlight. I was amazed to discover that the five-foot wide path wended its way along a steep ledge overlooking a thousand-foot drop!

Immediately I felt anxiety set in; my body became rigid and tense. I began to watch my steps carefully, and to keep myself from getting woozy I trained my sight on the path in front of me instead of the horizon. I found myself just waiting to arrive on solid ground, not enjoying the journey at all.

Just then we encountered another hiker. By contrast, this woman was as relaxed as I have ever seen anyone. Her gait was slow yet buoyant, and she was obviously enjoying herself immensely. I saw her stop occasionally and breathe in the glorious vista. Clearly she was on a self-nurturing holiday.

Seeing this hiker shifted my attitude enormously. Her easy-going energy was a clear statement that the situation was not necessarily a cause for fear or upset. (It is said that fear is not real, for if it were, everyone would be afraid of the same things.) I decided to try her attitude on for size. I breathed more deeply, dropped my shoulders, and stopped every now and again to drink in the view. It was magnificent indeed! By the time we hiked out of the valley, I felt exhilarated!

Consider the possibility that there is nothing that automatically causes stress. At another time I was sleeping at a retreat community in the mountains when I was awakened by a gentle knocking at my door. A soft voice called, "There's a fire in Jerry's cabin; come on over if you like." Still half asleep, I wondered why this person would come and wake me to attend a late night campfire. When I sat up to look out the window, I saw one of the cabins in flames. The members of the community had done all they could to put it out, to no avail. They cleared the area around the cabin, and just sat calmly and meditatively watched the structure burn. They seemed to be quite at peace with it, reflecting on the transformation as it occurred.

ACTIVATION:

THE EASE MAP

Situations in Which I Struggle

How I Would Be Doing this Differently if I Were Willing to Let it Be Easy

Career:

Relationships:

Financial:

Physical Well-Being:

Spiritual Path:

*If you need help, think of someone you know
who is a master of ease (friend, teacher, pet, etc.),
and consider how they might handle the same situation.*

We see every situation through the eyes of our belief system and emotional programming. We may not be able to change the situation, but we can change our attitude and the way we approach it. At any time we can choose peace over struggle. In fact, finding yourself in tension is a marvelous opportunity to reprogram subconscious fears that may have held you captive for a long time. If you notice yourself getting uptight in a traffic jam, for example, consider how you might be handling the situation differently if you were relaxed. Look for a driver who is calm, and use that person as a model. Remember a time when you were in a traffic jam and maintained your peace. This proves that it is not traffic that causes stress, but the way we filter it through our thoughts and emotions. I cannot overemphasize that situations have no power in and of themselves – it is the vision we choose to use, and our subsequent response that makes all the difference.

No Pain, No Pain

We have all heard and perhaps practiced the maxim, "No pain, no gain." This is a half-truth we need to lift to a broader understanding.

Painful situations certainly offer opportunities for awakening and growth. Pain is a signal that we are swimming against the current of life. When we are suffering in any way, the universe is trying to get our attention so we can make a course correction that will return us to our natural state of peace.

It is also possible to gain a great deal without pain. Some of the most rewarding moments of life are born of pure delight. To behold the majesty of a glorious sunset, to hold a newborn child against your bosom, to create artistically, to make love, to speak heartfelt truth to a dear friend, to sit quietly and feel the presence of the God within. Such peak experiences, and many like them, lift us to recognize and celebrate the wonder of being alive. These moments can be so profound that they alter the course of our entire life.

To believe "no pain, no gain," is to assert that we are here to suffer. Some people believe that life is just a big *Stairmaster* exercise machine, on which you work hard, sweat profusely, and get nowhere. But there is more to life than torture. What God would create a world in which Her children can learn only through anguish? And who but a cosmic masochist would enter a world in which he could gain only by travail?

To gain through pain is but a tile in the great mosaic of life; it is by no means the whole picture. Step back and open to a grander vista, and pain will reveal itself as but a part-time friend. Deny pain not, but neither worship it.

Love does not demand suffering. Only fear and guilt call for suffering. The universe is not a loan company. God does not deal in debts, guilt bargains, or punishments. God deals in forgiveness and release. Any view of God as other than loving is born of terror, and will not bring peace or success. Align your vision with God's, and be released from a lifetime of hardship.

The Best Rest

On the front page of the real estate section of my city newspaper, huge bold letters proclaimed, **"The Best Never Rest!"** Below the headline were photos of six realtors. The implication was that these salespeople were successful because they never stopped working. Looking at the photos, it showed. These men and women looked tired, tense, and burnt out.

What the headline failed to announce is that these people will probably die early through heart attacks or strokes, or nurse stomach or bowel disorders as they go. It is not true that the best never rest; to the contrary, *the best know how to rest*. The best love themselves enough to take care of themselves. The best value peace more than competition. The best know that a balanced life of outer activity and inner renewal will serve them and their clients more than feverish hustling. The best accomplish the best because they recognize themselves to *be* the best; they do not have to prove their worth to themselves or anyone else. Instead of trying to *obtain* self-worth, the best *proceed from it.*

The best *do* rest. The best recognize that there are more important things in life than wielding power or making mountains of money. The quality of their relationships, their sense of inner satisfaction, and their connection with Spirit are far more meaningful than making killings in the marketplace. The best recognize that *the only true measure of success is happiness.*

The best rest. The best take time along the way to catch the spirit in the eyes of their clients, have a laugh, and overlook temporary snags in favor of the big picture. The best put quality time with their families and friends at the top of their priorities. The best recognize that if they are empty inside, nothing they accomplish in the outer world is worthwhile. The best realize that they are here not just to do or to earn, but to *be.* The best have learned that as they proceed from creativity rather than competition, material success and achievement will come in miraculous ways that anxious struggle could not produce. The best recognize that they deserve the best, not because they posted the highest sales figures, but because their worth is innate, and no outer achievement or setback could add or detract from their wholeness. The best are the best because they rest not in outer accolades, but in God.

Listen to the Whisper

If you do not rest yourself, the universe will rest you. It is said that "the surest sign of a nervous breakdown is the feeling that your work is extremely important." Your work is important, but not as important as your spirit.

The Forced Rest Program is not pleasant or gentle, and you may end up wishing that you had chosen peace before life chose it for you. If you are overworked or overscheduled, you may be decked by an accident or illness that requires you to stop and find yourself. While this is a painful route to take, the long range results are invaluable. Those on the Stop Now Plan are given time to redevelop their relationships with themselves, their loved ones, and their spiritual source. They have the opportunity to read, study, meditate, listen to their favorite music, and enjoy valued company. They are able to spend more time in nature and learn the language of the wind. What began as an inconvenience or tragedy reveals itself to be a blessing and a gift.

Insights may also come in a more dramatic form. Descartes, considered the father of modern science, discovered the scientific method in a vision during a fever. The hardened prisoner Starr Daily beheld a vision of Jesus as he was hanging by his wrists in solitary confinement; he went on to give solace and encouragement to many thousands. Others meet angels or spirit guides at a moment of impending death. Whether our transformation curriculum is instant or long-term, the results are the same: we are moved to stop being driven by fear, and reclaim our spiritual essence.

We do not need to wait until we are out of commission to take the time to heed our inner voice. If we pay attention to messages of guidance when they speak to us gently, potentially painful situations will not escalate to the point at which we suffer. We have the capacity to hear and respond at any stage of the attention-getting process. If we hearken to the whisper, the universe will not need to punch us to get our attention.

A Wise Investment

While I was visiting a large successful bookstore in Virginia Beach, an employee told me that the staff is allowed (and encouraged) to take meditation breaks during their work day – on company time. Immediately I understood why the store is so prosperous: the management recognizes that clear and rested minds produce better results.

A peaceful countenance is a real asset in the business world. I am attracted to salespeople and business colleagues who are in harmony with themselves and maintain a positive attitude about life. I am turned off, not on, by high pressure or hyped-up sales pitches. Quality products or services do not require someone yelling in your face to get your attention. The strongest magnet for success is excellence. Cadillac and Lexus auto commercials are usually subdued and matter-of-fact; these companies do not need to resort to gimmicks or come-ons, since the calibre of the merchandise speaks for itself. By contrast, I occasionally tune in on television commercials for local car dealerships, pitched by an obnoxious rapid-rapping salesman whose voice is so loud and piercing that I have to put the TV on mute to escape it. Given a choice between buying a product or service from someone who is relaxed, and someone who sounds like he is strung out on amphetamines, I tend to gravitate to the peaceful being.

What most businesses have not realized, to their loss, is that ease is attractive and productive. Intra-company pressure and fear tactics may produce short-term results, but they exact a deadly toll in the long run. Employee morale, integrity, and commitment only increase when ease is an element in the atmosphere of the work place. I shop at a popular pet store at which the owner is a laid-back fellow. He never seems to be in a hurry, he always has time to chat with the customers, and he trusts his employees to be responsible when he is absent. As a long-time customer, I notice that most of his employees have worked there for years (an unusual feat in my region, which has a very high turnover). I noticed that one clerk worked there for a long time, left for a while, and returned. There is something about the store that is nourishing to the spirit of those who work and shop there.

At the mall just down the road from this pet store is another pet store in which the manager is a tyrant. He always seems frazzled, and his patience for employee errors is low. It is clear that he does not enjoy his work; he seems to live in a state of constant warfare. In that far less successful store, I rarely see the same employees twice. It is not a people-friendly environment; ease is conspicuously absent. This manager does not recognize that he would generate a lot more joy and success through taking it easier. He probably loses more efficiency through employee turnover than he gains through overbearing management. The two stores are just one block from each other, yet they are worlds apart.

Creative Loafing

The best contribution you could make to your career might be to relax and play more. When you are dealing with a lot of pressure, or have a big decision to make, one of your wisest strategies may be to take time off.

In his enlightening book *MoneyLove*, award-winning NBC radio broadcaster Jerry Gillies suggests creative loafing as a method to enhance productivity and success:

> *Self-reflection is one of the most productive things you can do with your creative imagination . . .When I was the director of the Biofeedback Institute, I demonstrated to some of the top executives of major corporations that by slowing down they'd be able to tap into deeper levels of their subconscious and come up with more valuable ideas. One publishing executive started taking Wednesdays off to relax and meditate. He reported back to me that he had gotten much more work accomplished in the remaining four days than he had ever gotten done in five!*[2]

To produce more and better results, step back and give the universe a chance to breathe life into you. When you take the time to renew your spirit, you open your psychic pipeline to a wellspring of intuition that you miss if you are preoccupied with continuous activity. Then you can pass your inspiration on to the world in the form of higher quality goods and services. Some of my most productive ideas come to me while I am showering, sitting on the toilet, or walking on the beach. Getting away from work gives us the perspective we miss if our head is buried in a project. Scientists tell us that we tap into the intuitive part of our mind when we are in the alpha brain wave state. One way to access the alpha state is to relax into an enjoyable activity, such as hiking, reading, sewing, playing golf, dancing, art, music, meditation, etc. Another way to get into alpha is to sleep. Great creative geniuses like Einstein and Edison were known for taking numerous cat-naps throughout their work day. For short periods of time they set aside their reasoning faculty and turned to the infinite for their guidance. Einstein declared, "I have not arrived at my understanding of the universe by means of the rational mind."

Entering the relaxed state awakens the right hemisphere of the brain, which is associated with intuitive knowing and non-linear guidance. Trying to figure out the answers to your questions through reasoning alone, is a very limited mode of problem-solving; it is but one element in a battery of skills that gets the job done. The most powerful approach to developing creative ideas is to combine the reasoning faculty with mystical knowing. Rather than working more feverishly, you may do better to play more regularly. Instead of staying late at the office to crunch a mountain of numbers, you may profit more by going to a movie. Strenuous work always hits a point of diminishing returns, and that is precisely the time to close up shop and head for the beach. Surfing, disco dancing, or dining at a fine restaurant, may be an extremely valuable contribution to the success of your career. Don't overlook the importance of play – it may prove to be the hidden key to your breakthrough!

To Stimulate Creativity,
Follow the Three R's –
Release, Relax, Reflect

If you look into the night sky for a particular star, it is easier to see the star if you gaze slightly to the side of it. Sometimes the most direct way to achieve your objective is the indirect way: let go of it temporarily and do something else. In a strain-free state, your superconscious mind can work for you more efficiently. The process is similar to trying to catch an idea that was "just on the tip of your tongue." The more you try to remember the thought, the more elusive it becomes, slipping away as soon as you are about to get a handle on it. Forget about it for the moment and go on to another thought. Soon the idea will pop into your brain without effort. This is how creative relaxation gets results.

I did some of my best writing when I lived in a farming community. I would write early in the morning, and then go out to work on a dwelling we were constructing. Throughout the day many fresh and exciting ideas would pop into my mind. In the evenings I would incorporate my day's inspiration into my book in progress. I found the balance of mental and physical activity to be a powerful formula for the generation of quality material.

Most successful people attest that their prosperity is a result of both work and play. Malcolm Forbes, affectionately known as "the happy millionaire," enjoyed his money and his friends. He was known for throwing sprawling exotic galas, such as a multi-million-dollar soiree at a sheik's palace in the middle east, to which he flew many of his friends for the celebration. When Forbes died, his will stipulated that he forgave all personal loans taken out by his employees. Even from the grave, Forbes knew how to have fun with his money and use it to make himself and his friends happy!

You do not need to be a multi-millionaire to start having fun with your money and your life. You just need to value peace more than struggle. You do not have to fly all of your friends to a sultan's palace; you just have to be emotionally present with them, and offer them a sense of refuge in your presence. In the end, it is not the achievements that our friends remember us for, or the accolades we obtained that make our life worthwhile. What we will value is the quality of our experience while we are here. Don't wait until you are sick or dead to discover that you would rather have played more while you had your life and health. Take the time now to do what you would really love to do, and you will have more time to do it.

The Trying Game

One of the most virulent enemies of success is *trying*. Trying is lying; trying is dying. Trying seems necessary only when we identify with the small self. The little "me" is the one who wonders if it can succeed. The vast "me" knows that I can do whatever I set out to do, in co-creation with Spirit. Trying implies that you may not be able to accomplish your goal; doing implies that you will. People who are not willing to take responsibility for their lives, try; those who are committed to success, do. Ken Blanchard, author of *One Minute Manager,*[3] describes the difference between involvement and commitment: "When you are involved in something, you do it only when it is convenient," Dr. Blanchard explains. "When you are committed, you accept no excuses – only results."

I spoke to a woman who was considering registering for one of my seminars. "I am trying desperately to get the money to come," Maggie told me.

The predominant element I heard in Maggie's voice was struggle. "Don't try desperately," I told her.

"Why not?" she retorted, startled.

"Don't try desperately," I reiterated. "Just do it. Or don't do it. Whatever you choose, don't make a struggle out of it."

I explained to Maggie that results always follow intention. If your heart is set on something and you are committed to having it happen, the universe will arrange itself around your vision – without you sweating to force it. Over the years I have seen many retreat participants draw to themselves miracle after miracle to mobilize funds and support to attend the programs to which their spirit calls them. Earnest participants have attracted gifts, raises, bonuses, inheritances, unexpected tax refunds, free airplane trips, the sale of old and unwanted possessions, and friendly loans. One participant won six million dollars in a state lottery. Another fellow sold a saxophone that had been sitting in his closet for years. An interior decorator received a bonus in frequent flyer miles that gave her exactly the number of miles she needed for the trip. There are an infinite number of doors through which our good can come. Our job is not to try to orchestrate the how of it; our job is to know our intention and keep moving ahead with the faith and trust that the universe is working on our behalf.

There is a masterful dialogue on the power of manifestation in the film *The Empire Strikes Back*. Jedi master Yoda is training Luke Skywalker to use telekinesis to lift his spaceship out of a bog.

Luke: We'll never get it out now!

Yoda: Always with you it cannot be done. Hear you nothing that I say?

Luke: Master, moving stones around is one thing, but this is totally different!

Yoda: No. No different. Only different in your mind.
You must unlearn what you have learned.

Luke: Alright, I'll give it a try.

Yoda: No, try not. Do, or do not. There is no "try."

(*Luke concentrates. He begins to raise the ship, then it falls.*)

Luke: I can't. It's too big!

Yoda: Size matters not. Look at me. Judge me by my size, do you?

Luke: No.

Yoda: And well you should not. My ally is the Force, and a powerful ally it is. Life greets it, makes it flow. Its energy surrounds us and binds us. Luminous beings are we, not this crude leather. You must feel the Force around you . . . in you. . . between you, me, the tree, the rock, everywhere. Yes, even the creek, the land, and the ship.

Luke: You want the impossible!

(*Yoda extends his hand and levitates the ship. Luke watches in amazement as the ship is carried across the bog and set gently on the land.*)

Luke: I don't believe it!

Yoda: That is why you fail.

I generally do not work with people who say, "I'll try." When I hear the word "try," I hear that they have not yet arrived at the state of awareness at which they know they can do. "Trying" is an excuse for not assuming responsibility for a result. A statement closer to the truth would be, "I do not wish to do this," or "I do not believe I can do this." But trying is denying. Trying implies that there is a force bigger than, or outside of yourself, against which you will pose your strength. There is no force greater than, or outside of intention aligned with truth. If the Force is your ally, you cannot fail.

When I began my study of metaphysics, my teacher told our class, "'Try,' 'if,' 'but,' 'maybe,' and 'impossible,' are the language of fools. Cross these words out of your dictionary."

The words "tried" and "tired" are composed of the same letters. If you are tired a lot, you are trying too hard. The remedy for tiredness is not to try more; it is to try less. *"Try not; do. Or do not."* Doing is easier than trying. Not doing is easier than trying. Don't let your spaceship get stuck in the bog between doing and not doing. Be at choice, not at effect. Be a creator, not a reactor. Be at ease, not at effort.

Play Now, Play Later

At a conference I had dinner with a well-known psychologist who told me, "Although I enjoy these retreats in the country, when I get back to my office, *I pay a price* – there is a huge stack of mail waiting for me."

I was struck by the model this man was holding – the belief system that joy requires payment. As children (or credit card mortgagees) we were taught "play now, pay later" or "pay now, play later." In either case we accepted a subconscious program that play demands pay. This is not so. Irresponsible play demands pay, for if we "play" in a way that is hurting ourself or another, sooner or later the universe will stop us, which is a great gift. Real play, however, is the celebration of the moment, which leaves us with no karmic debt, but in fact frees us.

It takes but a little introspection to see how self-abusive a "pay for play" thought system is. Children do not believe that play must exact a toll, and they are the happiest people on the planet. Play is the most efficient way to learn, rendering results far more productive than struggle. Observe little children mouthing their first words, modeling clay, or helping mommy bake cupcakes. It is all a game to them! They do not labor under a heavy "I better learn to do this right, or I will be a dweeb" attitude. The activity is an adventure in delight; even though they utter unintelligible syllables or their cupcakes flop, they laugh and do it again. Jesus emphasized that "to enter the Kingdom of Heaven, you must become like a little child." He did not say that you must struggle and pay for your happiness; he proclaimed that delight is our birthright.

Master Key:

Learning and Success Occur Naturally In a State of Joy.

This is not a Test

Many of us perceive our life as a series of trials. When a difficult experience comes our way, we interpret it is a test over which we must triumph. If we fail the test as we perceive it, we berate ourself, and if we pass it, we pat ourself on the back.

The notion of being tested proceeds from our conditioning as students. Studenthood, however, is a learned self-definition. Children do not show up on the planet with a self-concept prescribing, "I am a student; I must pass tests and learn." Babies arrive wide-eyed and eager to spontaneously express their inclinations. When children develop their walking skills, they do not cognize the experience as a test by some outside force – they have no concept of an outside force or failure. Such a thought is a trick of the mind, and a baby has not learned such tricks yet. The child falls down and gets up again; the process is a game, not a problem. The adventure of life is more exciting than the notion of constant examination.

Students get tested; masters are bigger than their experiences. Common understanding would define a master as one who has passed her tests. But it may more accurately be said that a master is one who has passed by the notion of being tested. If we, too, wish to be masters, we must pass our tests by passing them by.

When the perception of a test comes along, questions to ask are: *"Who is being tested?"* and *"Who is doing the testing?"* Typical answers might be, "I am being tested," and "God or life is testing me." Some reflection will reveal that such notions fall into a heavily dualistic framework. The idea that "God is testing me" assumes that God is outside of you, and you are a frail entity being submitted to an examination at least, and raked over the coals at worst. Here, as Ashleigh Brilliant notes, "Your reasoning is excellent; it's just that your premise is all wrong."[3]

You may have seen the *Far Side* cartoon depicting a television quiz show on which an ordinary man is competing against God. God is on an unbeatable roll, answering all the questions correctly, while the human contestant hasn't even had a chance to play. The scoreboard shows that the Supreme Deity has racked up 1065 points; the man's score is zero. The fellow, bored and frustrated, is just waiting for an opening to give even one answer. The show host announces, *"Yes! That's right! The answer is 'Wisconsin!' Another 50 points for God, and . . . uh-oh, looks like Norman, our current champion, hasn't scored yet."*[4]

We cannot compete with God – not because God is greater than we are, but because God is one with who we are. If you saw the cartoon above, with whom would you identify? Would you see yourself as a frustrated contestant, anxiously awaiting a chance to prove yourself? Or would you identify with God, who is having a field day of continual success? While on the surface we seem to be the stymied mortals, at the depth of our being we are one with the wise and powerful God.

Our nature is love, and love does not test. Love blesses and celebrates. Can you imagine being in a relationship with someone who is constantly testing you, trying to get you to measure up to a higher standard, grading you as you go, rewarding you when you pass the test, and punishing you when you fail? (Perhaps you are exclaiming, "I *am* in that relationship!") That is not much of a love affair (although some of us play "love" out that way); it is the Marine Academy. If your idea of heaven is the military, then carry on with your testing program. If you would rather be at peace, pass your tests by accepting your divine identity.

Every great religion affirms the oneness of God. The holiest prayer in Judaism is, "Hear O Israel, God is one." Jesus, in his mystically exalted state, declared, "I and the Father are one." Hinduism holds that at our core we are the Atman, the undifferentiated light. *A Course in Miracles* has us practice the lesson, "I am one self, united with all creation." Jedi master Yoda declared, "You must feel the Force in you, and everywhere."

One self does not test itself. The perception of a test proceeds from a split mind. There is no differentiation between "self" and "outside of self." *There is no "outside of self." There is only Self.* What we see outside of us is a movie on a screen, a reverie, a corridor of mirrors. The one you see in the mirror is not testing you; you but behold yourself. Do not, in frustration, take a hammer to the looking glass. Instead, love what is reflected. The mirror will disappear, and you will be left only with your wholeness, which you already embody.

When an apparent test comes along, reframe it as an opportunity to awaken from the dream of limitation. Ask, *"How can I look at this experience so it helps me to remember my spiritual nature? How would one who remembered his wholeness see this?"* Quickly the "test" will become a gift. You do not need to pass it; you need to embrace it. It is not what you thought it was. It is an invitation to love yourself more. Everything is an invitation to love yourself more.

Let it Be Hard

Sometimes the easiest way to move beyond pain is to let it be hard. While this may sound like a paradox, it is a masterful principle. Allow the difficult feelings to come forth, and be with them. The cause of pain is resistance; to resist pain only increases it. It is the battle against feelings that makes them seem overwhelming. Let them have their voice, and you will move to the other side of the pain. If you are constantly fighting against pain, your struggle will exact a more costly toll than to let the pain come up, feel it until you have gotten its message, and then get on with your life. Sometimes the way out is through.

I was asked to perform a memorial service for a young man who had been killed in a train accident. When I met the fellow's parents to confer with them before the ceremony, I asked his mother how she was faring with her son's death. "Oh," she answered, "I've just been so busy that I haven't felt too badly." It was clear to me that Mrs. Lawson was in heavy denial, avoiding her sorrow about this significant loss. While she implied that she hadn't been able to feel much because of her activity, I knew that the *purpose* of her busyness was to put a distance between herself and her anguish. But distance does not remove pain; it only drives it deeper, where it festers until it is faced and healed.

I needed to be direct with Mrs. Lawson. "I suggest that you take some time for yourself and allow yourself to grieve," I told her. "You need to feel your feelings. It may hurt for a while, but you will come out on the other side. This is an important time for you. Use it wisely."

Tears welled up in Mrs. Lawson's eyes, and within moments she was sobbing on my shoulder. I hugged her and encouraged her to allow the sorrow to come forth. This was the beginning of her healing process, one which she could not avoid, and needed to go through to find peace.

Henry Nouwen writes,

> *My own experience with anguish has been that facing it and living through it, is the way to healing. . .Our human suffering need not be an obstacle to the joy and peace we so desire, but can become, instead, the means to it. The great secret of the spiritual life. . .is that everything we live, be it gladness or sadness, joy or pain, health or illness, can all be part of the journey toward full realization.[4]*

A Higher Power

Letting it be easy does not mean running away from unpleasant or difficult situations. In the long run, standing up to challenges is much easier than living on the run from fear. It is not escapism we are encouraging, but liberation from the tyranny of smallness. Denial always exacts a costlier toll than honest confrontation. When faced, for example, with attending a funeral, dismissing an employee or tenant, or admitting an error I have made, my first impulse is often to put the unpleasant issue aside. But experience has shown me that turning my back on what I must confront only increases pain, and the longer I wait to deal with it, the harder it is. Once I move past the resistance and take action, doors to resolution are opened. The easiest way to handle a challenge may be to face it head-on. A moment of discomfort is a small price to pay for a lifetime of peace.

Neither does letting it be easy mean rolling over and becoming a lazy bum for the rest of your life. (When I first latched onto the principle of non-struggle, I posted a sign over my desk: *"I do nothing, yet all gets done."* When I walked into my office the next day, I found that my secretary had penciled in a few words of her own at the bottom of the sign: *"Yeah – by me!")* Ease is not a matter of level of activity, but a quality of energy. You can be extremely active and productive, while maintaining an attitude of play and delight. You can do what would appear to be hard work, but if you are loving it, there is no struggle, only the dance.

Ease masters are often among the most active change agents. Some are busy day and night, and they find only more energy to create and serve. Others, bound with resistance, become exhausted when performing the most menial act. We always have energy to do what we love.

You can liberate a great deal of peace and creative energy by dropping the thought that the welfare of the entire universe depends on you. If you believe you must do it all yourself or take care of people who are not taking care of themselves, you will quickly run down your batteries. Allow others to develop their own muscles, and you will serve them infinitely more than by trying to do for them what they can and must do for themselves. Then you will have the energy and enthusiasm to do what you are here to do.

Ease masters know that they are acting on behalf of a higher power. When we step back and let God work through us, we accomplish more than we ever would under the enslavement of ego. Successful recovery programs, such as Alcoholics Anonymous, are founded on turning one's life over to a higher power. Participants recognize that we all need help from a Force greater than the little self we have been trying to wield. One of the twelve-step mottos is "Easy does it" – a fitting affirmation for those who have been accustomed to making a struggle out of everything. Struggle is a key indicator of an insidious addiction called "hardoholism."[6] If you are accustomed to making everything hard, you will not extricate yourself from struggle by trying harder; the antidote to struggle is letting go.

Ashleigh Brilliant proclaimed, "Now that I have given up hope, I feel much better." If everything you have done has not worked, then you may do better to give up trying. Leaving the war zone does not mean you are a quitter; to the contrary, you are just quitting doing what isn't working. If something you are doing is not working, doing more of it will not work any better. Instead of working harder, you may just need to work smarter.

Do not be afraid to let go of a goal you are immersed in struggle to obtain. *You cannot lose what you deserve by right of your consciousness.* Affirm that struggle cannot be a part of the plan to get what you want and deserve. You may have to act, but you don't have to suffer. Letting go of toil may be exactly the opening the universe needs to arrange the situation in your favor. You might be pleasantly surprised to find that what you want is closer than you imagined.

One Frog per Hand

Country wisdom advises, "Never try to catch two frogs with one hand." Many of us have tried to do so many things at once, that we don't get any of them done well. I have sometimes identified myself with the circus entertainer who balances spinning plates on wooden sticks. With twenty plates whirling at once, his entire act becomes a race to catch teetering plates just before they fall and crash.

Many of us have slipped into what I call "Management by Emergency." Rather than proceeding toward our vision, we spend most of our time putting out fires. From the moment you walk into the office you field a series of emergencies as they arise. Your priorities are determined by the wheel currently squeaking the loudest, and which particular hassle is most obnoxiously in your face. Then you go home exhausted and wonder why you feel you didn't accomplish anything.

This can't be the way you were meant to work or live. If you have succumbed to Management by Emergency, there is a good possibility that you are trying to catch a lot of frogs with one hand. Such a predicament is a call for you to step back and ask, "What would it take for me to feel more peaceful and creative in this work?" You may need to say "no" more often to requests that come your way; you may need to delegate more; you may need to reestablish your priorities and choose to undertake only selected projects; you may need to ask for more help; you may need to take a break; you may need to quit and do something that doesn't stress you so heavily; or you may need to simply shift your attitude. Do not settle for a life defined by a series of emergencies. You are here to create, not react.

MASTER KEY:

Everything Always Works Out.

The Power of Trust

My friend Betty was a woman of enormous faith. After a traumatic health crisis, Betty decided to celebrate her time on earth and devote her energies to living with an open heart.

In the wake of her decision to see the world as a safe and friendly place, Betty trusted in many extraordinary ways, and she was rewarded with amazing results. Betty customarily left her keys in the ignition of her new car while it was parked at New Jersey malls, and never had a theft. One afternoon she picked up a young man hitchhiking. He explained to her that he had left his wife in a huff, and now he was going home to heal their relationship. Betty was so moved by the man's intention that she offered him her expensive auto to make the final leg of his journey. The fellow dropped Betty off at her house, took the car, and promised to return it in a few hours.

As the afternoon turned to evening, Betty started to wonder if she had made a mistake. Could she have trusted too much this time? Later that night the doorbell rang, and there stood the man and his wife. They came to thank Betty for her generosity. The couple had made amends and decided to go the distance in their relationship. Betty worked many such miracles as she made her life an adventure in proving that faith is a practical tool.

I know a student of *A Course in Miracles* who was meditating in his Brooklyn apartment before retiring one evening, when a burglar entered his darkened bedroom through the fire escape. Jack turned on the light and told the burglar, "You don't have to steal from me. I will help you if I can. What is happening in your life, and what kind of help do you need?"

The men began to talk, and after a while the burglar broke down and cried, describing the pain and horror of his life. Jack gave him some money and told him to call him if he wanted to talk. Jack didn't hear from the intruder again, but he did feel gratified that he had turned a potential disaster into a miracle.

Another person who assisted me to learn to trust was a car salesmen. When I moved to Hawaii, I went to the local Honda dealer to buy a car. After making my choice I realized I was not prepared to pay for the car. I told the salesman, "Since I have been on the island for only a few days, I do not have a bank account here yet. My money is still in my New Jersey account. If you will hold the car for me, I can give you a deposit and come back in a few days with a cashier's check."

The salesman conferred with the manager and returned to tell me, "No problem – you can pay for the car with your New Jersey check." On the spot I wrote a personal check for fifteen thousand dollars, drawn from a closed bank five thousand miles away. Then I drove a brand new top-of-the-line Honda Accord out of the showroom. For all the dealership knew, I could have had twelve cents in that account. As I turned onto Main Street, I said to myself aloud, "I don't think we're in New Jersey anymore, Toto."

I heard an even more remarkable story from a woman in Virginia who had just bought a new Toyota for over ten thousand dollars. Upon completing her deal late Friday evening, she discovered that she did not have her checkbook with her. When she asked the salesman if he would hold the car for her until Monday, he said, "That's O.K.– you can take the car and bring us a check on Monday." When she expressed her consternation that the business would trust her so implicitly, the salesman smiled and told her, "That's just the way folks are here in the [Shenandoah] Valley."

These accounts shed light on ordinary people creating extraordinary results by choosing faith over fear. Such people have challenged and gone beyond anxious defensiveness. I am not suggesting that you leave keys in your car, pick up hitchhikers, or entertain burglars, unless your spirit specifically directs you to do so. I am suggesting that there is a bigger pond that we can swim in, if we just open our minds to higher possibilities. Goldfish will grow to huge proportions if they are taken out of a little bowl and allowed to swim in a bigger area. We, too, will live as large as we allow ourselves to express.

The Two-Step to Peace

As many people have had a low success rate in keeping the ten commandments, here is all you need to remember:

1. Do what is nourishing to your spirit.

2. Do not do what is loathsome to your spirit.

If you practice these two principles, you will need no other advice or information to enjoy inner peace and outer success. You do not need to attend expensive seminars in which a Napoleonic facilitator tears you apart for your own good. You do not have to fast on wheat germ and brewers yeast. You do not have to wave crystal pendulums over your pantry to see what you are to eat for breakfast. You do not have to have your colon flushed out with a tincture of Dr. Bronner's peppermint soap, granola husks, and Mountain Dew. You do not have to consult your astrologer to ask what time to go to the bathroom, or wait until Mercury gets out of Taco Bell to phone your stockbroker. You will not have to spend years doing rectal contractions to try to lift your sexual energy above your navel, only to have it drop unexpectedly at the most inopportune moment in the check-out line at Safeway. You will not have to do long deep breathing exercises with a snorkel in your bathtub while listening to the Grateful Dead played backwards, in hopes of conjuring a personal visitation from John the Baptist or Jerry Garcia. You will not have to consult channelers to ask dead people how to live. You will not have to do anything unless your spirit so moves you. And you might just be happy.

> *Sitting quietly*
> *Doing nothing*
> *Spring comes*
> *And the grass grows by itself*
> – Zen proverb

FOLLOW YOUR SPIRIT

Go confidently in the direction of your dreams!
Live the life you've imagined.
- Henry David Thoreau

"**W**atch out for the goats!" a voice cried as I drove into the barnyard. I crooked my neck toward the farmhouse roof, where three gray goats were eyeing my open convertible. I gave the gas pedal an extra tap and slipped past the rough-hewn gate.

"Hi, I'm Sylvan," spoke a tall, bearded thirty-five-ish fellow in coveralls and an amiable smile. "Can I show you around?"

The East Maui Animal Refuge, tucked quietly into the wrinkled green hills on the windward side of the Valley Isle, is a homespun marriage of Old McDonald's Farm and Boys Town. The caretakers nurture animals that no one else wants, including the Humane Society. The staff nurses and rehabilitates sick, injured, and abused animals.

As I stepped out of my car, a large Australian sheep dog loped over and began kissing my hands. "Say hello to Mr. Magoo," Sylvan invited. "He's blind."

I followed Sylvan into the barn, where he was administering antibiotics to some cats. Speaking to me over his shoulder, he didn't miss a step in his rounds; it was clear that his priority was to care for these creatures; visitors were welcome, but the critters were obviously the stars of the show.

"We call these guys our 'Booboo Babies,'" Sylvan explained. "This cat has a feline version of AIDS. She's doing fairly well with these antibiotics."

My Adam's apple suddenly felt the size of a grapefruit; tears were wanting to well up. I was observing some very holy service.

"Over four hundred animals live here. Besides cats and dogs, we have ducks, pigs, birds, goats, deer, and a mongoose. Most of them would be put to sleep at the Humane Society; they just can't take care of them all. We give them another chance. If we can get them healthy, we turn them back into the wild or find them a home. If not, they have a place here for life."

There came those tears again.

"When the police find an animal injured on the road, they know to bring it here." Sylvan turned to a dog with an infected ankle. The caretakers had made a leather cuff to support Arnold's leg and keep him from biting the wound. Sylvan changed the bandage as I watched with awe and appreciation.

"Do you have any parrots?" I asked.

"Sure, let me introduce you to Blue."

Sylvan walked me into his living room, which was filled with cardboard boxes containing clutches of baby birds. His wife Suzie was feeding pablum through an eyedropper to the tiny amorphous fledglings. She looked up and smiled, then turned her attention back to the babies. A pig found its way through the open sliding door; after a quick introduction to me, he was curtly shoo'd out.

"This is Blue." Sylvan opened the cage door to let an Amazon parrot jump niftily onto his finger; the bird revelled in Sylvan's gentle petting. "Blue came to us after he had been kept in a closet for three years. His owners didn't know how to deal with him, so they penned him in the dark. When Blue came here, he had picked out all of his feathers. Now, after two years with us, most of them have come back."

Darn those tears.

By this time I was in a state of stun. These people were saviors of the animal kingdom. My mind lighted on St. Francis.

"How did you get into doing this?" I asked Sylvan, who was on his way out the door to the yard. Again I listened from a few paces behind him.

"Before I met Suzie, she was diagnosed with terminal cancer. When her doctor gave her six months to live, she came to Maui to die. That's when we met and discovered we shared a love for animals. She began to see a doctor of Chinese Medicine, who told me that, along with taking the herbs he was giving her, she would do well to find some activity that satisfied her soul.

"So I began to take Suzie to pet stores. If there was a sickly dog in the back of a cage, I would ask the shopkeeper if we could take it home. Suzie began to perk up while nursing such critters, and almost daily we would find or be given another animal needing love and care.

"I swear that some invisible force would send "Booboos" to us – cats that had been hit by a car, stray deer – you name it. Before long we had quite a scene going!

"We noticed that the more Suzie attended to her Booboos, the less pain she felt. She had found a purpose for which she was receiving joy and satisfaction. So she did it more and more, until she was spending most of her time with these animals.

"Then we went to a medical doctor, who took some tests and told us that her cancer was gone."

"How long ago was that?"

"Thirteen years."

We walked back through the house on my way to my car. On the desk I saw a stack of bills. "Do you have public funding?"

"No, we function entirely on donations," Sylvan laughed. "You saw that pile of bills. I'm not quite sure when or how those bills will get paid. Somehow we keep going. But the main thing is that we are happy. We love what we do. We do our part, and somehow the universe takes care of us.

" – Like Mister Magoo."

"Like Mister Magoo."[1]

Master Key:

Follow Your Spirit Without Hesitation.

Where's the Bliss?

Suzie Schwab went to the edge of death before she heard and acted on the voice that brought meaning to her life, and healing to her body. Like Suzie, you and I have a purpose and an inner voice guiding us to its fulfillment. If we listen and act on it, we will find our way home – and serve grandly in the process.

Life and death are not nets cast upon us by an alien force; they are choices we make. The life of the body proceeds from the vitality of our spirit; when we feed our soul, our physical health follows naturally. When we recognize our inner purpose, all else falls into place. The answer to outer challenge is to return to the river of self-knowing that flows within us; there wisdom abides.

You probably recall a popular television commercial in which an elderly woman steps up to the counter of a fast-food restaurant to order a hamburger. When she receives her sandwich, grandma peels away the bun to find a tiny hamburger buried in a stack of garnishes. Indignantly she demands to know, *"Where's the beef?"*

To get the most out of life, we need to ask a similar question: *"Where's the bliss?"*

Many of us have searched long and hard for true inner reward. In our quest, however, we may not have given due consideration to the voice of guidance that whispers to us from within our heart. The counsel has always been there, but we have looked for it in the wrong places, seeking outer authorities to answer inner issues. We are drawn to glittery substitutes for peace, which leave us feeling even hungrier after we have sampled them. Like customers in the inferior fast-food restaurant in the television commercial, many of us have settled for relationships and careers piled with condiments, accoutrements, and garnishes, only to face disappointment when we discovered that the main ingredient was absent. What is the use of a life with profuse amenities but no substance? As spiritual beings, our real food is joy. When we keep ourselves nourished from inside out, the outer world will follow suit.

ACTIVATION:

WHERE'S THE JUICE?

For one day base all of your decisions on intuitive guidance. Imagine that the voice of joy within you knows your best interests. Trust that this voice will answer your request for direction at any time.

When you have a decision to make, ask, "Where's the juice?" Where is the electricity, the passion, the joy, the empowerment? At every crossroads follow the path with the higher volume of joy. For one day give your intellectual decision-making faculty a rest as you turn your life over to Spirit.

At the end of the day, lie In bed and place your hand on your heart. Feel the energy, vitality, and peace that comes with living from your heart rather than your mind alone.

Master Key:

Tell the Truth Quicker.

To gain the benefits of following your spirit, *tell the truth and act on it as soon as you know it.* Many of us have gained some faith that the truth will work on our behalf, but we still do not trust it enough to act on it immediately and with confidence. There remains a lag between knowing the truth and making a stand for it. The game now is to cut down the time between the moment we recognize the truth and the moment we live it.

Years ago I struggled through a very difficult relationship.

After three months with Maureen, we found ourselves frustrated and disempowered. Maureen was wrestling with incomplete issues from her recently ended marriage, and she was not ready for a new relationship. I also harbored fears and resistances to opening my heart, and retreated to self-protectiveness. Neither of us was sufficiently self-aware to deal with our issues. Although we did not recognize it, we were settling for a very unhealthy relationship. Our chief stumbling block was poor communication; our mutual response to dissatisfaction was to say nothing and withdraw, which seemed easier than confronting ourselves and each other with the feelings that were "in our face."

But physical separation did not solve our issues, and we continued to psychically hold onto this excruciatingly ambivalent relationship. Maureen and I saw each other sporadically, sparking with the romance of being together after a hiatus, then becoming fearful and upset, and withdrawing for long periods of time. This was one of the most confusing and painful times of my life, as well as hers. Finally, after another nine months of momentary excitement and long-term loneliness, we acknowledged that we needed to let go of trying to have a relationship. At that point we both reclaimed our power and went on with our lives.

I look back on that relationship as a lesson in what happens when I don't tell the truth on time. Those nine months were agonizing because we were not communicating some very strong and important feelings. Both of us knew the truth after three months, but we were afraid to confront ourselves and one another. Now, as I have grown significantly since that experience, I could not stand to wait nine months to confront an issue. The time it takes me to deal with feelings and voice my truth has become shorter and shorter, and I am often speaking my truth as soon as I am aware of what I need to say. Now I am much more present in the moment, my communication is more direct, and my relationships are more rewarding. Waiting to tell the truth is hell, and heaven is living your truth as you know it.

ACTIVATION:

TELL THE TRUTH QUICKER

Make a list of the situations in which you have not said what you have wanted to say, and the people from whom you are withholding communication. How long have you known what you wanted to say?

Situation	Person to Communicate With	Truth I Need to Bring up to Date

Just Do It

It is said that "the heart has reasons that reason knows not of." Sometimes following your spirit will lead you along a path that seems foolish at the moment, only to be proven extremely wise as the bigger picture emerges. The sage moves with the inner voice, even if it leads her by way of strange means.

After a long and mentally tiring day in my office, I decided to pick up a video on my way home. Wandering through the maze of films on the video store racks, I found myself lost in movieland. The only film that attracted me was *Earth Girls are Easy*. The title and plot seemed silly, so I rejected it and kept searching. But no matter how many films I perused, *Earth Girls* jumped out at me. I thought, "This is ridiculous; I should get a more intelligent and redeeming film." But as I continued to feel drawn to this flick, I decided to follow my spirit and rent it.

After watching the film for a full hour and a half, I can tell you that there was not one shred of intelligence in it. The plot, clearly targeted for an audience with an I.Q. of twelve or less, portrayed three horny aliens whose space ship falls into the swimming pool of a Valley Girl. The Valley Girl rescues the E.T. dudes and takes them to her local boutique, where their green, purple, and brown fur is shorn and they turn out to be majorly cute guys. The Valley Girl gathers her girlfriends, who join the defuzzed horndogs in an outing to the local disco, where the aliens turn out to be truly bodacious dancers. The Valley Girl falls in love with one of the spacemen, and the couple goes back to live on the planet Zork. The Awesome End.

This plot had the redeeming value of Spam. But there was another kind of redemption that proved to be a real gift: by the end of the movie, I felt great. What I needed more than anything else was to shut off my mind. This movie assisted me perfectly, as there was nothing in it to stimulate thought in anyone whose brain had evolved beyond nurf. The movie served a divine purpose, and now whenever I see *Earth Girls* on the video store shelf, I smile and think of it with great fondness. Party on, dudes!

Destiny Strikes Again

If we do not follow our spirit without hesitation, we will receive a memo from the "Wake Up and Get Your Butt in Gear Department." Usually such experiences are not pleasant, as life has to pry us away (often kicking and screaming) from our notion of how it should be. New York Governor Mario Cuomo noted, "Every time I do something that does not feel right, it ends up not turning out right." But such experiences do get the job done; when the dust has settled, we have undergone a major course correction, and once again we are destined for heaven in spite of our efforts to stay in hell.

I received a touching letter which eloquently described this process:

A few years ago I accepted a position in England. In preparation for leaving, I quit my current job, moved out of my house, and got rid of my car. I withdrew my savings to complete any outstanding debts, and allowed an ailing relationship a decent burial. With just two suitcases I was primed and simply awaited my departure date from my new British employer.

Instead of a working permit, I received a telegram. The whole thing was off! Once the initial shock was over, I remembered that my heart's desire was always to become a physician. The only way the Boss would ever get me to do it was to help me clear away a few minor details (house, car, furniture, money, job, lover). The initial shock lasted twenty-four hours, and I was in medical school four months later.

I will be an M.D. on February 22. In thinking back on it, I would never have done it if those things hadn't happened. My friends and family watched with awe as God weaved Its magic through the life of a thirty-one-year-old woman who lost everything, but went on to live out a dream. Yea for me!

A Zen maxim notes, "Now that my house has burned down, I have a much better view of the sky." This is grace. When we are too asleep or afraid to give ourselves what we want and need, the universe will step in and take care of us. We may then choose the path of ease or resistance, and either way we will ultimately arrive at the same destination. The choice of how we will get there is ours.

Whose Spirit are You Following?

As I watch my pet parrots, I notice that these zany creatures operate under a herd mentality. If I walk into the aviary to feed or play with them, one bird sets the standard for how the others will relate to me. If the first parrot who sees me is friendly and welcoming and jumps onto my arm to play, quickly the others follow suit. If, however, one of the birds decides to snarl at me and tries to peck me away, they all line up and act tough. They do not have much of a mind of their own.

My parrots are not so different from people. If we do not exercise our inner wisdom, we fall into herd consciousness, or "race thought," as metaphysicians describe it. We will think not with our own thoughts, but with those of the masses. A good question to answer is, *"If you are not using your mind, who is?"*

In many relationships one person sacrifices following her own spirit to follow that of her partner. This is never healthy, and always bears painful repercussions. One partner shuts down on heeding her own intuition in order to please or keep peace with the other. While many people convince themselves that they are dutifully acceding to their partner's wishes in the name of love, self-abuse is not loving. To deny who we are and deafen our ear to the inner guide, is worse than physical death. To die bodily is one thing, but to die spiritually is quite another.

Self-sacrifice inevitably snowballs into a boulder of resentment. After one has spent years putting aside her own heart's desires in favor of her partner's, upset hits the fan and she undergoes an angry and radical shift. (Remember the Jill-Out-of-the-Box housewife in *Fried Green Tomatoes* who, in her newfound liberation, took a mallet and skillsaw to her house and rearranged a few walls before her oppressively complacent husband came home from work one day?) The pendulum of self-sacrifice must eventually swing to the end of its tether, and as it sweeps back, the rebel explodes and goes off to assert her independence. (For a delightful portrayal of this process, see the film *Shirley Valentine*.) This is often a healthy act of self-honoring, as it vents the steam that has built perhaps over many years. But an even healthier thing to do is to not give away your power in the first place.

When I first got together with my partner Carrie, I was delighted that she wanted to do all the things that I enjoyed. She worked in my office, travelled with me, decorated our house as I wished, and in general mirrored my tastes. While I did not force any of these decisions on her, I was very pleased that she had the same wishes and tastes as me.

Not!

After several years Carrie had a violent reaction to following my lead, and became angry at me. We later discovered that she was really angry at herself for giving her power away to me. She then had to take off and purposely do her thing for a period of time. (The definition of her thing was anything that was not my thing.) Her shift was a natural reaction to self-abrogation. Eventually the pendulum swung back to the middle, and we recreated our relationship to honor her interests as well as mine.

Be wary of any relationship in which both partners want all the same things in the same way at the same time. While it is a blessing when two people share mutual interests, it is unnatural, unhealthy, and unrealistic for two people to be exactly alike all the time. When both people in a relationship seem identical, usually one person has sacrificed following his or her spirit in favor of a partner's. This will not last forever. Sooner or later the person who has denied himself will either psychically die of soul-starvation or blow up in resentment. To avoid such a dire destiny, pop the fantasy balloon before that point and honor individual differences as a source of color and artistry in a wholesome relationship.

The most successful relationships are those in which both partners are true to their own inner direction. If you are each following your spirit and find yourselves together, you will enjoy a divinely empowered relationship. If your spirits draw you in different directions, it will only hurt you to try to cling to a form that is not alive. Your prime responsibility is to listen to your heart and act on the deepest guidance you can feel. Put essence before form, and trust.

If you have to lie to maintain a relationship or a job, what good is it? To lie is to die. Good relationships can stand the test of truth. If both of you can live fully in your truth and be together, you've really got something going. If telling your truth destroys the relationship, the coupling lacks substance, and you would do better to recreate the relationship so it will stand the test of truth, or establish another one on more solid ground.

Have the courage to live your truth in relationship. To sell yourself out to keep another body next to yours is a poor bargain indeed, one which you will regret. You may have gained a partner, but you have lost your soul. As Meryl Streep declared in the film *Out of Africa*, "I don't want to come to the end of my life and find that I have lived someone else's dream."

Keep your soul, and you will attract a partner who will honor it. Or at the very least you will be able to sleep at night, knowing that your life is an expression of who you are, not who another is. Fear not – you will not walk alone.

ACTIVATION:

THE JOY SCALE

Call to mind an important choice before you, and narrow the decision down to two primary paths.
   Choice A:

   Choice B:

Close your eyes, take a deep breath, and imagine you have just committed to choice A. Visualize that you have just signed the contract, bought the property, or committed to the relationship. Notice the strongest feeling in your gut. It may be excitement, constriction, enthusiasm, or depression, for example.

   The strongest feelings elicited by Choice A:

Close your eyes again and try choice B on for size. You have just left the relationship, said "no" to the job, or called the realtor and told her that you will not be buying the property. Again search your inner sensation. Do you feel released, disappointed, empowered, or saddened?

   My strongest feelings elicited by Choice B:

You probably noticed that one choice made you feel more alive, free, or peaceful than the other. This path feels empowering, not constricting. Follow your heart.

Where's Waldo?

It is not unusual for people in service positions (and those in the public eye) to lose their identity in their role. Parents, teachers, health practitioners, psychotherapists, ministers, entertainers, and political figures often lose sight of their own self in an effort to please their clients or live up to the expectations of their family or followers. Then, after years of raising children or ministering to patients, Mr. Do-It-Well wakes up one morning horrified as he realizes, "I don't know who I am! I know the role into which I have been cast by my wife, children, and patients, but in the process I have lost myself." There is no greater shock than to realize that the one element missing from your life is you.

There is one way to regain and stay in touch with your personal destiny – *follow your spirit without hesitation*. The self you miss is not lost; it is just buried under adopted identities. To shed the layers of not-self, begin to tell the deepest truth you know about who you really are and what you would really love to be doing. Do not delay. He who hesitates is not only lost – he is dead. In *Dead Poets Society*, inspirational teacher John Keating cautions his students, "You must find your voice – for the longer you wait to begin, the less likely you will find it at all." *A Course in Miracles* advises us, "Delay means nothing in eternity, but in time it is tragic."

There is a popular series of children's books called *Where's Waldo?* Through a succession of clever cartoons, the reader traces the adventures of a fellow named Waldo who disappears in crowds. Each page of the puzzle book shows a densely populated scene, such as a huge beach or city park where hundreds or thousands of people are busily engaged in a myriad of activities. The reader's game is to find Waldo amidst the teeming throngs.

As I played *Where's Waldo?* I realized that the reader's challenge is not unlike our quest in life. We must find ourself in the midst of a crowd. We must keep sight of who we are as a unique individual and stay true to our chosen destiny even as millions of others are about their business. Sometimes our path is similar; sometimes it is different. Only you can know your personal calling.

Albert Einstein declared that "Few is the number of those who think with their own mind and feel with their own heart." It takes faith and courage to crane your head above the herd to see a broader horizon. If you look closely at herd behavior, you will see that it is not about living. It is about surviving, protecting, and adapting. As a divine being you deserve more than a fearful, guarded existence. You deserve a life of creative self-celebration. Be sure that you are thinking with your own mind and feeling with your own heart. Then you will be able to consistently find Waldo in even the largest crowds.

Enough to Say "No"

Cogent examples of those who follow someone else's spirit rather than their own are children who do not know how to say "no" to their parents, and parents who do not know how to say "no" to their children. In giving way to a child's demands, such parents discount the importance of heeding their own inner voice. In the long run, both parents and children lose in such a situation, and eventually they will each have to retrace their steps to the moment they stepped out of integrity, and then make another choice. *Self-worth and service to others are not mutually exclusive; they are one.*

Children, parents, students, patients, and friends need to hear "no" when "no" is the truth. If they do not hear it, they will not know how to say it, to themselves or others. My friend Lara visited me with her three-year-old son, who, the moment he entered my house, began to throw mushy bananas at the windows. In the name of teaching the boy freedom, his mother rarely set boundaries for her son, and she had a hard time getting him to stop. When I later discussed this genre of training with my counselor, she told me, "This is not true freedom; the child is not free to *not* throw bananas."

One of the primary trappings of codependent relationships is the inability to set boundaries. In a society in which many of us have suffered because we did not know how to maintain healthy limits, we are coming to recognize that we do a great service by claiming our sovereignty and upholding it. To not set limits with children, students, or business associates is a poor model of self-esteem. The statement behind your actions is, "I do not value myself enough to take care of myself." If, however, you demonstrate self-respect, your affirmation will serve your child or partner infinitely more than acceding to manipulations or tantrums that play on your sense of unworthiness. When you know what you are worth, you are impervious to fear-based political power-plays. An expert on self-actualization noted, *"It's important to let people know what you stand for. It's equally important to let them know what you won't stand for."*

Musician Scott Kalechstein[2] sings a stirring song about a woman who was sexually abused as a girl. The refrain commends her for eventually learning to love herself "enough to say 'no.'" Many of us have had a hard time saying "no." The key to learning to say "no" is remembering that a "no" to one thing, means a "yes" to another. A "no" to that which would hurt you or move you away from your right place is a "yes" to what will heal you and keep you on your purpose. When we are true to our spirit, we are true to others and all of life.

The "Yes" Behind "No"

Your spirit would not inspire you to ask for something unless you need it and the universe is able and willing to provide it. How, then, can you reframe "no" to find the "yes"?

1. *You may not need it.*

You may have asked for something that would not serve you to receive it, and so the "no" you hear is actually the voice of grace saying "yes" to your higher good and pointing you in its direction. St. Theresa noted that "more tears have been shed over answered prayers than unanswered prayers." Oscar Wilde echoed, "I have lived long enough to thank God for not answering all my prayers." Be thankful that grace intercedes when we are tempted to force something that might hurt us.

2. *Your package may be delivered by another carrier.*

The individual you have asked may not be ready or able to deal with your request. Perhaps he is caught in fear or misunderstanding, and cannot see clearly enough to know that your request is a worthy one. Perhaps he is not capable of handling the energy and ramifications of what you invite him to do; acting on it would overload his circuits. The person may give you a mundane reason for their denial, but more likely there is a benevolent spirit guiding them at a level of which both of you are unaware. The refusal, then, is not a statement about your lack of deservingness; it is a statement about the refuser's unreadiness, unconsciousness, unwillingness, or inappropriateness.

The delivery service is not as important as the item to be delivered; as long as it gets to you, the mission has been accomplished.

Consider these demonstrations of the above principle:

• The sculptor Rodin's father complained, "I have an idiot for a son." Described as the worst pupil in the school, Rodin failed three times to secure admittance to the school of art. His uncle called him "uneducable."

• After Fred Astaire's first screen test, the memo from the testing director of MGM read, "Can't act. . .Slightly bald. . .Can dance a little." (Astaire kept that memo over the fireplace in his Beverly Hills home.)

• The Beatles were turned down by ten recording companies before Capitol took them on. (Obviously the Beatles had a destiny on the planet; they were ultimately to affect billions of lives with their music and their consciousness.) They just kept knocking on doors until the right one opened.

• Richard Hooker's humorous war novel, M*A*S*H* was rejected by twenty-one publishers before Morrow decided to publish it. It became a runaway bestseller, spawning a blockbusting movie and one of the most successful television series of all time.[3]

What a loss it would have been if these gifted artists (and many like them) gave up because they were initially turned down! In light of the great entertainment and upliftment they brought to so many people, it is clear in retrospect that their rejections were not the result of their lack of talent, but a lack of vision on the part of those who judged them. Consider that your creative efforts may be just as (or more) valuable as those above, and do not let the small thinking of others stand between you and your destiny!

3. *You may not be willing to receive it.*

You may be harboring some ambivalence about your request; you may not be sure you want it, or you may hold some fear or sense of unworthiness about receiving it. (Sometimes the only fear that outweighs the fear of failure is the fear of success!) If you are less than fully confident about your request, the universe will mirror your doubt; you will "hire" someone to give you the answer you expect. If you believe you deserve "no," someone will say it to you. If you know you deserve "yes," that is the response you will receive. Your experience is not the result of external factors, but your own consciousness. As Emerson illustrated, "The sower may mistake and sow his seeds crookedly; the peas make no mistake, but come up and show his line." James Allen echoed, "Circumstances do not make the man – they reveal him."

If what you have requested is yours *by right of your consciousness*, keep asking, and it will come through another door. Sometimes the only difference between failure and success is persistence. Jesus told the parable of a woman who beseeched a corrupt judge to fulfill her petition. Finally he gave in, just to get her off his back. Jesus used this example to teach that if you pray for anything with enough fervor, the universe must supply it.

While travelling, I needed to change a plane flight on short notice. At that time airlines had many rules against changing tickets after they were issued, and I was having a hard time getting booked on the flight I needed. I spoke to several reservation agents, all of whom gave me a flat "no." As the situation was urgent, I just kept calling back until finally I got a reservation agent who said "yes." (Michael J. Fox later summarized this success principle in his film *For Love or Money*: "Nothing is impossible; 'impossible' just takes a few more phone calls.") No matter how many times you hear "no," sooner or later someone will say "yes." It is said that "the only time you fail is the last time you try." Say "yes" to your own good, and watch life line up to take care of you as you honor yourself.

Master Key:

Do What You Are Here to Do.

I keep in mind a motto that helps me stay on purpose:

The main thing is to keep the main thing the main thing.

During Paul Simon's historic *Rhythm of the Saints* world tour, his band experienced violent resistance on the eve of their concert in South Africa. The joining of black and white musicians posed a threat to fearful minds of those in that country who believed that the races should be separate. Several anarchistic groups announced bomb threats, and horrific rumors ran rampant. The concert made international newspaper headlines as tension mounted to an excruciating degree.

The day before the scheduled concert, the band met to search their souls and decide if they would go ahead with the program in the face of possible violence. Round and round the debate went, with strong arguments for and against each viewpoint.

Then a proud black drummer stood and spoke: "I am a musician. This is what I am on earth to do. I would rather die on stage playing music than live in fear offstage, without fulfilling my purpose."

The man's truth rang deeply in the hearts of his colleagues. The group agreed to go on with the program. Remarkably, the entire concert was free of violence, and the event was a milestone in the culture. The voice of Spirit spoke loud and clear; it was truly the rhythm of the saints.

Pull the Plug

You cannot be doing what you are here to do while continuing to do what you are not here to do. Many people tell me, "I want to follow my spirit, but what am I supposed to do if I can't hear my inner voice?" Others report, "I do not know what I am supposed to be doing, but I do know that what I am doing is not it." But if you know that this is *not* it, there must be a place in you (though momentarily shrouded) that knows what *is* it. That's an excellent starting point.

The next step is to stop doing what is *not* it, so you can make a space for what *is* it to show up. This is where a leap of faith is required. Begin to release anything in your life that does not fit, serve, or honor you. Start with the simple task of going through your closets and removing any clothes that do not fit, you do not like, and have not worn. (Just because you used to like something does not mean that you must keep it now.) This is a good metaphor for the broader process of releasing anything in your life that does not befit you.

Walt Whitman boldly advised, *"Dismiss whatever insults your soul."* In letting go of what is not you, you may stir up some uncomfortable issues within yourself and others. Some may complain that "you are no longer the person I thought you were," and that is true. You are no longer the person *you* thought you were, either. There is more to you than you were expressing, and the time has come for you to step forward in courage and confidence. The caterpillars look up at the butterfly and mutter, "You'll never get *me* up in one of those things." What the earthbound creatures do not realize is that they *are* one of those things. One day, when the time is right, they will look down amidst free flight and understand the entire process from a grand overview.

As you extricate yourself from a fishbowl existence, you may make waves around you – but that is far better than drowning in the kiddie pool. If those who complain about your changes are at risk of drowning with you, you may be doing them a far greater service by standing up and walking out, than by doing the dead man float with them. Go ahead and make some waves – an entire ocean awaits!

ACTIVATION:

GETTING FREE OF WHAT IS NOT ME

Rate your activities on a joy scale of 1 (least) to 10 (highest).

Activity	Joy Value	Activity	Joy Value
1.		11.	
2.		12.	
3.		13.	
4.		14.	
5.		15.	
6.		16.	
7.		17.	
8.		18.	
9.		19.	
10.		20.	

Considering the activities you rated 3 or less:

Activity	Next Step I Could Take To Release

Considering the activities you rated 7 or above:

Activity	Next Step I Could Take to Increase

Responsible Living

"But if everyone followed their spirit without hesitation, the world would be swallowed up in chaos!" you might reasonably contend. "Self-centered egomaniacs would go around raping and pillaging. There would be no integrity, no commitment, nothing would get done, and the world would fall apart."

The scenario just described is exactly the world engendered when we do *not* follow our spirit without hesitation. The message is to follow your spirit, not your fear, anger, desire to run away, current bodily sensation, or mass hysteria.

As spiritual beings, our nature is loving, and so to follow your spirit is to live in the constant expression of love. Love does not go around raping, pillaging, or hurting others. Love seeks to serve and create peace and harmony.

To follow your spirit is to be fully responsible. Responsible means, "able to respond." Who knows better how to respond in any situation than God? And by what means would God speak to you except through the deepest inclinations of your heart?

Those who purport to be following their spirit, and then launch out on bizarre campaigns causing pain and confusion, are not following the voice of love. Neither does following your spirit mean running away from what you are afraid to face. To the contrary, Spirit delights in transforming painful situations by moving beyond separateness to establish unity. It does not indulge behaviors that are out of integrity. To follow your spirit is to be constantly moving toward clarity and resolution.

Your spirit is infinitely more responsible than any personality could possibly be. Spirit is very practical when it comes to keeping things running smoothly and efficiently; the God within you recognizes that human affairs usually work best when we do what we say we are going to do. We empower ourselves and others when we follow through on our word. In so doing we bring integrity to our affairs, and bolster trust and confidence in our relationships.

If, however, you made an agreement in unconsciousness, and keeping that agreement would hurt you or others to go ahead with it, you will only serve yourself and others to take another course. Our commitment to truth must supersede any agreement we make on the plane of human affairs. Spirit will not ask you to undo a commitment unless there is a really good reason.

Sometimes our spirit asks us to break a smaller agreement to keep a greater one. If you meditate on a situation and you keep receiving guidance to take a different course, you must act on it. Even if you do not see the whole picture at the time, there is a reason that Spirit is speaking to your heart. Communicate honestly and directly to the person with whom you have made the agreement, and tell them of your desired plans. At such a time the sincerity of your conviction is your best friend; do not fabricate other reasons or feign apologies. If the other person loves and supports you, they will recognize and honor the truth of your being. (They may even acknowledge that they were having a similar inclination.) You may be able to suggest an alternative arrangement that will leave the other person feeling satisfied and cared for, and still allow you to move ahead as desired. Simply stating your feeling may move the situation to the next level; you may then choose to continue what you were doing, or find a previously unseen option. If you are true to the voice of Spirit, at a later time everyone involved will realize that the change came for the good of all concerned.

Tango and Waltz

Ken Keyes Jr., author of *Handbook to Higher Consciousness*, likens our interactions to couples dancing at a grand ball. If you are immersed in a tango and someone invites you to waltz, it would be foolish to accept; you would end up tripping over one another's feet, and neither of you will enjoy the dance. When someone in your daily life asks you to perform a function that is distasteful to your spirit, or you find yourself fox trotting with someone who is doing a samba, the greatest service you can offer is to acknowledge that you are doing different dances. Then both of you are free to join with other partners who will be aligned with the steps you enjoy taking.

There is nothing wrong with doing different dances; both the tango and waltz are lovely and worth undertaking for the sheer joy of the ball. To acknowledge that two dances are not compatible does not imply judgment or rejection. Two people can maintain tremendous love and mutual appreciation as they agree that their steps do not match at the moment. It is a statement of honor and respect to acknowledge that both of your dances are worthwhile, and you deserve partners who match your energies. Perhaps you will come together at another time in another way, to enjoy another kind of dance that is more rewarding than crunching each other's toes.

This principle applies not simply to romantic or marital relationships; the great dance includes *everything* – friendships, careers, and the simple act of deciding where we will eat for lunch or what movie we will attend. One foundation principle composes the dance floor: you must trust that your inclinations and intuition are good and valid. You must know that you are worth being happy, and so is everyone else. And you must hold the high vision that even if things do not seem to be merging at the moment, there is a grander plan that will find everything in its right place for the right purpose and highest results.

Ideally, if everyone followed their spirit without hesitation, agreements, commitments, and future plans would be unnecessary. In such a world each person would be so attuned to the will of God that everyone would always be in their right place at the right time, everything would be taken care of, and everyone would be happy. While we may live in a world that does not currently reflect the manifestation of such intrinsic self-trust, we can begin to create it by taking steps to live our outer life in accord with our inner vision.

Write for You

I attended a writers conference headlined by an impressive array of literary luminaries. Some of the world's most prominent authors, publishers, screenwriters, agents, and publicists delivered outstanding addresses on what it takes to be a successful writer in today's market. I was astounded that every distinguished lecturer, without exception, bore the same message: *follow your passion; write from your heart; say what you personally have to say; do not write for mass appeal – write for yourself.* When an audience member asked the editor-in-chief of one of the world's largest publishing houses, "What kind of material are you looking for?" the publisher answered, "We are not looking for any particular kind of material; we are looking for what *you* have to offer. Write what turns you on, what is meaningful to you, and that will be your best ticket to success."

Everything happening on the planet now is calling us to take our power back from outer authorities and return it to the God within, where it belongs. No one knows better than yourself, what you need to do in any situation. Others can counsel, advise, and inspire, but ultimately you must act on the guidance that resonates in your soul. You are the one who is going to have to live with your decision, and therefore you are the only one who can make it. But you will not be alone. There dwells within you a guide to support and comfort you. Go within for your answer, for there it awaits.

A Win-Win Universe

The universe is set up to serve everyone simultaneously; the Bible tells us that God knows every sparrow, and every hair on your head. If you are attuned to the will of love, you will find that your blessings are joined with those of others. You cannot be happy at the expense of another, and another's happiness can never take away from your own. If you can find the courage to trust and act on your intuition in spite of appearances, in the long run you will be amazed at how well your act serves everyone.

I received a letter from a woman who believed I was her soulmate. After searching my heart for an honest and loving response, I told her that while I respected her feelings, I did not believe that I was her mate. I explained that I appreciated who she was, as well as our friendship, but I did not feel moved to pursue the kind of relationship to which she was inviting me. At the personality level, I feared that I might hurt her or lose her friendship, but at a soul level I knew that I had to speak the deepest truth I knew.

A year later I received a touching letter from this woman telling me, "Thank you for pushing me away gently. It was exactly what I needed to dismantle my fantasy and reclaim the power I had given away to you."

The whole situation was a blessing to both of us. She needed to express her heart's prompting, and I needed to respond with mine. The interaction drew the best out of both of us, and we both won.

Following your spirit requires trust in God. You must have faith that there is a bigger plan than meets the eye, deeper principles running the universe than the rules dictated by society, and a grander destiny than your past conditioning. It means that the thinking mind is not the sole or final arbiter of what will serve the highest good. It means extricating your behavior from the expectations of others, and transferring authority from outer demands to inner knowingness. It means living a life infinitely more free and alive than the one that most people on the planet have settled for. It means launching out as a pioneer of freedom in a world where imprisonment has become the norm. It means releasing preconceived notions in favor of the knowing of your heart. It means being *you* and living as what *you* are, without apology or explanation.

The personality is little more than an adaptive defense system to protect the tiny bit of life force that remains with us after we have withdrawn our spirit because we decided that this world is not a safe place. To consult the personality as an authority on truth and right action is tantamount to walking into a mental institution and asking the first patient you see what you should do with the rest of your life. Your personality is your mask of choice in a play of madness. How much truth and comfort can it give you? Just the tiniest amount to adapt to an insane world. Is this a worthy guide to direct you to the peace and power of heaven?

A guide is available, and It lives within your heart. The voice of Spirit speaks to you as you read these words. It whispers to you throughout the day and into the night. To hear the call of love, you must listen. You must turn your attention away from feverish dreams and sit quietly before the altar of peace. You must be open and willing to receive the counsel of strength, and act on it. The wisdom of God can do no more for you than it can do through you. Listen, and you shall hear. Act, and you shall see. Be, and you shall live.

Stop this day and night with me
and you shall possess the origin of all poems,
You shall possess the good of the earth and sun. . .
You shall no longer take things at second or third hand,
nor look through the eyes of the dead,
nor feed on the spectres of books,
You shall not look through my eyes either,
nor take things from me,
You shall listen to all sides
and filter them from your self. . .

I know that the hand of God is the promise of my own.
— Walt Whitman, *Song of Myself*

CARPE DIEM!

If you were going to die soon and had only one phone call you could make, who would you call and what would you say? And why are you waiting?

– Stephen Levine

"*C*arpe diem – Seize the day!" I told a large seminar audience. Then I asked the assembly, "What dreams are you waiting to put into action?"

A woman named Cindy raised her hand and admitted that she had been wanting to invite a certain man to an upcoming party, but out of fear of rejection she kept putting off calling him.

I turned to the sponsor of the program and asked, "Can Cindy use the phone in your office?"

"Certainly."

"Would you call him now?" I invited Cindy.

"Now?"

"Now."

"Yes, I will," Cindy answered. "This is my moment."

As Cindy stood up to go to the telephone, an outburst of excited applause surged through the auditorium. The group was rooting for Cindy – they appreciated the courage she mobilized to make her vision a reality.

When Cindy returned about ten minutes later I asked her, "How did it go?"

"I got a date!" she announced with a huge grin.

The assembly burst forth with a round of cheers and a

standing ovation – the most enthusiastic swell of spontaneous group support I have ever experienced in such a program. The people in that room were electrified by Cindy's triumph over her sense of limits; her courage wakened in many the possibility that we do not have to wait to ask for what we want.

When I returned the following year, Cindy excitedly introduced me to her new husband – the man she had called the night of our seminar! There is a reason for our inner promptings, and we must give the universe a chance to fulfill them. Now.

ACTIVATION:

MAKING NOW COUNT

Imagine that you have 24 hours to live.
Who would you call, and what would you say?

Name of Person   *What I Would Say*

Continue on a separate sheet of paper, if necessary.

Too Young to Settle

My friend Lisa was telling me about her divorce. "What was the key factor that moved you to leave?" I asked her.

"One day I woke up and realized that twenty-five was too young to settle for a life without passion," Lisa answered.

I thought about it. Twenty-five *is* too young to settle for a life without passion. Thirty-seven is too young to settle for a life without passion. Eighty-three is too young to settle for a life without passion. *Any age* is too young to settle for a life without passion.

Life is like a post card on which we write trivial messages in big letters and then squeeze what we really want to say in little letters around the margins. It's also like a telephone answering machine on which you have just so much time to leave a message. Have you ever left a message on someone's machine, and been cut off by a loud annoying beep right in the middle of a sentence? Then you had to call back to record what you really wanted to say. After that happened to me a few times, I realized that I may not have unlimited time to talk on someone's answering machine. Now I give the most important information first, just in case I am cut off. If I have time left, I leave more casual information.

We never really know how much time we have to leave the message we came to impart to the world. It may be one year or a hundred. It's a very wise practice to do first things first; write the most important things in big letters first, and record what you really want to say before you are interrupted. Sing your most cherished song now, and if you have some extra time you can sing some variations on the theme. Then you won't have to call back to finish your message.

ACTIVATION:

DO IT NOW

Go back to the list you made in the *Making Now Count*
Activation above. Put this book down, go to the telephone, and call the appropriate people. Remember that
your purpose is not to elicit a particular response, but to
tell the deepest truth you know.

Just Be Here

I have a ten-year-old mentor who keeps me honest. One day
as Shanera and I were driving home from our visit to Parrot
Jungle, she was playing with a little stuffed bunny I had bought
her. Feeling bored during the long drive, I decided to make some
conversation in hopes that Shanera would say something humorous or profound.

"So, Shanera, how about if you tell me the story of your
life?" I invited her.

Without looking up, she answered seriously, "Right now the
story of my life is getting this price tag off of this bunny's ear!"

Out of the mouths of babes. . .

I asked another young friend, Tasha, "What is the purpose of
life?" She thought for a moment, giggled, and suggested, "Just
be here!"

We are attracted to children because they live in the kingdom
of heaven, even while their feet touch earth. They do not stake
their joy on future plans. They are fully present, and we love to
bask in their joy.

At the other end of the spectrum, some older people have
transcended the illusion of age and limitation, and have come full
circle to live in the glory of the moment. My friend Amalia

Frank, at over eighty years of chronological age, is a minister with a youthful and vivacious spirit. While having lunch with Amalia, I told her that she reminded me of my eighty-three-year-old friend Tensie, who showed me a video of her recent attendance at an underwater wedding.

"Now that's a good one!" Amalia laughed. "An underwater wedding!. . .I have performed weddings on boats, but I haven't done one underwater yet."

Yet! Now there it is, I thought. *Yet.* At eighty-two, most people are packing it in or living in the past. But here Amalia is open and looking forward to more outrageous experiences. Age is not a weight to Amalia. She lives today, and she is free.

How Old are You?

Hall of Fame baseball pitcher Satchel Page asked, "How old would you be if you didn't know how old you were?" Think about that for a moment. Close your eyes and mentally release any sense of age associated with what you have been told. How old do you feel?

The concept of age is a hypnotic hype that has kept humanity downtrodden throughout history. Age has no reality or power except that which we give it. Time is an illusion, an invention of the separated mind, and any offspring of the concept of time, such as age, is equally unreal. I saw a bumper sticker declaring, "Time is what keeps everything from happening at once." Stated metaphysically, we might say that "without time we would exist in a state of eternal oneness."

Buckminster Fuller noted that "human beings are the only creatures on the planet who tell time and believe they have to earn a living." While time assists us to make and keep agreements on the worldly plane, it does not point us to our real identity, which is far beyond time. When my teacher Hilda was asked, "How old are you?" she answered, "I was never born and I will never die." Hilda was not referring to her physical body, which came and went. She was affirming her spiritual identity, which cannot be ravaged or touched by physical elements. Perhaps that is why Hilda was such a powerful teacher. Over her lifetime she taught and healed many thousands of people, and the students ultimately affected by her teachings number in the millions. Indeed the effects of her service span far beyond one lifetime.[1]

If we wish to soar beyond age, it is very helpful to observe people who are empowered, not limited by their physical years. In her ninth decade, my friend Tensie is more vibrant and alive than most people in their twenties. When I recently ran into Tensie in a restaurant, she winked at me from beneath her trademark straw hat, and apologized for not being able to sit with me longer; she was on her way to macrame class at the local artists' collective. Then she would have dinner at the gourmet deli before going to her evening class on "writing your autobiography as a therapeutic tool." Tensie's list of classes to be taken, trips to be set off on, and dreams to be fulfilled is longer than the medical dossiers of most people her age. Instead of filling the book of her life with diseases and infirmities, she has filled it with passionate adventures and golden memories. It is said that "lovers make a fool of time," and those who simply love life do the same.

Are You as Happy as Your Dog?

A fellow at one of my workshops confessed, "For years I was so miserable that I prayed to God daily to let me wake up as happy as my dog!"

I went home and thought about it. Am I as happy as my dog? Hmmmm.

I began to observe my dog Munchie, who is happy all the time. This seven-pound fuzzball is the most joyful creature I have ever seen. He lives in a state of constant delight. Deducing that this furry creature knew something I didn't know (or at least didn't remember), I decided to study Munchie's attitude and activities in the hope that I, too, might one day wake up as happy as he is.

The key to Munchie's happiness is that he lives entirely in the here and now. He has no sense of the past or future, and he is fully present with whatever is happening. You will not find Munchie at the local bar nursing a beer over lost love. He has no lost love. He loves whatever is in front of him.

Munchie regularly shows up at the front door asking to come in and play with me. Depending on what I am doing and how muddy his feet are, sometimes I let him in. The moment I open the door, he *charges* in. He doesn't give me a moment to change my mind. He knows what he wants, asks for it, and seizes his opportunity the instant it is offered. Munchie is a master of *Carpe Diem*.

When I arrive home, Munchie greets me enthusiastically. As soon as he hears my car pull up to the garage, he drops whatever he is doing anywhere on the property, and *zooms* to meet me. He is so delighted to see me that he barks and cries simultaneously, wags his tail so hard that he wipes up the garage floor with his furry butt, and he pees. (Munchie taught me the meaning of the phrase, "I could hardly contain myself!") This dog *lives* the attitude of gratitude.

Munchie offers me the same whole-hearted greeting no matter how long I have been gone. Whether I have been away for an afternoon or a month, he gives me the full red carpet welcome. When I come home after a long time he doesn't sit on his haunches with his arms folded and soberly announce, "I think it's time we discussed your commitment to our relationship." No, he is just happy to see me, and he lets me know it.

When I am not home Munchie finds plenty of other amusements. He chases cats, sniffs dead critters, naps, and tries to mount the German shepherd next door. (He's a possibility thinker!) Munchie, as far I can tell, is an enlightened being. Perhaps, if I play my cards right, one day I will wake up as happy as him.

ACTIVATION:

ARE YOU AS HAPPY AS YOUR DOG?

Observe your dog, cat, bird, or other pet, and note below what they teach you about how you might live your own life more fully:

Pet's Activity   *What My Pet is Teaching Me*

106

Don't Wait Until You Wish You Had Done It

One of the most powerful ways to deepen the quality of a relationship is to imagine that today is the only day you have with that person. When feeling upset with a friend or family member, ask yourself how would you be feeling and acting differently if you knew that you would not see this person after midnight tonight. You would probably experience more appreciation for the gifts they brought you, and be less interested in the things they did which disturbed you. And you would probably tell them of your love for them.

Don't wait until someone is on their deathbed before you express your love for them. I learned a tremendous lesson in priorities when my mother was passing on. During her life she had a number of habits that annoyed me. She was a heavy smoker, and in spite of my objections, she would ask me to go to the store to buy her cigarettes. She criticized my eating habits, accusing me of living on "bird food." When we went to the supermarket together, she would stand at the check out counter and check each item against the receipt to make sure she wasn't overcharged. (After years of being embarrassed by this, I would just go to the car and wait for her.)

As my mother lay before me during her final days, the life force waning from her tired body, all of my upsets seemed so trivial and unimportant in the face of the depth and breadth of my love and appreciation for her and our relationship. I would have traded everything in those last aching moments for the chance to take her to the supermarket or sit down to one of her homemade meals. I would have gladly gone to the store to get her some cigarettes; even my criticisms of smoking felt petty in the light of the life we shared. Later, when I saw the movie *Ghost*, I was touched by Patrick Swayze's final line before he merged into the light: *"It's amazing. . .We take all the love with us."*

Right now there are perhaps many more things you would like to say to those who are or have been close to you. You may have all kinds of reasons and rationalizations about why you cannot be fully in your truth with them now. But we never really know how much time we have with a dear one. Quality living is a paradox: *to make this moment last forever, act as if it is your last.* Don't wait until someone has left your life before you recognize the importance of communicating with them. The telephone call you have been putting off, may be the most important call you will ever make.

The Door Is Still Open

In my seminars I do a lot of work with people who wish to complete communications with loved ones who have left their life through death or separation. Some of the most powerful healings I have observed are those which occur when we speak from our heart to those who are important to us – even if they are not physically present.

Because the real issues of relationships live *within* us rather then between us, it is possible to heal incomplete relationships even after the other person is physically unavailable, or departed. Since we are spiritual beings, it is possible to call anyone to us in spirit at anytime and communicate with their essence. Remember that life is not so much about bodies as it is about soul. Speak the words that will bring release to your soul, and you will have mastered the great invitation of the relationship.

ACTIVATION:

COMPLETING COMMUNICATIONS WITH LOVED ONES

1. Make a list of the people no longer in your life, to whom you have more to say. Include those who have passed on and those from whom you have become separated physically or emotionally. Your communications may be expressions of love and gratitude, or upsets you have denied or withheld.

Write a letter to each one, telling them <u>everything</u> you want to say. Do not leave any thoughts or feelings uncommunicated. You may or may not send the letter. After you write it, you will know what to do with it.

2. Sit with a good friend or therapist and imagine that they are, one by one, each of the people on your list above. Tell them everything you would like to say. Your friend's role is simply to listen lovingly; they are not to respond with words.

3. <u>When appropriate</u>, find the people you need to talk to. (Sometimes wisdom dictates that we simply express ourself for our own sake, and we release the other person to live their new life, as well as ourself.) If you feel moved to contact the person directly, hold a prayerful vision of peaceful completion and tell them what is in your heart.

Mastering the Moment

If you are going to change your life for the better, the only time to do it is *now*. Time and again I have seen ordinary people mobilize extraordinary courage to make their dreams come true. We are masters at finding all manner of excuses and rationalizations for postponing our joy and fulfilling our purpose. Now let us take the power we have offered to procrastination, and re-channel it into action. Every one of us has the ability to live our vision, and we will. The question is not *if*, but *when*. The timing of our destiny is up to us. There is no power outside of us that can stop us from doing what we came here to do. All power and all love reside within us.

Our one responsibility is to lift this moment to the highest and celebrate it with all our heart. It is said that "the past is like a cancelled check, the future is like a promissory note, and the present is cash in hand." Take what you have, and make what you want. Now is the moment you have been waiting for, and you are the one you have been waiting for to live it.

If not now, when?
                                                    – The Talmud

THERE AIN'T NO FUTURE
IN THE PAST

*The only wholly true statement that can be made
about the past is that it is not here.*
– A Course in Miracles

From Nowhere to Now Here

"I'm sorry sir; we don't show a reservation for you." I couldn't believe I was hearing the hotel clerk utter the frequent traveller's most dreaded greeting.

I turned to the sponsor of the program I had come to present. Upset, she engaged the clerk in a polite but thinly-veiled argument over whose fault it was that the reservation had been lost. For several minutes the sponsor told the clerk where and when and how the reservation had been made, and the clerk kept defending herself and the hotel, reiterating that they had no record of my reservation. The conversation slipped into a tailspin.

Finally, I interrupted the debate: "Do you have a room for me now?" I inquired. A startled look washed over both women's faces. The clerk checked her computer. "Yes, we do." We all laughed as we realized that we had become more fascinated with the problem than the solution.

Within minutes I was stretched out in a comfortable bed. As my head nestled into the soft pillow, I considered the vanity of the "blame and defend" conversation I had beheld. I have been involved in many of them. They go round and round, centered on what went wrong and whose fault it was. Guilt is traded, blame is shifted, and usually both parties end up feeling worse than when they began.

Breakthrough success experts tell us that problems persist because we ask the wrong questions in attempting to solve them. The critical shift, they suggest, lies in formulating a question that will lead us ahead to the answer rather than back to the error. Instead of "What went wrong?" a more practical question is, "What do we need to do *now* to accomplish what we want?" Such refocusing can make all the difference between floundering in the past and succeeding in the present.

Psychic Cryogenics

Cryogenics is the science of freezing dead bodies with the hope of reviving them at a later time. When we keep ourselves and our friends frozen in our mind (holding one another to our mental pictures of what we *were* rather than what we *are*), we engage in psychic cryogenics. We keep our old images of self and others frozen, and do not thaw them out. Surely none of us want to be limited by what we were; we want the freedom and power to be new and known as our current self, not our historical image.

A long-time friend of mine attended one of my seminars. The last time I had seen Cora was a year before the workshop, when she had literally died in the hospital and was revived. My predominant memory of Cora was that of a weak, heavily-medicated chronic asthma patient with a Medusa-like tangle of tubes and electrodes piping her vital signs in and out of a massive medical mainframe.

When Cora showed up at the retreat, I was amazed to see that she had made a remarkable recovery. She had lost a great deal of weight, gotten free of her medication, and she looked more vital and radiant than I had ever seen her. Cora was a walking miracle.

Our retreat included a hike up a mountain. When we arrived at the trailhead, I became concerned about Cora; images of her asthma machines, medications, and mortifications came to mind; I remembered seeing her labor just to walk from her living room couch to the bathroom. I worried that this moderately steep hike would be too much for her. Not wanting to single Cora out, I diplomatically announced to the group that anyone who felt that the climb was too rigorous could take an easier walk around a lake at the base of the mountain.

To my surprise, no one chose the lighter hike, including Cora. Instead, Cora began to lead the group up the mountain! "This is amazing!" I thought, as the middle-aged woman set a rigorous clip. I hustled to second place in the line of hikers, right behind Cora, thinking that I could support her if she got winded. But she didn't get winded, and she didn't even look tired. Cora kept the same dynamic pace until we reached our destination after half an hour of trekking.

I kept looking at Cora in disbelief. Was this the same woman whose doctors had not long ago advised her immediate family to call the relatives to come and say their goodbyes?

No, it was not the same woman. The sick woman I remembered had died and been resurrected as healthy. It was only in my thoughts that I maintained the image of an ill Cora. I was trying to stuff a new and expanded being into a tiny box to which I consigned her in my mind.

Walking down the hill (still trying to keep up with Cora) I realized that I had just seen a most profound model of the way that we keep each other bound to our past – and can liberate ourselves to be entirely new in the present. We must be open to seeing new and being new. Otherwise we freeze our friends and ourselves as we were, and we die to the new life of the moment.

Dead or Alive?

When I taught spiritual development classes in adult schools and colleges, one of the first comments my students would make after a short time was, "I'm losing my old friends!"

My response was, "Congratulations! It's only when you keep your old friends forever that you know you are in trouble."

We do, of course, have some dear lifetime friends with whom we walk and share quality experiences for many years. In such relationships, we usually grow side by side and support each other through inner and outer changes. The kind of friendships that are no loss to lose are those in which we try to maintain the status quo at the expense of new realities that want to emerge. This is not true friendship. Real friendship is like canoeing down a river with a buddy; each of us has to navigate our own canoe, while we ride near one another and help each other if we fall out. Frozen relationship, on the other hand, is like two people anxiously clinging to the shore out of fear of the journey.

Thinking further about Cora's resurrection, I realized that if unchecked, psychic cryogenics leads to spiritual necrophilia. Necrophilia is a sexual perversion in which someone has sex with corpses. While this image is downright repulsive to most people (although you may argue that in your marriage you have been making love to a corpse for years) it is an appropriate metaphor. To engage in any way with the dead past is a form of necrophilia. From the ego's point of view (the motto of which is "maintain the known at all costs, even if the known stinks") such behavior is sound; the past is familiar and seems safer than launching out to deal with real life, which requires risk to navigate. But life in the now offers us something the past cannot – wondrous opportunities to feel the power of the moment and become even more alive. To negotiate lovemaking with a living being may be more challenging than cavorting in mortuaries, but it is our only hope to truly live. Since I saw Cora master that mountain, I realized *anything* is possible. We need to keep open to reap the rewards of possibility, not past, thinking.

ACTIVATION:

RADICAL PASTECTOMY

Get rid of anything in your life that ties you to the past.

1. Go through your closets and dressers and remove any items that you have not worn in one year. Give them away, sell them, or throw them away.

2. Go through your papers, cards, letters, books, photos, and gifts, and discard everything that does not empower you in the present moment. Hold the object in your hand and feel the energy It evokes within you. If it brings you happiness, keep It; if it does nothing or depletes your energy, get rid of it. Let everything in your personal environment strengthen you to be the highest self you can envision.

3. Make a written list of your relationships, noting any relationships that are built on who you were rather than who you are. Do certain friendships draw you into an old way of life that you are no longer living? After you have noted them, lovingly release them.

No Regrets

Indulging in the past robs us of the delight of the moment. Regret depletes our precious life force when we look back on mistakes we made and berate ourselves for not doing it right or better. We may even wax melancholy or become depressed as we wonder how much happier our life might be if we had made better choices.

We can, however, replug the holes in our bucket of aliveness out of which regret drains our sense of fulfillment. We must realize that *if we could have done it better, we would have.* In any given situation each of us does the best we can with what we know at the time. If we knew better, we would have done it. Perhaps the whole situation arose to open us to a more rewarding way of doing it. Sometimes we learn by doing something right, and sometimes we learn by doing it wrong; the result is the same. When learning to ride a bicycle, sometimes you learn by falling, and sometimes you learn by balancing. Every experience during the learning process ultimately leads to mastery. It is only the little mind that does not see that errors, as well as successes, contribute to learning.

If you knew how to do it all perfectly you wouldn't be here in the first place. The earth assists us to learn by graphically manifesting the results of our beliefs, sometimes quite rapidly.

The human experience allows us to develop and refine our divine qualities. If only perfect people were allowed to be born, none of us would be here. Fortunately, mastery is not a prerequisite for arriving on earth; it is the goal of our journey. Learning by doing is the way evolution progresses. If parents had to be perfect before they had children, no more children would be born. The way to become a good parent is to be a parent. You learn as you do. If teachers had to wait until they knew everything to teach, there would be no teaching. We learn as we teach. And we master as we live.

Another antidote to regret is to understand that *missed opportunities will come again.* Opportunities show up because our consciousness is ripe for them. If you are inwardly ready to draw a new level of experience into your life, and a particular opportunity passes you by, don't worry – it will show up again. This principle is called *The Right of Consciousness.* Everything that comes to you, and everything you have, is drawn to you by the magnetic strength of your mind and heart. Particular avenues for the events may come and go, but as long as you hold the same consciousness, you will surely have another chance.

If you deserve something or need it, it will be there. You do not have to struggle or manipulate to get it or hold onto it. Another door will open. Just be sure that you show up to walk through it, and do not miss the next opportunity because you are bemoaning missing the last one.

A third answer to regret is to *bless and release the people and experiences that no longer serve us.* While certain experiences will come to us again by right of consciousness, there are other experiences that will not come to us again, precisely because our consciousness has grown beyond them. You do not want to demand to repeat or continue an experience from which you have graduated. You have mastered that plateau of life, and now you are ready for something better. Do not weep over your lost good. *There is no such thing as lost good.* If something is good for you, it is available now. Just because something was good for you once does not mean it would serve you now. Don't sit around and dream about yesterday's dessert; it is stale now. There is a new treat in store, if you will but open your eyes to see it, and expand your heart to accept it.

Romancing the Bone

Another way we distract ourselves from the power, magic, and potential of the moment is by nostalgically *romanticizing the past.* "That was such a great time in my life," we sigh. "I wish I could get that feeling back now." Or "Maybe I should have held onto that relationship!"

When the perfume of wistful longing wafts into your psychic domain, you must be able to discern between *fantasy* and *reality*. Fantasies are not confined to the future; they also color the past. Just as we delude ourselves with imaginary future relationships, we lose ourselves in romantic overlays on the past.

When I was in relationship with Maureen, she regularly broke our dates. Nearly every time we were to get together, she phoned me at the last minute and told me that an emergency had come up and she needed to drive one of her children somewhere. Or she would show up hours late with the same apology. Looking back now, I see that Maureen was using her children as an excuse to avoid intimacy and the issues of our relationship. (I also had my fears and resistances.) After a long and frustrating year, Maureen and I agreed to let go of trying to have a relationship. We lovingly blessed each other and parted.

During the following six months I began to wonder if I had made a mistake in saying goodbye to Maureen. I remembered the romance we had enjoyed at the beginning of our relationship, as well as a few moments during which Maureen and I seemed fully present with one another. (Meanwhile I entirely disregarded the other ninety-five percent of our time together, which was painful). I fostered Hollywood-scale fantasies that Maureen was indeed my soulmate, and I had missed my opportunity to be with her. Subsequently I was distracted from being present in any new relationships because my reveries were with Maureen.

Finally I found the courage to call Maureen and tell her, "I really miss you and I would like to get together with you."

"Yes, I miss you, too," she replied. "I want to see you, too."

We made a date for Thursday evening, until which I spent most of my time humming *"Back in the Saddle Again,"* anticipating the rekindling of our love.

Late Thursday afternoon I received a telephone call from Maureen. "Gee, I'm sorry," she told me; "Kevin needs a ride to karate school, so I guess I won't be able to make it tonight."

After we hung up I sat back and had a good laugh. The light of reality flooded over the screen of my romantic movie as I remembered why we hadn't been able to have a relationship.

I was glad I called Maureen. Our last interaction dashed my remaining fantasies – which was exactly what I needed. I was then able to truly release Maureen and get on with my life.

Romanticizing past relationships often stems from a deeper pattern of romanticizing our parent of the opposite sex. As John Bradshaw explains, we idealize this parent in our memory as we fail to acknowledge their human shortcomings. This can be a serious hindrance to being open to participate in quality relationships, as we compare our human partner to an angelic ideal with which it is impossible for them to compete.

If we are to enjoy rewarding relationships, we must be fully present with them. We must tell the truth about our past, let the dead rest in peace, and not superimpose fantasies or idealized parents over the face of our present loved one. Then and only then will we see them as they truly are.

The Past Isn't What it Used to Be

Dr. Jerry Jampolsky defines forgiveness as "giving up all hope for a better past." The most powerful way to release ourselves from a painful past is to *reframe* situations that have occurred. To reframe, take a situation which is distorted by regret or fantasy and ask, "Is there another way I can look at this? Can I see this experience in a way that brings peace and empowerment?" Look at the story from another angle and you will see another picture, often radically unlike the one you saw when you first looked at it. The facts of the situation remain the same, but seen in a new light we may recognize an altogether different purpose than the one we originally assigned to it. Perhaps the experience helped bring us to a place in life that we now value. Instead of cursing us, the experience ultimately blessed us. *A Course in Miracles* brings us the refreshing news that "All of your past is gone except the blessing it has left you." Thus we can say with honesty, "the past isn't what it used to be."

ACTIVATION:

BEAUTY IN THE BEAST

Reframe your past by holding it in the light of a higher vision.

My Most Difficult Experiences   *The Gifts They Bestowed*

Look in the Right Nest

Miguel de Cervantes, creator of the beloved *Don Quixote*, advised, "Never look for the birds of this year in the nests of the last." We cannot afford to use the past as a referent for our future. *Our history is not our destiny.* When we become fascinated with what was, we lose sight of what is, and what could be. If we compare now with then, we will not see either clearly.

I know of an innovative computer word processing program for creative writers. The program does not let you see what you have just typed. Although the words are recorded and available to be reviewed later, they are invisible while the new writing is emerging. The effect of this process is that the writer has no choice but to stay in the moment. She cannot look back to compare or edit. She must live on the cutting edge of her current thought.

Here we have a magnificent metaphor for all creative endeavors. If you truly want to move ahead, you cannot afford to mess around with the past. You cannot simultaneously edit and innovate. You can't fix the past, tempted as you may be to try. Many artists are haunted by their earlier work; they are tempted to go back and improve their past renderings so they reflect their current level of expertise. When I read my earlier books, I sometimes reach to get out a red pen and start editing my printed text so it says more of what I want to say now. But I am happy to report that I have never changed it. I recognize that the earlier work is a pure and perfect expression of who and where I was at the time, and I must honor it as such. I further see that this work appeals to people at a particular stage of the path, and the work I do now appeals to readers at a different stage. If I were to revise that work, I would erase an important contribution. I would also divert the energy now moving into my new work. So I leave what was, and release it like a dear child to go out and make its own way in the world; then I turn my full attention to my new direction.

As you read these words, the scientific world of physics is

undergoing a major revolution. For hundreds of years physicists explained the universe in terms of Newtonian physics. Within the last few decades, however, an entirely new paradigm, quantum physics, has replaced the old model. The implications of this shift are phenomenal! Physicists are discovering that energy, matter, and consciousness function in *an entirely different way* than the old "laws" indicated; they were not laws after all – they were simply a belief system reinforced by popular agreement. (James Harvey Robinson noted, "Most of our so-called reasoning consists in finding arguments for going on believing as we already do.") Amazing as it sounds, physicists are in many ways starting all over with a new understanding of how the universe operates. The key principle here is that *the new way has nothing at all to do with the old way.* There is no linear connection; quantum physics did not evolve as an extension of Newtonian principles. Just as the new title implies, there was a quantum shift between what was, and what is. We had to look at the game from an entirely different angle to see more of what is happening. We are playing in a new ball park with a brand new set of rules.

I find this new development very exciting! It means that no matter what we thought, or what "laws" under which we believed we were bound, the whole slate can be cleared in an instant and an entirely new paradigm can replace it. As *A Course in Miracles* declares, "The past is over. It can touch me not."

If we rely on the past as a referent, we will only keep recreating it. The touching film, *The Joy Luck Club,* traces the evolution of several Chinese families as they go through the labor pains of shifting from an old patriarchal society to a new world in which strong women reclaim their power to live as whole and worthy beings. In one poignant scene a mother tells her daughter, "For generations our people went back and forth; the daughter was the opposite of the mother and her daughter was again like her grandmother. But that way we got nowhere. One generation went down the stairs, and the next generation went up – but all the while we stayed trapped on the same staircase."

This wise woman was underscoring the importance of

breaking the karmic chain of reactive, rather than creative, living. This principle is one of the laws of the old physics: "Every action has an equal and opposite reaction." But just as Newtonian physics gives way to quantum physics, the "law" of karma gives way to Grace. For aeons the seers of the Orient have been telling us that we need to get off the wheel of karma. But you cannot end karma by making more of it; even good karma will not get you off the wheel. The way to be done with karma is to expand your vision to behold a universe that is bigger than karma. The law of Grace tells us that we, God, and life are bigger than our notion of karma, cause and effect, action and reaction, sin and punishment, life and death. Grace supersedes sin and error. When you sincerely say, "I forgive" or "I release," *the past is instantly nullified.* No matter how limited or obligated you believed you were under the laws of karma, Grace tells you that there is a broader vision, and you are free the moment you step into it.

It is time to claim Grace and live the great life. You were born to be grand, and littleness does not befit you. The past is always smaller than you are now, because the past is an illusion and you are real.

I heard a man on a radio program describe a mystical experience he had. In a vision, the man saw himself walking down a country lane. Suddenly the entire scene rolled up "like a window shade." All that remained was brilliant white light. His world had no more reality than a piece of canvas; all that was left was an eternal morning.

Our past is like that window shade. It is but a picture we carry and refer to when we fear or do not recognize the power available in the present moment. Now is the time to roll the shade up and welcome the morning.

Keep your eye on the road,
and use your rear view mirror only to avoid trouble.
— Daniel Meacham

A HEART ACT TO FOLLOW

Make love now, by night and by day, in winter and in summer. . .You are in the world for that and the rest of life is nothing but vanity, illusion, waste. There is only one science, love, one riches, love, only one policy, love. To make love is all the law and the prophets.
                                    – Anatole France

Love is the great need of this world. While we have achieved all manner of material success, human beings on this planet daily cry out – and die – for love. If only we could love, how quickly would our problems dissipate!

In a small town in Spain, a man named Jorge had a bitter argument one morning with his young son Paco. When he arrived home later that day, Jorge discovered that Paco's room was empty – he had run away from home.

Overcome with remorse, Jorge searched his soul and realized that his son was more important to him than anything else. He wanted to start over. Jorge went to a well-known grocery store in the center of town and posted a large sign that read, "Paco, come home. I love you. Meet me here tomorrow morning."

The next morning Jorge went to the store, where he found no less than seven young boys named Paco who had also run away from home. They were all answering the call for love, hoping it was their dad inviting them home with open arms.

She Gave Me Everything

During a lecture tour I was invited to stay in the home of an eminent academician. When I arrived at his house I felt quite tired and wanted to rest. To my chagrin, Richard was eager to engage in conversation. Why, I wondered, did I not stay in a hotel?

Richard introduced me to his wife Martine, who ushered us to a colorfully-set dining room table. As Martine artistically placed a casserole before us, Richard kissed his wife and announced, "Fifty years – that's how long we have been together . . .and I love this woman fifty times as much as I did when I met her."

Both smiled, and Richard gave Martine an affectionate hug around her hips. They really did love each other. I flashed on the kindly older couples in the movie, *When Harry Met Sally*. I have seen few mates in love for so long. "What is their secret?" I wondered.

I awoke early the next morning and seized a welcome quiet moment to write. I was just into my second paragraph when I felt two strong hands on my shoulders. One massaged deeply, the other held a photograph.

"Do you recognize this woman?" Richard asked me.

I surveyed the photo. No, I did not know her.

"Perhaps you will realize who she is if I show you her book."

He handed me a hardcover volume; I recognized it immediately as a classic bestseller. There was her picture on the jacket. Of course I knew who she was.

"She was my lover," Richard confessed.

"But I thought you were happily married?"

"I am – and I was," my mysterious yet strangely familiar host confided. "But when I met this authoress, I felt irresistibly drawn to her."

"What did you tell Martine?"

"I tried to hide it for a while, but quickly I realized that there was no use trying to keep it a secret. Martine knew. I told her I wanted to spend time in San Francisco with this woman."

I was stunned. Here was one of the most happily-married men I have ever seen, telling me a heart-rending tale of infidelity. "What did Martine say?"

Richard's eyes softened as his mind drifted to a sensitive memory. "She thought for a moment, took a deep breath, and answered, 'Then go to San Francisco.' Martine told me, 'I can't give you everything. If this is what you want, then go do it. There is not enough love in the world. I can't and won't stop you. I want you to be happy.'"

I was amazed. I had never heard such surrender spoken so gracefully.

"So what did you do?"

"I had my affair with this woman, and after a time I knew that I wasn't to see her anymore. I came home and fell into Martine's arms. I put my head in her lap, wept, and looked into her eyes. There she was, loving me as she always had."

Tears brimmed in Richard's eyes, then trickled in tiny rivulets over his high cheekbones onto his white moustache. I, however, had no moustache to catch my tears. I reached for a tissue.

"I remembered Martine's words, 'I can't give you everything,'" Richard reiterated. "But in that moment she gave me everything."

Kahlil Gibran affirmed:

Love gives naught but itself and takes naught but from itself.
Love possesses not nor would it be possessed;
For love is sufficient unto love. . .
Love has no other desire but to fulfil itself. . .
To wake at dawn with a winged heart and give thanks
for another day of loving. . .
And then to sleep with a prayer for the beloved in your heart
and a song of praise upon your lips.[1]

Far Greater than Money

The beach town of Kihei, Maui has burgeoned with tourism over the last ten years. What once was a sleepy romantic getaway has become a mini-metropolis teeming with time-share condominiums and strip malls.

In the shadow of rampant development, there remain a few aromatic breezes scented with the spirit of old Hawaii. A handful of natives have chosen not to cash in on what have become million dollar properties, and retain the charm and dignity of their lifestyle rooted in love of the land.

Auntie Martha ("Auntie" is a Hawaiian term of endearment and respect for an elder) has lived in elegant simplicity for over eighty years. Her leathery brown skin, white hair, slightly glazed eyes, and unabashed toothless smile paint a classic portrait of a colorful era nearly gone by. In striking contrast to the mega-pricey condos that have mushroomed on either side of her charmingly unkempt lot, Auntie Martha still lives in her ramshackle house just down Ili'ili Street from Kamaole Beach. There, in her own quiet way, she lives the ancient spirit of *aloha* (literally translated, "the breath of life").

I first met Auntie Martha when I was parking my car across the street from her house. Before I even opened my door Martha approached me and asked, "Do you have any cigarettes?"

I smiled and shook my head.

We chatted for a while, and she told me, "You can park in my yard if you want to. I like to have friends." She took my hand and looked into my eyes. Her eyes glistened, and she was very present. "My grandsons may try to charge you, but don't pay them. Tell them that you are my friend and I invited you." Auntie Martha smiled. "Aloha is far greater than money."

Aloha is far greater than money. That about covers it. Aloha is far greater than money – and being right, and holding grudges, and protecting your image, and just about anything else. Aloha – love – is the only thing worth living for. I know, because Auntie Martha told me so.

Deep Instead of Fast

We have lost our sense of purpose. In our mad quest to acquire objects, accolades, and experiences, we have forgotten how to live. Our obsession with doing has cost us our being; the race to get there has blinded us to what is here. We have allowed our intellects to strangle our hearts, forgetting that the source of life emanates from within us, not out there somewhere.

At a crucial point in our soul's journey we realize that the quality of our life is more important than any material activity or possession. Gandhi declared, "There is more to life than increasing its speed." When we discover that our journey home is an *inward* one, our value system shifts, and our life takes on a new and infinitely more rewarding purpose. A friend told me, "Last year I took the biggest step of my life. It was but eighteen inches – I bridged the chasm between my head and my heart."

At one of my seminars an endearing man named Bernie came onstage and told the group that he was a medical doctor who had had a heart attack. "I realized that it was not my heart that attacked me; *I* had attacked my heart," Bernie confessed.

The room was silent; Bernie had captured everyone's attention instantly.

"In retrospect," Bernie went on, "I am not surprised. I was living a hurried, frazzled, heartless life. My existence was about achievement, money, status symbols, and accolades. It was not about people or spirit." Bernie's voice started to crack as his eyes welled with tears that once might have threatened him, but now cleansed his soul.

The audience was riveted; everyone wanted to hear more.

"During my recovery I had a lot of time to evaluate the quality of my life. I recognized that I had come to put self-importance before service. I remembered Leo Buscaglia's words, 'We were born to love people and use things; instead we love things and use people.' That day I made a commitment to put love first, and practicing that vow has changed my life." Bernie's sincerity was gently commanding. "Today," Bernie added, "I am a new man. I have rekindled my relationship with my wife and children, and my life is a thousand percent more rewarding. I thank God for more time on earth to discover the depths and joys of living from my heart. My life now is dedicated to loving."

The audience rose with thunderous applause in acknowledgement of Bernie's touching testimony. Bernie completed his account by revealing that his practice of medicine has now taken a back seat to his new love – ballroom dancing.

Henry Seidel Canby wrote:

"We live in the midst of details that keep us running round in circles and never getting anywhere but tired, or that bring on nervous breakdowns and coronary thrombosis. The answer is not to take to the woods, but to find out what we really want to do and then cut out the details that fritter away what is most valuable in life. *Live deep instead of fast.*"

Master Key:

Live Deep Instead of Fast.

An episode of the television show *A Different World* centered around an argument between a young artist and a medical student. The doctor-to-be was criticizing the impracticality of art. "While you are out painting," he scoffed, "I will be saving lives!"

The artist retorted, "But what will you be saving them *for*?"

Jesus asked the same question: "What shall it profit a man if he gains the whole world, but loses his soul?" Gaining mastery in the material world is meaningless unless we hold our sense of loving above it all. (A sign in a pottery shop in England read, *"Please report any breakage so we can forgive you."*) If we have everything but love, we have nothing. If we make love our foundation, all else shall be added.

The Choice for Love

Any activity in life can be elevated to the level of blessing. Nothing in this world is outside the power of transformation by way of a loving heart.

Alice is a heart-centered executive who had a chance to test her belief in the power of unconditional blessing. As she was writing checks to pay her bills last April, Alice penned a note of blessing on the memo line of each check, as is her custom. When Alice came to the check due to the Internal Revenue Service for her tax payment, she wondered, "Do I really want to bless the I.R.S.? Would anyone there receive the gift?"

After some reflection, Alice decided that there are no exceptions to the law of love. "Perhaps," she reasoned, "the I.R.S. is in greater need of blessing than most of the other people and companies I am paying." On the memo line of her check Alice inscribed, *"Peace and joy be with you."*

Several months later as Alice was going through her cancelled checks, she noticed the check she had sent to the I.R.S. On the back of the check, below the institutional stamp, she read these words, written by hand: *"And with you, too!"*

Somehow Alice's blessing found its way to someone's heart. Consider what a gift this was to the person who received it! The I.R.S. is probably not the most delightful place to work. Hardly anyone enjoys paying taxes, and I expect that I.R.S. employees are not the recipients of many blessings from their constituents. (The turnover rate for I.R.S. employees is the highest of any government agency.) Can you imagine the pleasant surprise of the person who processed the check? Perhaps it changed his entire day. Perhaps that person went on to offer some extra kindness, caring, or forgiveness to the next person he dealt with. I am certain that Alice's blessing went a long way. The situations we encounter are templates upon which we imprint our heart's intentions. Every moment we make the choice between love and fear. When we choose love, we bring the world closer to heaven. Fear makes the world hell. The choice is ours.

131

More Love to Life

I am fascinated by the ways that ordinary people bring more heart to life. Every encounter is an opportunity to create separation or joining. When we make the choice to care, we set into motion a snowball effect that touches many people, most of whom we will never know about. On my way home one night, my car broke down, and I decided to hitchhike. As it was late in the evening and I live in the country about half an hour outside of town, I wondered about my chances of getting a ride close to my house. I decided to make the experience an adventure in faith, and allow Spirit to take care of the details.

After a few minutes, a fellow in a rusty old Ford pickup truck stopped. To my delight he told me that he lived on my road, and he drove me to my door!

En route, Jack told me that he was coming home from work at the airport. He was the ground crew member who stands in front of the airplanes as they pull up to the gate, and directs the pilots to park on the marks.

"How do you like your job?" I asked. (I held a covert judgment that his must be a boring job. I hoped I had not invited him to consider a day he wanted to forget.)

"It's actually pretty interesting," Jack answered. "You get to work with all kinds of pilots."

I was surprised. I didn't think there would be much more than a brief mechanical interaction between him and the cockpit crews.

Jack elaborated, "Some of the pilots are really cold and unappreciative. They treat me like a machine. As soon as they are parked, that is the end of our interaction. That's when the job is a drag."

Then Jack's face brightened. In the dim glow of the dashboard lights, I could see the sides of his mouth turn into a slight smile.

"Then there are other pilots who really acknowledge me for my service. They smile, thank me, and some of them even give me a short salute. That makes me feel like a million dollars!" Jack turned his head my way and underscored, "It's no fun standing out there in all kinds of weather, breathing in jet exhaust all day. When a pilot, who most people probably consider the most important person in the airline, acknowledges me, that makes my day."

I sat quietly and drank in this fellow's sharing. I recalled the line in *A Course in Miracles* reminding us, "A miracle is never lost. It may touch many people you have never met, and produce undreamed of changes in situations of which you are not even aware."[2] Every human interaction is important, and may contain a gold mine of blessing if we are willing to give and receive the good that is available. The energy we pass along in our encounters goes much farther than we can see in a given moment. A slight salute can lift a tired soul above the jet fumes, and make his day worth extolling to a stranger.

Master Key:

Never Underestimate the Importance of a Kind Act.

A Heart Act to Follow

As I was returning a rented car at the San Francisco airport, I was greeted by a short Hispanic man waiting to check my car in. In a rush, I exited the auto and hurriedly headed toward the trunk to grab my suitcase.

As I handed the attendant my keys, he asked me, "You liked the car, sir?"

"Yes, it was fine."

"That's good!" he laughed. "I'm glad you liked it."

Suddenly I realized that this fellow, Manuel, was not just offering me a canned company spiel. He was speaking from his heart, making contact; he was genuinely glad I was pleased with the vehicle.

I thanked him for his service, and started toward the shuttle bus.

"You come back again," he called to me. "We give you another nice car!"

Sitting on the bus, catching my breath and feeling more relaxed, I had a chance to reflect on the gift that Manuel had bestowed upon me. I felt nurtured and cared for. In a busy, impersonal, and often heartless environment, Manuel remembered that his job was about people more than cars. While some would consider his job the lowest on the company's totem pole, this fellow was acting with the grace, hospitality, and personal investment one would expect from the company president. I wondered if the president of that company knows that Manuel is doing more to develop reliable business for them than any ad they could conjure.

I surmised that Manuel's attitude is no accident. Positivity and job satisfaction filter down from the top of the organization. In an era when "trickle-down economics" has become a political catch-phrase, I wonder if we should pay even more careful attention to "trickle-down service." I imagine that his company creates a nourishing environment for their employees, and this fellow was passing his sense of well-being along to me and other customers.

Looking back on that day, I wish I had taken the time to shake Manuel's hand and tell him how much I appreciated his thoughtfulness. In my hurry, I caught up with my heart only in retrospect. If I had it to do over again, I would have told Manuel that he made my day. He taught me that no job is unimportant; that caring and service make a difference at every echelon of the business world; that no interaction is too menial for meaningful contact between human beings.

But I'm sure I will have the opportunity again. Perhaps not with Manuel, but there will be another hidden saint in some car lot or news stand. I won't miss out on a heart act to follow.

Gibran declared:

> *When you work you fulfil a part*
> *of earth's furthest dream,*
> *assigned to you when that dream was born,*
> *And in keeping yourself with labor*
> *you are in truth loving life,*
> *And to love life through labor*
> *is to be intimate with life's inmost secret. . .*
>
> *[To work with love] is to weave the cloth*
> *with threads drawn from your heart,*
> *even as if your beloved were to wear that cloth.*
> *It is to build a house with affection,*
> *even as if your beloved were to dwell in that house.*
> *It is to sow seeds with tenderness*
> *and reap the harvest of joy,*
> *even as if your beloved were to eat the fruit.*
> *It is to charge all things you fashion*
> *with a breath of your own spirit. . .*[3]

More Lovers, More Soul

I share these stories as demonstrations of real people elevating mundane or adverse situations to a divine level of expression. Perhaps many people would not notice Manuel's extra caring, or a pilot's salute, or the friendliness of an elderly Hawaiian woman. Hardly anyone would think to include the Internal Revenue Service in their broadcast of blessings. But these are the gifts along the way that make life worth living. They dispel dreariness and drudgery from daily activities, and restore human relations to the godly status they are intended to express.

We need more lovers on the planet, more people who sincerely seek to paint brighter colors on the pallet of their days.

We need more kind souls who are willing to take an extra moment to offer a word of thanks, or an extra minute of patience for the older fellow taking a longer time to gather his papers from the teller's window at the bank. We need more entry-level employees who are willing to be as responsible for customer satisfaction as the CEO. Simply put, we need more heart in a society that has lost much of its own.

More directly, we need to *be* the lovers we wish we would encounter more. It will do us no good to hope we meet more Manuels and friendly pilots; to wait for other people to take better care of us is to miss the opportunity to be the Christ or Buddha ourselves. No, it works the other way around. We need to take better care of the other person first. We need to imagine that our position is the pivotal one of the day for everyone who passes through our field of influence, which goes much, much farther than we realize.

Perhaps each of us needs to go down to the local store and post a sign inviting, "Paco, come home." We may not have a wayward son named Paco, but there is a Paco in each of our lives. There is someone who is needing our love, someone to whom we might have said, "I love you," before they lost faith that we did. It is not enough to just feel love for someone, and it is not enough to reserve telling them for a special occasion. I don't believe it is possible to say, "I love you" too much. Those three precious words, sincerely spoken, are the food our souls crave. Perhaps, just perhaps, if we post our sign, "I love you," in a conspicuous place, we will feed not only our own Paco, but the others who hoped that it was their dad inviting them home.

What can you do with each moment of life
but love 'til you've loved it away?
— Bob Franke

THE BIG PICTURE

You are a child of the universe,
No less than the trees and the stars;
You have a right to be here.
And whether or not it is clear to you,
No doubt the universe is unfolding as it should.
    – Max Ehrmann, *Desiderata*

Once upon a time in a tropical land there lived a king who had an optimistic advisor. This lieutenant was so positive, in fact, that the king was often annoyed by his practice of constantly finding good in everything.

One day while the king and the lieutenant were on a journey through the jungle, the king was chopping a fresh coconut for breakfast, and his machete slipped, cutting off his toe. The aching monarch limped to show his misfortune to the lieutenant, who exclaimed, "That's wonderful!"

"What did you say?" asked the king, astonished.

"This is a real blessing!"

Hearing this response, the king became very angry; this man was obviously poking fun at his mishap.

"Take it from me," the lieutenant exhorted, "behind this apparent accident there is some good we do not see."

That was the last straw! Furious, the king picked up the lieutenant and hurled him into a dry well. Then he set out to find his way back to his castle.

En route, the potentate was apprehended by a band of headhunters who decided that he would make an excellent sacrifice for this month's offering to the volcano. The warriors took him to the tribal priest, who prepared him for the dubious honor.

As the holy man was anointing the reluctant sacrifice, he noticed that the king was missing a toe. "I'm sorry," the priest informed the king, "we can't use you – the volcano goddess accepts only full-bodied sacrifices; you are free to go."

Overjoyed, the king hobbled out of the tribal camp. Suddenly it dawned on him that the lieutenant had been correct – there was indeed a hidden blessing behind this seeming misfortune!

As quickly as he could, the king found his way back to the well where he had left the lieutenant. To the ruler's delight, his companion was still sitting in the well, whistling happily. (He was indeed a positive thinker!) The king offered the lieutenant a hand, pulled him out of the well, and apologized profusely.

"I am terribly sorry I threw you in there!" the king confessed, as he dusted his advisor's shoulders. "I was taken prisoner by some wild natives who were about to cast me into the volcano. But when they saw my toe was missing, they let me go. It was actually a miracle, which you foretold – and I so thoughtlessly cast you into this pit! Can you ever forgive me?"

"No apology necessary," replied the lieutenant. "It was also a blessing that you left me in the well."

"Now how are you going to make something positive out of that?" queried the king.

"Because," the lieutenant explained, "if I was with you, they would have taken *me* for the sacrifice!"

When a Minus Becomes a Plus

There is a bigger picture to life than the one we see when we judge only by the obvious. Real faith is remembering that there is a beneficent plan behind the events at hand. During times of trial, we must not be fooled by appearances. Love is the only reality, and all else is an error in perception.

On the eve of my departure for a lecture tour I bought a portable computer. As soon as I arrived at my hotel en route I unwrapped my new toy and began to program it. Within a few minutes I programmed it so well that it didn't work at all! All I could see on the screen was a blinking cursor; the machine would not allow me to access even the simplest program.

Immediately I began to criticize myself for making such a foolish error. My judgmental mind reared its unforgiving head, chastising me, "You don't know how to do *anything* right. . .here you buy an expensive new state-of-the-art device, and you break it before you even get to use it. . .This just proves what a clumsy jerk you are," and on and on. Amidst the warped soundtrack of this torturous litany, I kept trying to restore the computer to function. After many unsuccessful attempts, I gave up and went to bed with a tired mind and heart.

The next morning I phoned the sponsor of the program I came to present and asked her if she knew anyone who could help me remedy my software gaff. Within a few hours a kind man named Tom came to my room, inserted a remedial diskette in my computer, and in minutes my machine was up and running. I was grateful beyond words.

Then Tom suggested, "I have some software that will help your work. Would you like me to install it? Of course I would. He loaded three programs which have proven very valuable.

As Tom left my room, I realized I was way ahead of where I would have been if I hadn't made my mistake! What began as a minus ended up as a plus. Yes, I made an error – but the error turned out to be a thread in a tapestry larger than I could see at the time. There was a bigger picture than met the eye.

Maybe God Brought You Here

In her hilarious movie *Sister Act*, Whoopi Goldberg plays a streetwise woman who, while escaping from gangsters, hides in a convent and impersonates a nun. It is not long before Deloris finds monastic life a real stretch for her, since she is used to nightlife, men, and constant action.

After a short time in the cloister, Deloris complains to the Mother Superior. Deloris asserts that she does not belong in the cloister and does not need the place, cockily claiming, "my life is working just fine."

"Your life is *not* working just fine," the elder sister replies. "You are in a dangerous relationship with a married mobster, your life has been threatened, and you are running from hit-men. That doesn't sound like a very fine life to me. Perhaps God *did* bring you here."

Sometimes the place in which we find ourselves seems all wrong, but in the big picture it is all right. *A Course in Miracles* reminds us that we do not perceive our own best interests, and "you cannot be your own guide to miracles, for it was you who made them necessary in the first place." The *Course* notes that chance plays no part in God's plan, and we do not really know what anything is for, as we do not have the perspective to accurately assess situations on the basis of appearances. Our refuge, the *Course* recommends, is to ask to see the situation from a higher perspective than the one that fear would show us.

Love always offers a clearer vantage point than upset, and peace is a more powerful guide to action than separation. We need not fear, for Spirit is with us wherever we go, and we do not walk alone.

There Must be a Miracle in Here Somewhere

On my way to the airport in Puerto Rico my car had a flat tire and I missed my plane by ten minutes. I was especially vexed by this mishap, for I was on my way to present a workshop in Florida that evening and I wanted time to rest before the program. The next available plane would land me just a short time before the workshop. Taking the later flight, I grumbled to myself for most of the trip, blaming myself and others.

In an attempt to somehow salvage the day, I told my travelling companion, "There must be a miracle in here somewhere." I must admit that I did not believe my own words at the time; I was trying to convince myself.

When I arrived at the event, I was greeted with tremendous love and appreciation. The sponsors welcomed me profusely, and the hall was overflowing with an eager and enthusiastic audience. From the moment I walked through the door, I was hugged and blessed with a great outpouring of heart.

In the presence of such a warm reception, my energy quickly returned. My upset gave way to exuberance, I felt no sense of fatigue, and I went on to present one of the most dynamic programs I have ever offered. By the end of the workshop I had a great deal more energy than I had when I began.

A miracle had indeed occurred. The experience showed me that my energy and effectiveness do not depend on things I do in time or space, but on being in the presence of joy. Emmet Fox declared that "love has the power to heal anything," and *A Course in Miracles* teaches that "love waits not on time, but on welcome." I experienced a dramatic demonstration that no matter what has gone on beforehand, love, enthusiasm, and caring can nullify the past entirely, and make way for ecstasy now.

I was very glad that I was wrong about the cause and the purpose of the delay. God had a bigger plan than I could imagine. There *was* a miracle in there somewhere, and I was closer to the truth than I realized when I suggested that good may have been operating behind the scenes.

Between the Swings

Many of us are going through many changes in a short time. As we evolve rapidly, we are being asked to let go of our old life before a new one is fully in sight or manifested.

Such a time calls for *faith* and *trust*. Imagine that the life you are leaving is like a trapeze swing. You went back and forth so many times that you finally got tired of the rat race and said, "That's it – anything must be better than this treadmill – I'm outa here!"

Then you let go, and you find yourself hurtling through space in uncharted territory with no apparent safety net. Looking back, you see that the swing you left is too far behind to grasp. (Or you may grab it, and quickly remember why you chose to let go.)

Ahead in the distance you see another trapeze bar, representing the new life awaiting you. It is swinging toward you, and there may even be someone hanging onto the swing with his hands outstretched. But it is still too far in the distance for you to grasp.

So what do you do? You fly through the air with the greatest of ease (or a reasonable facsimile thereof). You may not fly very gracefully, but you just keep on going. Eventually you will find your next resting place; the outstretched hands will find yours, and you will be ahead of where you were.

Many of us are being drawn to a new life that is attractive, but unfamiliar. (Some of us have been cast forcibly out of our old life, and we don't perceive anything attractive about where we are or where we are headed; we just know that the old has gone, and nothing has taken its place.) We may grasp for some familiar rock of security as we find ourself amidst a journey with an unknown destination. We may demand guarantees and assurances that we will be taken care of in what feels like deep space. We, too, may utter, "I don't think we're in Kansas anymore, Toto."

But there is no such thing as a safe adventure. Adventure implies risk, stretching, and pioneering new territory. No one in the world can give you a guarantee. (It is said, "If you want a guarantee, buy a toaster.") But there is a Source that can give you a guarantee, and that is Spirit. God's guarantee is that if you trust, follow your heart, live your truth, and love, you will be taken care of. You will be led to the right people and the right circumstances at the right time. You will not be left comfortless.

During manned space flights, there is a period of time before landing when astronauts lose radio contact with ground control. This occurs when the spacecraft is passing through a dense layer of the atmosphere, and static impedes clear communication. During such a blackout, the pilots must trust that they will regain the connection. This momentary separation is not a problem for the astronauts; they have been told about it in advance and they know they will re-establish contact when conditions are more favorable.

You, too, will regain contact. Just because you cannot hear the voice of God does not mean that It is not speaking to you, or that love is not present; it just means that you are momentarily out of position to hear. The voice speaks and you will recognize it. The next trapeze swing will meet your hand at just the right moment. Be patient. Breathe. Your trust will be rewarded. The course you are travelling has been trod by many before you. It is not a mystery. There are roadmaps of consciousness. Those who have gone before you extend their hands to assist you. Don't worry. Just keep flying and trust.

The psalmist affirms, "Yea, though I walk through the valley of the shadow of death, I will fear no evil." The key word here is *shadow*. The journey through the valley seems frightening only because the light is being blocked. The light is there; it is just obscured from your view at the moment. The light will be there when you are ready to see it again. You will arrive at the mountaintop safe and whole. You are loved. God takes care of Her own, and you are Her own.

We all sit around and suppose
While the secret sits in the center and knows.
                                   – Robert Frost

DOORS TO THE LIGHT

In the middle of every difficulty lies an opportunity.
                                                        – Albert Einstein

Take Away Another Chair

A problem is not the worst thing that could happen to you. The worst thing that can happen to you is to stay asleep in the world of fear and miss the love that is available. Problems exist only to pry us from our slumber. What we perceive as problems are simply invitations to think with a greater mind and remember our wholeness.

The level at which a situation seems to be a problem is just one aspect of a much broader purpose. When young eaglets reach a certain point of maturity, their mother gradually decreases the amount of food she brings them daily, and she begins to remove straws from their nest. The mother makes the babies hungry to find their own food, and undoes their resting place. From a limited perspective her actions surely seem cruel, but when understood, she is giving her children the greatest gift possible – their own strength and freedom.

When we have graduated from a particular station of life, the universe will push us to fly at a higher altitude. We have mastered the awareness available to us at one level, and we no longer have a function there. A loftier purpose calls. To facilitate our flight, the rewards of the old level are withdrawn and its support system begins to collapse. At the time this may seem unkind, but that would be so only if there were not something better to replace it. The mother eagle is not weakening her children; she is empowering them. She knows they have wings they have not tested.

If you have gone through a painful divorce, illness, financial stress, or death of a loved one, it certainly may appear as if the universe is out to hurt you. But appearances are not the same as reality. Temporary discomfort pales in the face of long-term awakening. At such a difficult time, it seems that your world is falling apart – and it is. But that is not the end of the story. A new world awaits – but first the old one must be undone to make space for the next level of expression. To expedite this process, your old source of nourishment is removed (sometimes abruptly) and you are forced to flap the wings you have not yet used. You may not see how and when your next comfort will come, but rest assured it will be there.

The fastest way to your new home is to release the past as quickly and gracefully as possible. Feel your feelings, acknowledge the pain, take time to grieve if you need it, and then get on with your new life. Use the experience to grow, rather than reinforce your sense of powerlessness or victimhood. As you discover the greater purpose, you will find strength you never would have exercised if life had not forced you to leave a crumbling nest in search of higher ground.

A Better View of the Sky

What seems to be the worst thing that could happen may actually be the best thing. A Gallup Poll found that eighty-seven percent of those interviewed felt that the most difficult events of their lives turned out to be among their most helpful experiences, and now they appreciate that the events had occurred. *A Course in Miracles* echoes that what we perceive to be triumphs are often setbacks, while apparent disasters may be gifts in disguise.

A Zen master noted, "Now that my house has burned down, I have a much better view of the sky." When we get our feared experiences behind us, we can enjoy what the fears were blocking us from seeing. When I took a white water rafting trip in Bali, I dreaded the possibility of falling out of boat into the rapids. As the instructor gave his preparatory lesson, I silently prayed that I stay safe in the boat. To my chagrin, the inner response I heard was, "Just have fun."

Less than one minute into the trip, our raft got caught up against a wall of rocks on the side of the river and overturned. As calmly as possible, I allowed myself to float down the river, where I was soon picked up by another raft. After I was returned to my boat, I enjoyed the rest of the trip far more than I would have if I had been worrying about capsizing. The "worst" had already happened, and it was not as bad as I had feared.

Innovate!

Conflict is not our natural state; our true nature is peace. The purpose of a sense of conflict is to get your attention so you will change something you are doing that is hurting you. You may have to let go of a self-defeating position that you are holding, or become more assertive. In either case the conflict is asking you to be more true to who you really are, or ask for what you really want.

When you accept trouble as a way of life, or remain in pain with a sense of sacrificial resolution, you do yourself the greatest disservice possible, for you deny your right to live in joy. "Right to Life" lobby groups have attracted much attention; perhaps we might develop within ourselves an internal "Right to Light" lobby. But before you can exercise a right, you must be aware that you deserve it. If you accept darkness as a condition of life, you will not reach for the light. It is only when you are sick and tired of being sick and tired that you say, "there must be a better way." Then the universe will answer the question you have asked, and show you the way you have requested.

Conflict is a call to innovate. If you are involved in a

conflict, internally or externally, there is an answer you have not yet seen. The tension you experience is a call to look at the situation from another angle, or do something differently. We must not run away from conflicts when they arise, for they are doors to a new dimension of creativity. Your desire for peace is the voice of God speaking to you through your heart. The conflict is *supposed* to go away. The crucial factor is *how* we make it go away. We can deny conflict, run away from it, or increase the force we are using until our side "wins." But "winning" is not the same as resolution. We can cream our opponent, but that does not mean we have solved the conflict. Sooner or later there will be another opponent, and at some point the use of force will fail.

The presence of conflict calls not for greater force, but for broader consciousness. If something you are doing is not working, doing more of it will usually not work any better. True resolution asks us not to act stronger, but to think bigger; not to fight harder, but to work smarter; to keep innovating until we find a solution in which everyone wins.

Master Key:

The Answer Is Always at a Higher Level than the Problem

Carl Jung recognized that "conflict exists strictly as an opportunity to raise our consciousness." If we do not wake up as a result of pain, we will only act out the same scenario in a more intense form. Most pharmaceutical medications do not make the problem go away; they simply mask the symptoms. Unless we have a change of consciousness, the symptoms will probably reappear. The symptoms are not our enemy, but our friend; they are calling our attention by saying, "look deeper and discover what you need to change to live happier."

When nature hits a set of limits, it innovates. Millions of years ago there was no oxygen in the atmosphere of the earth, and living things on the planet functioned without oxygen. When green plants showed up in the course of evolution, a great quantity of oxygen was introduced into the atmosphere. Amazing as it may sound, oxygen started out as a poison – many living things were not able to process it, and they died in its presence. Some life forms, however, were able to adapt through mutation, and that was the beginning of gills and lungs, which are now standard fare for breathing creatures on the planet. While our rudimentary biological forerunners could not imagine a world with oxygen, now we cannot imagine a world without it. We innovated, and that has made all the difference.

We are all familiar with the expression, "survival of the fittest." Usually we think of "the fittest" as the biggest and the strongest. Look again at the word "fit," and you will see an altogether more practical meaning. The "fittest" are those who are the best at fitting in. Sometimes that means big and strong, but more often it means the most adaptable, flexible, and versatile. Water would seem weak when compared to a formidable rock, but send water over a boulder for a long enough time, and the water will wear away the boulder. It has an entirely different kind of power than the rock – fluidity – and so the water endures while the rock does not.

Dinosaurs were once the largest and strongest creatures on the planet, but they became extinct because they could not adapt to rapid climatic changes. I sometimes wonder why dinosaurs have become a commercial craze during the last decade. (*Jurassic Park* is the largest grossing film in history, and dinosaur toys are among the most popular.) I believe that we are at an evolution-ary point on the planet similar to that of the dinosaur era. We are being faced with intensely rapid evolutionary advances that call for us to adapt, perhaps even mutate, quickly. Those who cling to the old order, no matter how big, strong, and powerful they were in the old value system, will have to let go of the past regime to live successfully in the new world that is forming around a higher vibrational level. The force of evolution is stronger than any personal or institutional ego. If we understand, however, that the next evolutionary step is infinitely more rewarding than the old one, there is no reason to try to hold on to the old way. The changes are not a wall, but a door. It is only when you see change as a threat that it seems frightening. Change is a blessing; Remember the *Course in Miracles* teaching, "All change is good."

Beyond Challenge

To master our problems, we must reframe them as opportunities. We must also redefine our identity to see ourselves as capable of deftly handling what is before us. *A Course in Miracles* tells us that the word "challenge" is a misnomer, as the word implies a possibility that we may fail. As divine beings, created in the image and likeness of an omnipotent God, we *cannot* fail. We can delay success, hold on to self-images of failure, and repeat errors, but ultimately we will emerge triumphant. Every apparent problem before us will sooner or later be resolved, and we will be left only with gifts. The *Course* encourages us, "A happy outcome for all things is assured."

It is very useful to eliminate the word "problem" from your vocabulary. Here again we see that relanguaging is an important transformational tool. Whenever you are inclined to define a situation as a problem or challenge, stop and substitute the word "project" or "opportunity." These descriptions are closer to the truth, and they will provide you with a perspective from which to find solutions rather than reinforce the problem.

A God of Only Love

If we perceive difficulties as punishments from God, we keep our problems big and ourselves small. This archaic, superstitious, and self-defeating notion must be rejected without compromise if we are to live in the dignity we seek and deserve. God does not punish; God loves and forgives. The concept of punishment is a human invention, manufactured by a mind clouded by guilt. The French philosopher Rousseau quipped that "God created us in His image and likeness, and we returned the compliment." The God of Love, who lives far beyond our warped projections, would never hurt any of His children. The real you could never be hurt, and you cannot be deserving of that which you are incapable of being.

Karma is the concept generally used to rationalize suffering. Instead of blaming God for our current difficulty, we ascribe its cause to our past misdeeds, which occurred in a former life. But our previous life, whether in this lifetime or another, is ours only as we hold onto it. Our past is not part of the present, and bears no relationship to who we are now – unless we carry it with us in our thoughts.

I am not the same person I was last lifetime, last year, or last week. I am not the same person I was when I began to write this sentence. You cannot step in the same river twice. I am not limited by what I have done. I can be limited only by my thoughts. *All limitation is self-imposed*, and the concept of karma is no exception.

If we must speak of karma, let us recognize that it is instant; every situation we experience is the manifestation of the thought held in mind at the moment. Karma is not horizontal, stretching over time and spanning lives; it is vertical: we think a thought in a given moment and the world we see outpictures that thought.

To change our world, we do not have to pay off our past. *We have no past.* God knows no debt, and as godly beings we cannot owe. To change our world, we must approach it from a fresh perspective. We can look through the eyes of fear, which shows us a world of guilt, owingness, and punishment; or we can look through the eyes of love, which shows us a universe of grace and forgiveness. The choice is ours, and we can change it at any given moment.

If we must speak of God, then let us know the God of only love. The altars of the Lord of Wrath and a God of Grace stand before us. Either one will give us its "gifts" as we bow down to it. Where do you choose to worship?

The Invincible Summer

Albert Camus declared, "In the midst of winter I discovered within me an invincible summer." Adversity is the soil in which seeds of greatness are grown. Every great person has achieved mastery not in spite of their challenges, but *because* of them. Difficulties are not boulders to crush us, but stones to build a stairway to the stars.

As I was walking with a medical doctor on his property in northern California, he picked a few leaves from a bush and offered me one. "Would you like some poison oak?" he asked.

"Why would I want some poison oak?"

"I used to be so allergic to the plant that I would break out in awful rashes if I even came near the stuff," he explained. "Once I was hospitalized for it."

To my astonishment, he placed the leaf in his mouth and started munching on it. "Now I eat a leaf every day to build my resistance to it. It hasn't bothered me in years."

The principles of homeopathy and vaccination demonstrate that ingesting small doses of poisons actually strengthens our resistance to them. This is how the experience of hardship can become our friend. In the popular video game, hungry ghosts chase Pac Man around a maze, seeking to gobble him up if he is caught off guard. If, however, Pac Man is prepared for them (by eating power nuggets along the way) Pac Man eats the ghosts and gains points and stamina. Then the remaining ghosts have to run from Pac Man.

Amazingly, the ancient Buddhist tradition contains a legend that remarkably resembles the modern Pac Man principle. The story is told that when a band of demons came to eat the Buddha's flesh, they were unable to destroy him. Instead, as they came into his presence, they became enlightened and were transformed to become his disciples. This parable demonstrates that the light is always more powerful than the darkness. Light has substance and presence; darkness is simply the absence of light. What is not, cannot be more powerful than what is.

We must devour the ghosts and demons that have haunted us. I refer not to the spooks that stalk our physical houses, but old, lingering, wispy fears that suck our life force from the beauty and wonder of the present moment. We must gobble up archaic self-images that hold us hostage as weak and worthless. The attics and basements of our minds are populated with ghoulish guilts and sardonic self-doubts, false definitions of ourselves as impotent addicts and selfish fools.

None of this is true, and we cannot afford to feed such vampires in our divine abode. We must transform them before they sap our dignity and undermine our noble purpose. We must march into their lair, while holding high the torch of truth. When touched by the light of dawn, illusions must disperse.

With every fear we overturn, we walk in a bigger world. Tiny pathways widen to become sweeping thoroughfares. With every awakening we clear the way for many more to walk at our side. We are much farther along the path to enlightenment than we realize. The voice of fear would tell us that we are still small and limited, and no progress has been made. But beware the prompting of lack; illusions are hard-pressed to acknowledge truth. The seeds of greatness, sown long ago within you, are blossoming. You shall not be small again. The big picture reveals that love has guided us thus far, and it shall not stop now.

I am your friend and my love for you goes deep. There is nothing I can give you which you have not got; but there is much, very much, that, while I cannot give it, you can take.

No heaven can come to us unless our hearts find rest in today. Take heaven! No peace lies in the future which is not hidden in this present little instant. Take Peace!

The gloom of the world is but a shadow. Behind it, yet within our reach, is Joy. There is radiance and glory in the darkness, could we but see – and to see we have only to look. I beseech you to look.

Life is so generous a giver, but we, judging its gifts by the covering, cast them away as ugly or heavy or hard. Remove the covering and you will find beneath it a living splendor, woven of love, by wisdom, with power.

Welcome it, grasp it, and you touch the angel's hand that brings it to you. Everything we call a trial, a sorrow, or a duty, believe me, that angel's hand is there; the gift is there, and the wonder of an overshadowing Presence. Our joys too; be not content with them as joys. They too conceal diviner gifts.

Life is so full of meaning and purpose, so full of beauty – beneath its covering – that you will find earth but cloaks your heaven.

Courage then to claim it; that is all; but courage you have, and the knowledge that we are pilgrims together, wending through unknown country – home.

And so, at this time, I greet you. Not quite as the world sends greetings, but with profound esteem and with the prayer that for you now and forever, the day breaks, and the shadows flee away.

– Brother Giovanni, 1513

IF YOU CAN'T FIX IT,
FEATURE IT

Trust your hopes, not your fears.
— David Mahoney

After beseeching his parents for a long time, eight-year-old Richie was given a baseball and bat. Quickly he ran into his back yard to play with his new equipment.

From the kitchen window Richie's parents watched him throw the ball in the air, swing at it, and miss. Again and again Richie tried to hit the ball, and missed. To his parents' chagrin the child failed to hit the ball every time.

After about ten minutes of wincing at watching only strikes, Richie's dad decided it was time to cheer up his son. He walked out to the boy, put his hand on Richie's shoulder, and in a consoling voice told him, "I guess maybe you're not cut out to be a hitter."

"Hitter?" Richie responded. "Who cares about hitting? – I'm on my way to a great pitching career!"

Consider the possibility that what you thought was wrong with you may actually be what's right with you. If this is so, you have made but one mistake: judging against yourself. You have arrived at a faulty conclusion based upon erroneous or insufficient evidence. It is easier to correct this one error – in perception – than to attempt to remedy the thousands of things you thought you needed to change to become perfect.

Master Key:

What You Thought was Wrong with You May be What's Right with You.

After I delivered a lecture on this theme, a young man asked me how his long-term shyness could possibly be right with him. I told him that shy people are extremely sensitive, easily affected by energies around them, vulnerable to the pain and feelings of others. This is not a character deficit, but a mark of psychic attunement and deep compassion. Shyness is the personality's way of protecting a sensitive being from being overwhelmed by energies that could overload his system, a defense mechanism established in wisdom to protect the emotional body from being frazzled. I told the fellow that his shyness could assist him to be supportive to others. Shy people, after learning to honor their sensitivity and set boundaries, often go on to become highly successful counselors, teachers, parents, and even motivational speakers, political leaders, and media personalities. Their sensitivity and compassion may eventually prove to be their greatest assets in rendering true service and finding inner reward.

A woman in another seminar stood up and tearfully shared her most vulnerable experience: "For over thirty years my most terrifying dragon was my epilepsy," Allisa confessed. "My fear of unpredictable seizures nearly paralyzed me. I never knew when an episode would overtake me, and I lived in constant anxiety and embarrassment. Once I had a seizure while driving over a bridge, and it took a lot of courage for me to drive again.

"After living in fright for many years, I became involved in a group at a center which offered counseling and support for epileptics. I gained so much from this service that I became a volunteer at the center, and eventually I was put on the paid staff. Now I run the support groups myself, and I am a sought-after speaker on the topic of epileptics adapting successfully in families and the workplace. This work has brought me fulfillment beyond description. Today I am an extremely happy person, and I thank God for bringing me to this place. Now I see that my epilepsy was not a curse; it was an arrow that shot me to my highest vocation."

You Just Have to Know Where to Put It

Everything in creation has a purpose. There is nothing in the universe that does not serve in its right time and place. (Even a clock that is stopped is right twice a day.) To judge against something is to deny God's hand in creating it.

Manure is an earthy example of how what's wrong in one context is extremely right in another. Nobody likes to be around manure (unless you are a farmer and know its true value). Manure is repulsive to the senses and unhealthy to touch – and that is perfectly in line with its function. If we spent too much time in its presence, we would become sick and set into motion a chain reaction of disease. So the only reasonable thing to do with manure is to get it out of here! We toss it into a field, away from where people are living.

Once manure gets into the field, it begins to go to work for us. Through natural processes it decomposes and becomes a primary nutrient for growing crops. In the time of a season, manure is transformed into glorious golden wheat, from which appetizing piping hot fresh bread is baked. To look at the bread, smell it, and enjoy its delicious taste, one would have no idea that manure was a prime factor in its creation.

So is manure good or bad? It is bad if used improperly and good if put in its right place. Was it made by God? As surely as fresh delectable bread.

Garbage and Gold

Most famous world change agents had to turn a lot of manure back into the soil. Here are a few examples of good soul farmers:

• Beethoven handled his violin awkwardly and preferred playing his own compositions over practicing technique. His teacher called him hopeless as a composer.

• Before he was elected to the presidency, Abraham Lincoln lost nine public elections, declared bankruptcy twice, and weathered a nervous breakdown and the death of a fiancée. He said, "You cannot fail unless you quit."

• Alfred Nobel, the namesake of the Nobel Peace Prize, was the inventor of dynamite. After seeing the destruction his invention wrought, he was inspired to devote his efforts to world peace.

• Babe Ruth, famous for setting the home run record, also holds the record for strikeouts.

• Albert Einstein did not speak until he was four years old, and didn't read until he was seven. His teacher described him as "mentally slow, unsociable, and adrift forever in foolish dreams." He was expelled, and refused admittance at the Zurich Polytechnic School.

• Eighteen publishers turned down Richard Bach's *Jonathan Livingston Seagull* before MacMillan finally published it in 1970. By 1975 it had sold more than seven million copies in the U. S. alone.

• Walt Disney was fired by a newspaper editor for lack of ideas. Disney also went bankrupt several times before he built Disneyland.[1]

Master Key:

Every Minus is Half of a Plus, Waiting for a Stroke of Vertical Awareness

Here are some other ways what you thought was wrong with you could be what's right:

Apparent Negative	Positive Potential
Apprehensive	Cautious, vigilant, reasonable
Class clown	Tension reliever, lighten-upper
Controlling	Leadership, take charge, stay on purpose
Daredevil	Risk taker, overcomer of fear, dispeller of perceived limits
Dark past	Preparation for higher service in the world, advocate for the downtrodden
Demanding	Claiming rights based on worthiness
Disabled	Overcomer, shift focus to unusual areas of ability, inspire others
Dreamer	Visionary, poet, mystic
Judgmental/ critical	Discerning, discriminating

Miserly	Prudence, self-control, wise dispersement of energy
Misfit	Independent, inner-directed
Naive	Innocent, virginal, pure heart
Non-committal	Willing to live the truth in the moment, adaptable to change
Obsessive	Thorough, detail-oriented, well-organized
Oversexed	Passionate, sensual, erotic
Reclusive	Inner-directed, contemplative, independent
Rebellious, argumentative	Challenger of status quo
Stubborn	Persistent, demands rights; perseveres to get job done

Every so-called negative trait holds the seed of a positive potential that goes far beyond the judgments we hold about it. "Character deficits" are simply character assets in the early stages of development. Directed wisely, the energy behind most undesirable personality traits can be turned into the greatest gifts of a lifetime.

The limited mind sees smallness; divine vision beholds present or inherent greatness. At any moment we have the choice of which vision we will choose to employ, and we will reap the results of the sight we accept.

ACTIVATION:

FROM MINUS TO PLUS

**Consider how what's wrong with you
may actually be what's right:**

Negative Trait or Act	*Positive Potential*

Shining the Light on the Shadow

Dr. Abraham Maslow is affectionately known as the father of humanistic psychology. His classic book, *Toward a Psychology of Being*, lifted modern psychology from a world view of assisting broken patients to cope with their illnesses, to that of elevating creative human beings to express their highest potential.

After twenty-five years as a practicing psychologist, Dr. Maslow came up with a revolutionary notion: instead of studying sick people in order to learn the anatomy of dysfunction, why not study healthy, productive, and successful people to discover what promotes self-actualization? If we want to learn how to make our lives work better, let's focus our attention on what *is* working instead of what isn't.

Many of us are well-versed in what is wrong with us. Given the invitation, most people could rattle off a long list of their problems, impediments, and shortcomings. As a society, we are very deficiency-conscious. We glorify our defects and play down our successes. We have become masters of disaster; we know our dark side as if it were our best friend, and clutch it as if it were our self. If we knew and championed our divinity as adamantly as we glorify our frailties, we would quickly transform our lives and the planet.

Our limits are but one facet of the masterfully sculpted beings we are. When characterizing yourself, be sure not to stop with your limits. That would be like defining an exquisite piece of property by its borders only, and ignoring the mansion built upon it. Yes, the limits are there, but there is also something else there, and the something else makes all the difference.

The key to rapid transformation is to *take what you have judged against, reframe it, and make it work for you.* You may be shy, argumentative, oversexed, or spaced out; that may be a fact of life which we are not disputing. Consider the possibility, however, that this characteristic is *not* the whole story of who and what you are; it is but a piece of a larger jig-saw puzzle. By itself it makes no sense and seems inappropriate, even damaging.

162

Seen in the context of your life's greater purpose, however, it may make perfect sense and prove to be a crucially significant element in your destiny and that of those you affect.

Part of your purpose in overcoming a difficulty may be to serve others who are still struggling with the same hardship. Consider, for example, Bill Wilson, one of the founders of Alcoholics Anonymous, or Dr. Helen Schucman, the scribe of *A Course in Miracles*. Both of these courageous individuals struggled for a long time to overcome their personal difficulties. Neither of them had any idea that the mastery they gained in their individual awakening would ultimately help many millions of people. When you move beyond an apparent limitation, you do so not just for yourself, but for many whom you will perhaps never see or know about. *A Course in Miracles* reminds us, "When I am healed, I am not healed alone."

Real Alchemy

The invitation before us is to get our head out of deficiency consciousness and begin to see possibilities where we once saw obstacles. A problem is simply an opportunity that has not been seen in its wholeness. Shift your vision from the part to the whole, and the problem will give way to a solution.

There is nothing that the spirit of love cannot take and turn into an asset. The next time you are inclined to label a person or situation "a pain in the ass," stop and rename it "a pain in the asset." Yes, there is a pain, but yes, there is an asset. There is an opportunity here which will empower you if you can discover and make use of it.

We are learning spiritual alchemy – taking the lead of life and turning it into gold. The secret of alchemy is to recognize that you *are* the gold. It is useless to make gold (material or metaphoric) out of any substance in the outer world unless you realize that the true treasure lies within. We are spiritual beings, born in the image of a whole and loving God. Know this basic truth, and the life you manifest will reflect your knowledge of your true identity.

The motion picture *The Dark Crystal* powerfully underscores the crucial value of joining *all* the components of the big picture. The film centers on a dying world reduced to two separate factions – the strong but vicious *Skeksies*, and the gentle but powerless *Mystics*. The Skeksies are mighty warriors, but have no integrity. The Mystics, on the other hand, are quite wise, but lack motivation. Both camps spend most of their energy attempting to stay separate and protect their private interests.

As their world is coming to an end, the Mystics and Skeksies must come together in one place, where a miraculous transformation occurs. Both groups mystically merge and meld into one another; the old degenerated beings in each faction disappear and become new and different creatures of brilliant light and strength. Separate, they were impotent. Together, they form an entity that far surpasses any they could imagine in their protected territories.

As a result of this psychic merger, their dying world returns to life. The parched and barren desert blooms again, flowers and animals return, and their formerly hopeless existence is resurrected as a realm of majestic beauty.

In becoming greater, neither of the groups had to give up what they were; each faction contained a unique element crucial to the creation of the whole being. The separation of their world into polarities was exactly what weakened it and caused it to die, and the bringing together of the polarities restored it to life. The weaknesses of each group were magnified as they pulled apart, and their strengths were amplified in their unity.

The Dark Crystal is a perfect symbol of the way we got ourselves into our current predicament, and the way we can and will find our way out. In separating ourselves into polarities and identifying only with what makes us different, we lose sight of the contribution our individuality may offer to the whole. We tend to put ourselves down for exactly the things we should be putting ourselves up for. We have criticized ourselves out of heaven, and in so doing cast ourselves into hell.

But that is not the end of the story. Even during our sojourn in darkness, we have been developing the qualities and traits that will once again open the door to a heavenly existence. We need to acknowledge the goodness of who and what we are, so we can make use of it, and heal the old world so we can find a new one.

We will not receive any new gifts to create the world we desire. We have already been given all we need. Our only need now is to use what we have; to capitalize on the power that lies within us, which has remained untapped because we have overlooked our strength and denied the power vested in us. Alchemize your most prominent weakness by peeling away the mask of deficiency to reveal and honor your greatest strength. It is waiting for you now. Let your life become a magnificent reflection of what you already are. There is no stopping those who have discovered the wonder at the core of their being. Live your destiny now, and you will bless everything Love created you to be.

> *Welcome is every organ and attribute of me. . .*
> *Not an inch nor a particle of inch is vile. . .*
>   – Walt Whitman

THE ATTITUDE OF GRATITUDE

Love cannot be far behind
a grateful heart and thankful mind. . .
These are the true conditions for your homecoming.
– A Course in Miracles

Samantha is my little guru who has a way of opening my heart like no other. She lives in the body of a child, but teaches me like an ancient sage. Samantha inspires me when I feel uninspirable. She is a gift from God.

One Saturday after our excursion to Pizza Hut, the mall, and a movie, I drove Samantha to her family's new residence. As we turned off the highway onto a dirt road that led to her house, my heart dropped to see that she and her parents were living in an old school bus in a field.

As Samantha showed me around her family's quarters, I began to feel sad that this little girl whom I love so much, was growing up in such a shoddy environment. As my eyes painfully fell upon rusted seams on the metal walls, cracked windows, and a leaking roof, I realized that her family had fallen into bare subsistence living. I wanted to rescue her from such a barren plight.

Looking up at me with her big brown eyes, Samantha asked me, "Would you like to see my room?"

"O.K.," I answered hesitantly.

The child took me by the hand and guided me up a makeshift staircase that led to a small wooden addition which had been superimposed over the roof of the bus. I shuddered to observe

167

that her room was in the same condition as the rest of the place, just barely livable. Looking around, I noticed one fairly attractive element of her abode, a colorful tapestry hung over the one section of the room that could be called a wall.

"How do you feel about living here?" I asked Samantha, waiting for a glum response.

Instead, to my surprise, her face lit up. "I love my wall!" she giggled.

I was stunned. Samantha was not kidding. She actually enjoyed the place because of this colorful wall. The child found a touch of heaven in the midst of hell, and this is what she chose to focus on. She was happy.

I drove home in a state of awe. This ten-year-old saw her life through the eyes of appreciation, and that made all the difference. I began to consider all the things in my life that I have complained about. I realized that in my preoccupation with what isn't there, I have been missing what *is* here. While focusing on rusty metal, I have overlooked some colorful tapestries. I made Samantha's statement my meditation: "I love my wall!"

Master Key:

The Attitude of Gratitude Brings Altitude.

The Big G's

While we have searched for therapists, gurus, spirit guides, and channeled entities to show us how to live, two paramountly powerful allies stand ready to deliver all the fulfillment we desire. The two "Big G's"[1] are *Gratitude* and *Generosity*.

Gratitude and generosity are inseparable sides of the same divine coin. If you are grateful for what you have received, you will naturally and joyfully want to share your blessings. Then, as you extend your love to others, you open the door to even greater abundance to flow into your life. The more you give, the more you will be given, and the more you will have available to give. The principle is the heaven-on-earth inverse of the fearful mind's notion of a vicious cycle; we might call it a "delicious cycle."

The most generous people in the world are also the most grateful. Those who understand the dynamics of abundant living know that joyful givers are also willing receivers. The divine circuit flows as we accept blessings with one hand and pass them along with the other.

A charming Japanese story captures the essence of the power of gratitude:

A hundred and fifty years ago there lived a woman named Sono, whose devotion and purity of heart were respected far and wide. One day a fellow Buddhist, having made a long trip to see her, asked, "What can I do to put my heart at rest?"

Sono said, "Every morning and every evening, and whenever anything happens to you, keep on saying, 'Thank you for everything. I have no complaint whatsoever.'"

The man did as he was instructed for a whole year, but his heart was still not at peace. He returned to Sono crestfallen. "I've said your prayer over and over, and yet nothing in my life has changed; I'm still the same selfish person as before. What should I do now?"

Sono immediately said, "'Thank you for everything. I have no complaint whatsoever.'"

On hearing these words, the man was able to open his spiritual eye, and returned home with a great joy.[2]

Gratitude, like faith, is a muscle. The more you use it, the stronger it grows, and the more power you have to use it on your behalf. If you do not practice gratefulness, its benefaction will go unnoticed, and your capacity to draw on its gifts will be diminished.

To be grateful is to find blessings in everything. This is the most powerful attitude to adopt, for there *are* blessings in everything. In the book of Genesis, we are told that after God created each new element of nature, He declared, "And this is good." If we want to know God, then we must become like God; to become like God is to celebrate beauty everywhere. In being grateful we return to our true nature, which opens the door for us to enjoy the bounty of heaven, even while on earth.

To accelerate your experience of abundance, begin to name it all "good." Find a way to reframe every situation until you can see the blessing in it. The highest use of the mind is that of a "blessing extractor." You have probably seen or used a juice extractor, which operates when you insert a carrot into a funnel atop the device. The extractor grinds up the vegetable, and soon rich golden juice gushes out of a spout, while the raw pulp is expelled through a chute on the side of the machine.

The blessing extractor works the same way. Into the funnel of higher consciousness you insert your experience. Flip on the switch by calling for a more empowering way of seeing the situation. As the machine whirs, allow pain, sorrow, and upset to be released out the side chute. Then open your mind to see the blessing you were missing as you were absorbed in the pain. The good is there if you are willing to find it.

Once you receive the gift of an experience, it will take on an entirely different meaning. You will not be tied to your past through resentment, and you will be free to take your next step toward your greater good. Toss the pulp in the compost heap (to be recycled as fertilizer for the next crop of carrots) and enjoy the juice. In other words, take the best and leave the rest.

Don't Worry, Be Happy

As long as human beings have looked for a higher answer to the mysteries of life, spiritual traditions have identified judgment as the primary necromancer of peace. Judgment ravages the gifts that gratitude would lay at the doorstep of the heart. You cannot sit in judgment and be happy.

In the Garden of Eden, Adam and Eve were told that they could eat of any fruit in the garden, including the Tree of Life. The only tree they were to stay away from, God instructed, was the Tree of the Knowledge of Good and Evil.

The story is, of course, a metaphor. Adam and Eve are not remote historical characters; they are *us*. The Garden of Eden is the abundant universe in which we live. The Tree of Life represents our right to be fully alive and vital in spirit, mind, and body. The Tree of Knowledge of Good and Evil symbolizes the separation of life into concepts of good and evil, seen arrogantly through the limited rational mind asserting that its heavily-shrouded perception is the sum of wisdom. The moment we introduce judgment into a situation or relationship, its purity is plundered. Perhaps you have had the experience of meeting someone wonderful, to whom you were deeply attracted. You enjoyed a blissful honeymoon period during which you saw them as a fantastic person, perhaps even faultless and godlike. Then you began to notice little flaws about them. At first their foibles seemed tiny, perhaps even cute or lovable in the face of their overall magnificence. Then the voice of judgment grew louder and stronger, until their faults seemed overwhelming, and the good you originally saw in them diminished to a mere trickle, or disappeared. You complained that they had misled you, changed, or they were not the person you thought they were. Then you parted angry, or disappointed at least. Afterwards you retreated to loneliness or self-protection, wondering how you could have made such a mistake.

This is the fall from the Garden of Eden. The expulsion from the Garden did not happen historically millions of years ago; it happened in your lifetime and mine, and it continues to play itself out daily. It was not God who expelled us; it is *we* who banish ourselves from paradise by seeing through the eyes of fear rather than love. The Creator told Adam and Eve exactly what they needed to do to stay in bliss: enjoy life and avoid judgment (in other words, "Don't worry, be happy.") It was only when Eve and Adam lowered their vision from unity to separation that they could no longer see the graced world into which they were born.

To keep separating life into good and bad, right and wrong, friendly and threatening, life and death, is to continue to take poisoned bites from the apple that cast us out of paradise. (The notion of "forbidden fruit" is an oxymoron. The fruit of judgment is not forbidden; it is rotten. But no one would believe that "rotten fruit is always sweeter.") There is life beyond opposites, but we will fail to recognize the perfection in and around us if we are preoccupied with judging, comparing, and competing. Born of one source, we will find our way back to the Garden only by seeing through the single eye of love.

The Journey Home

Since we ate the apple with the worm in it, we have spent most of our time trying to find our way back to the Garden. It is said that we spend nine months trying to get out of the womb, and the rest of our life trying to get back in. The womb to which we are seeking to return is not a physical one; it is our spiritual home. We all know that it is there; it's just how to get back that we are trying to figure out.

The good news is that our expulsion from the Garden was in *consciousness* only. Even while we have labored under the onus of judgment, we have carried heaven within us. We have had it all the time; we just didn't know it was here. *The cure for hell is not geographic; it is attitudinal.* We don't need to go anywhere; we just need to see from a clearer perspective. Hell is not an eternal dispensation from which we need to escape; it is a bad dream from which we need to awaken. As Emerson noted, "We may search the world for happiness, but unless we carry it within us, we will find it not."

Your awakening is already in process. You have begun the journey back to the Garden, and you are well along your way to reaching it. The final step to enter paradise is the recognition that you never left it. All external journeys but reflect our inner longing to remember that we are eternally free and infinitely loved. Once you recognize your identity as a spiritual being, nothing in the outer world can give you more than you already have, or make you more than you already are. You already live in Eden, and going anywhere else will not get you any more here.

The most direct route out of hell is to undo the way you left heaven: *drop judgment*. Return your mind and heart to the peace that proceeds from the vision of oneness. Release thoughts of an evil world trying to injure you. The level at which evil seems to exist is far beneath the dignity you were created to express. (The amount of consciousness contraction required to see an evil world is incredible!) The universe *is* trying to get you, but its motivation is not torture; it is liberation. Be at peace and fear not. Love is the only reality.

Swords into Plowshares

A Course in Miracles offers a prescription for healing the mind that has been tormented by painful thoughts. The *Course* suggests we practice the attitude, "I will judge nothing that occurs today."

ACTIVATION:

THE CRITICISM FAST

For one day resolve, "I will criticize nothing that occurs today. I will imagine that everything that happens is for my good and the good of others. I will release myself from the judgments I have laid upon myself. I will see myself, my motivations, and my actions as pure. I will not agree with the critical or judgmental words or attitudes of others. I will not deny the good within and around me. I give this entire day to the celebration of good."

If you can release judgment for one day, even one hour, even one minute, you will be well on your way back to the Garden of Eden. You will discover that criticism – especially self-criticism – has forged the links in the chain that has kept us bound in fear and pain. *Converting the focus of your energy from criticism to gratitude will change your life forever.* Imagine, for example, how dramatically the world would be transformed if governments took the trillions of dollars now invested in weapons and defense, and used the money for creative service projects such as health care, education, social services, and the endowment of the arts and sciences. In a short time the amount of human happiness and effectiveness on the planet would make the world an entirely different place.

On a personal level, the energy we invest in criticism is our internal defense expenditure. The more time we spend cutting ourselves and others down (even mentally) the less energy we have to heal ourselves, be creative, and enjoy life. Our preoccupation with what is wrong with us, is exactly what keeps us from seeing and enjoying what is right with us and life. There is much that is right – if we are but willing to see it.

The Divine Fool

In the Tarot deck, a fascinating card called "The Fool" depicts a young man walking gaily over a cliff, smelling a bouquet of flowers as he goes.

There are two classic interpretations of this symbol: the Fool could be the lowest card in the deck, or the highest. At face value, the man looks like an idiot, so oblivious to danger that he is about to plunge to his death. On the other hand, The Fool could represent one who is stepping out on faith. Perhaps he is not an idiot, but a sage. The precipice may symbolize not a physical cliff, but the unknown. When we launch out on an adventure we step off familiar solid ground into uncharted territory. While there may be danger in such a move, there is also the opportunity for discovery and attainment. Great geniuses and world change agents have usually appeared the fool at the outset of their undertaking, and are later considered heroes. The Divine Fool trusts so deeply that he is willing to walk innocently past apparent threat while appreciating the beauty of the flowers as he goes.

In the film *The World According to Garp,* Robin Williams portrays a divine fool. In his own offbeat way, Garp consistently finds good wherever he goes. Sometimes he looks like a jerk, but in many ways he is a sage in disguise.

The movie contains a marvelous scene in which Garp and his wife are inspecting a house they are considering buying. As the realtor is showing them the grounds, a plane flying overhead sputters, goes into a tailspin, and crashes into the second story of the house, where it lodges. The pilot climbs out of the cockpit, dusts off his flight jacket, and nonchalantly asks the realtor, "May I use the phone?"

In the wake of the destruction to the dwelling, Garp's wife gets into their car to leave. When Garp does not follow, she asks him, "Are you crazy? You're not still considering buying this place, are you?"

"Of course I am!" he answers enthusiastically. "The chances

of this happening again are infinitesimal!"

We can look at any experience two ways: through the eyes of fear, or the eyes of love. Fear sees limits, while love sees possibilities. Each attitude will be justified by the belief system you cherish. Change your allegiance from fear to love, and love will sustain you wherever you walk.

Judgment and Discernment

Many on the spiritual path have difficulty distinguishing between judgment and *discernment*. In our attempts to avoid judgment, we have gotten ourselves into painful situations because we have not exercised discernment. God told Adam and Eve not to judge, but He did not tell them not to discern.

The difference between discernment and judgment is the same as that between innocence and naivete. One blesses us as our natural faculty; the other fails to utilize our innate wisdom.

Judgment is the shroud that obscures true vision. Thoughts of lack, victimization, and separation smudge the lens through which we view life. We see, as the Apostle Paul described, "through a glass darkly." We miss the joy of living because we are not acknowledging the good before us.

Discernment is the ability to choose wisely on the basis of intuitive wisdom. If I went along with every proposal offered me, I would be sorry indeed. I have been invited to participate in unethical projects as well as activities that are quite legitimate, but do not belong to me to do. I would only be hurting myself as well as others if I said "yes" to something that is out of integrity or not in accord with my purpose. If someone is headed over a cliff in their car, you do not assist them by jumping into the car with them. Or perhaps they are not going over a cliff, but they are simply driving north while you are going south. You serve best by declaring, "This is my right place or direction, and I must be true to it." We do not need to make the other person wrong for going in their direction, but neither must we invalidate ourself for walking the path to which we are guided.

One way to know whether you are exercising judgment or discernment is to observe the kind and amount of emotion accompanying your action. Judgment sets up a disturbance in the emotional body; anger, conflict, and distress muddy the situation at hand. (Sometimes these energies are not obvious; if there is a tinge of upset, however, be sure that fear is calling the shots behind the scenes.) There is the sense that the other person is wrong, and they must be corrected, punished, or escaped. Actions proceeding from judgment leave you feeling ill-at-ease and unresolved. There is a lingering sense of victimization, bitterness, or resentment. You do not feel whole, nor do you see the other person as whole. You are haunted by a sense of incompletion. The incompletion, however, is within you. You have chosen a guide other than peace, and sooner or later you must go back to the point at which you stepped into separation, and make a different choice before you can move on with integrity.

Discernment, on the other hand, proceeds from peace; centered in the strength of your heart's resolve, you move clearly and calmly, trusting that all is well. You proceed from action rather than reaction. As you are inspired to serve, the universe lines up to support you. You can say "no" without ire or apology, for you realize that as you are true to your course, grace enfolds you and everyone involved. When judging, you attack the person rather than the action. When discerning, you may not approve of another's action, but you respect and hold compassion for the person behind the act. Dr. Eric Allenbaugh, author of *Wake-Up Calls*, [3] uses the motto, "Tough on issues, soft on people." Acting with discernment leaves you with a sense of peace; having heeded your inner voice, your heart is free.

All judgment must eventually give way to discernment. No matter how much separation or strife has come between you and another, it must eventually be resolved and healed. Neither you nor the universe will rest until you see and act on the truth behind the appearances. Love will have its way.

Lifestyles of the Rich in Spirit

John Robbins, author of the Pulitzer Prize-nominated book, *Diet for a New America*,[4] has made some strong choices to follow his intuitive wisdom. John has attracted a great deal of public attention in the wake of his renunciation of the fortune offered him by his father, who founded the Baskin-Robbins Ice Cream empire. Instead of ascending to the throne of the dynasty, as his father had planned for him, John became a vegetarian and activist for the humane treatment of animals, and for raising awareness about food choices that affect the entire planet.

The television show *Lifestyles of the Rich and Famous* invited John to be interviewed on the program. "I told their production staff that I am not rich (I live in a rented house) and I am not as famous as many of the people on the show," John confessed, "but they said they were interested in me anyway.

"The crew came and I showed them around my modest abode in the mountains of northern California. Afterward, several of the staff approached me with tears in their eyes. They told me that this was the most rewarding shoot they had ever done. They said that they felt an ease and a joy here that they had not experienced at the homes of the fabulously wealthy people they usually interviewed. They hugged me and thanked me profusely. Perhaps I planted the seeds for a new show called, *'Lifestyles of the Rich in Spirit.'*"

John's testimony reminded me that real abundance is not about money, things, or productivity. Real abundance is *an appreciation for enoughness*. Many people who have millions of dollars feel broke, and many people with no money feel rich. Abundance is not a situation – it is an attitude.

When I visited the island of Bali, I found the happiest people I have ever seen. The Balinese are among the friendliest and most easy-going people on the planet. When I asked my Balinese hotel waiter, who seemed to be smiling constantly, "Are you happy today?" he lit up and answered, "Always!"

I find it poignant that the Balinese have very little in the way of material possessions. They live in agrarian villages without electricity; old women still work bare-breasted in the rice fields, and wash their laundry on rocks by waterfalls. Spry elders smile and say hello as they carry huge pots of water on their heads, scaling rough-hewn steps up valley walls from streams. Only a small percentage of the Balinese own cars, and hardly any own property. Yet while they have very few possessions or material comforts, the Balinese live in a state of constant gratitude for the beauty of nature and community. They believe that the reward of good karma in past lives is to be born in Bali. They have pride in their island, their children, and themselves. They take care of one another and visitors. In continual celebration, these gentle people retain the consciousness of heaven, and thus live in it.

Seeking and Claiming

Harville Hendricks' masterful book *Getting the Love You Want*[5] has become a popular manual for many people seeking greater depth and reward in their relationships. I believe that the first step to getting the love you want is to *appreciate the love you have. The universe always gives you more of what you are focusing on.* Jesus taught, "To him that hath, more shall be given; to him that hath not, more shall be taken away." At first this axiom would appear to define a cruel God who rewards the rich and punishes the poor. To the contrary, Jesus was elucidating a paramountly important metaphysical principle, the very key to the manifestation of abundance. Jesus was teaching the importance of focusing on what we have or want, rather than on what we lack or do not want.

Master Key:

Fascination Is Fertilizer.
Whatever You Pay Attention To, Grows.

The physical universe, for all its apparent complexity, is simply a manifestation machine. Plug in your picture of reality, feed it with your thoughts and feelings, and *voila*, you have constructed the psychic (and subsequently the physical) environment in which you live. It is said that "we walk in the atmosphere of our own believing." Jesus declared, "As ye think, so shall it be."

The element that attracts substance to our lives is not just our thoughts and feelings; it is *fascination*. You will get more of whatever you are fascinated with. The universe observes the object of your attention and then says, in effect, "She is really fascinated with that – send some more her way!"

It is important to understand that *manifestation is an impersonal principle*. Even if you are fascinated with something you don't like, the universe will give you more of that, just as readily and willingly as it would give you something you desire. Attention, no matter what its object or motivation, is a magnet. It will pick up rusty old junk cars as well as brand new steel construction girders. Your job is to be careful where you point the magnet. The Universal Studio has given you the funding to produce a movie, and you are free to make any production from *Friday the Thirteenth* (including a long series of inane sequels), to *It's a Wonderful Life*, and anything else in between the poles of horror and ecstasy. There is no power outside the one within us; our destiny is what we make it.

If you don't like what you are getting, the most direct way to transform your results is to *change the object of your fascination*. Focus your thoughts, words, and attention on what you want more of, rather than what you do not like. Define yourself and act on what you are for, rather than what you are against. Being against something always creates more of it. What you resist, expands and persists. When Nobel Peace Prize recipient Mother Theresa, considered by many to be a living saint, was invited to speak at an anti-war rally, she declined, explaining, "If you want me to come and speak for peace, I will do that; but to speak against war is just another form of war."

Consider this striking example of misdirected fascination: In a restaurant I noticed a woman wearing a white sweatshirt with the word *Pornography* splashed across the front in big red letters. Printed in tiny black letters below the red were the words, "is not the will of God." The latter phrase was written in such small type that I had to be quite near the shirt to read it. "Pornography," however, was easily visible from across the street.

It occurred to me that while this woman was intending to campaign against pornography, she was advertising it. The moment I read the huge word on her sweatshirt, images of pornography came to my mind. She would have been more effective in her campaign if she wore a shirt advertising what she wanted to *create*, not destroy. She might have worn a shirt with an image depicting two people embracing lovingly, or some phrase that would have reminded onlookers of healthy sexuality. This woman did not understand the metaphysical meaning behind Jesus' instruction to "turn the other cheek." To improve our lives, we must look in the direction of that which serves us rather than what hurts us.

If you are fascinated with the ways the universe doesn't support you, how people let you down, or how there is not enough time, money, sex, or available men, you are giving the universe a clear and strong message to send you more of the same experience. If you would like a different result, you must feed the universal manifestation machine a different starter material. Give Spirit something else to grow for you. Apple seeds will not grow oranges, and fascination with lack will not produce abundance. If you want to demonstrate greater prosperity, you must think prosperity thoughts, speak prosperity words, and take prosperity action; if you want more rewarding relationships, you need to become engrossed with what is working in your relationships, rather than what is not. If you want to live a life of constant celebration, start by appreciating the gifts already given instead of complaining about the lack of those you await.

Already Home

The most powerful prayer begins with "Thank you." Many of us bring God long lists of things we want (and that is fine, as it affirms that we can have what we want and there is a higher power that can deliver it). But there is an even more potent method to bring about greater manifestation: *give thanks now for what you already have.* To bring about the most specific demonstration, give thanks for what you already have in the same area of life as the things you desire. (For example, if you desire more fulfilling communication in a particular relationship, begin to pay more attention to the areas in which you are already communicating well, with this person or others.) You will be amazed at how *appreciation accelerates manifestation.* The difference between a prayer of "I want" and "Thank you" is like that between a propeller-driven airplane and a jet. More exactly, it is the difference between getting somewhere and already being there. There is no bridge to cross; you are already home.

A famous basketball player was asked how he consistently maintained his status as the highest scorer on the team. "It's simple," he explained. "The ball is in the basket before it leaves my hand." This athlete may not have recognized that he was using a principle suggested by Jesus: "Give thanks for the answer to your prayer before you even receive it." Two millennia after Jesus, Jonathan Livingston Seagull's teacher Chiang echoed the precept: "To fly as fast as thought, to anywhere that is, begin by knowing that you have already arrived."[6]

What desire seeks, gratitude already claims. All that your heart yearns for is already yours. To claim your greater good, see yourself as already whole and blessed. When you bless what you have, your sense of blessing will quickly and naturally expand until you recognize that you already have it all. When you recognize that you already have it all, your life will manifest the demonstration that this is so.

Gratitude is much more than an act of etiquette or spiritual discipline. It is a mystical key to the manifestation of abundance, the door to heaven on earth. All that you seek is within you now. Jesus invited us into the kingdom of wholeness: "Come, for all things are now ready." He told the disciples, "You say that it is four months until the fields are ready for harvest. I say look now, and see the fields are already white with harvest."

Master Key:

Appreciation Accelerates Manifestation.

ACTIVATION:

THE ATTITUDE OF GRATITUDE

For a month, keep a journal of everything for which you are grateful. Record everything that comes to mind, even the slightest thought or experience of appreciation. Speak of your gratitude as you become aware of it, especially to people to whom you are grateful. Tell them exactly what they have done, and how you feel.

At the end of the month (if you are still on the earth plane), note which objects of gratefulness you received more of, as a result of your appreciating them.

The Crucial Shift

While many astounding changes are now occurring on the planet, the most crucial shift is in *consciousness*. More important than our strides in being able to communicate more quickly, genetically engineer our children, and extend the life span of the human body, is the fact that we are learning to think with a higher mind and see with brighter eyes. Sending rockets to the far reaches of the universe is an infinitesimal accomplishment in comparison to our minds piercing beyond previously accepted barriers, embracing larger possibilities for our destiny as divine beings. Plumbing the depths of the sea is a tiny feat in light of the discovery of the treasures that lie within the hidden recesses of our souls. Regularly, now, skilled physicians are replacing failing hearts with donor transplants. Yet even more auspicious is the healing of broken hearts as they awaken to the love that once lay dormant.

Behind all of these monumental advancements, there rests one awakening which will ultimately lead us to all the good we yearn for: we are learning to live with grateful hearts. Innocent simplicity will lead us back to the heaven we lost in the wake of our sophisticated social engineering. We are learning to love ourselves and our lives. We are remembering that we deserve good because our nature is good. At the heart of all success is gratitude, and at the heart of all gratitude is gentle love.

Out of the determination of the heart the eyes see. . .
Better to lose count while naming your blessings
than to lose your blessings while counting your troubles.
                                        – Maltbie D. Babcock

GRACELAND

The quality of mercy is not strained;
It droppeth as the gentle rain from heaven.
— Shakespeare, *The Merchant of Venice*

The man sitting next to me on the airplane was not used to waiting, and it showed. Our departure had been delayed several hours, and finally we boarded the aircraft – only to sit on the runway for another hour. To offset his uneasiness, my fidgeting seatmate plunged himself into obsessive doingness, making several calls from the airphone and nervously rearranging the magazines in the pouch in front of him. He was one anxious traveller.

Finally the pilot announced that we were just waiting for clearance to push back from the gate. "For those of you who would like to listen to our communication with air traffic control," the gravelly voice on the loudspeaker announced, "I will pipe those transmissions onto channel nine of your inflight audio."

My neighbor quickly donned his headset and listened intently. After a minute his eyes lit up and he pressed the button to call the flight attendant.

"May I help you, sir?" the attendant came and asked.

"You can tell the pilot we can leave now," the man firmly commanded. "We just got clearance."

"I'll be sure to do that right away," the attendant smiled. Perhaps my seatmate did not realize that the pilot was well aware that we had been cleared to take off. An entire cockpit of professionals was tuned to the same channel, their ears perked just as keenly for the news. The man, however, designated himself responsible for the plane leaving. But the airplane did not need his permission to leave. There was a pilot in charge.

As we lifted off the runway I began to consider the times in my life when I have tried to put myself in the Pilot's seat. How much unnecessary energy I have invested in manipulating to keep myself safe, attempting to control other people's lives and the world! Instead, I could have sat back, enjoyed a magazine, and let the Pilot fly the plane for me.

Perhaps you, like my fellow passenger and myself, have designated yourself *General Manager of the Universe*, responsible to make sure that everything always goes right, everyone does what they are supposed to do, and everyone is happy. And perhaps you have struggled with disappointment, anguish, fatigue, or illness in the wake of your frustrated attempts to steer the universe in the direction of your choosing.

The good news is that you do not need to run the universe. There is a brilliantly orchestrated system in operation, which goes far beyond the comprehension of the mind that believes it is in control. Fortunately, life does not depend on human understanding for it to unfold in wisdom. The fearful mind is fooled by appearances, while Spirit abides in trust. Love is always present, even when the small self experiences limited visibility. If you need to do something to serve the plan of good, you will be told (from inside out) what it is. Otherwise, relax and enjoy the ride. Be at peace. The world will not fall apart if you release your anxious control. To the contrary, you might be surprised at how masterfully your life comes together when you let go of the notion that something terrible will happen if you do not constantly protect yourself. Perhaps the situation is a call for love, rather than control. Perhaps something wonderful will happen. Perhaps, instead of the disaster you fear, a miracle is in the offing. Let the Pilot fly.

A Tale of Two Cities

While the billions of people on the planet seem to be living in many different cities and countries, there are really only two places to live:

Scare City is a frightening, threatening place to live. It is the home of those who choose fear as their guide.

In *Scare City* there is never enough of anything. Money is always in short supply, goods and services are overpriced, and you cannot trust the people who provide them. You have to be very careful who you associate with in *Scare City*, for there you are susceptible to all kinds of diseases, intrusions, and violations of your well-being. At every crossroads you have to guard yourself from villains who will use and abuse you. You never know what threat lurks behind someone's apparent good intentions; they must have some hidden agenda which they will ultimately use against you.

The driving motivation in *Scare City* is survival. "Take care of yourself, and let everyone else do the same" is the name of the game. Why risk your well-being to help someone else? You have it hard enough as it is. If the world took better care of you, you might be able to do something for it – but until that happens you had better cling to what you have, for nice guys finish last and only the strong survive.

Relationships in *Scare City* are always disappointing. While some people seem to be your ally at first, when you get to know them you find they have major character defects and cannot be counted on. Then you have to leave or get rid of them to protect yourself. When someone comes along that you really like and want to continue to associate with, they leave you. While many have made promises to extricate you from the pain and sorrow of *Scare City*, each pledge has been broken. With every disappointment you vow that next time you will be more wary to trust.

Hourly, newscasts and newspapers in *Scare City* splash headlines of disaster and mayhem before the eyes of already terrified observers. It seems that no matter how hard people try to stay safe, there is yet another more horrifying report of massive layoffs, poisons in the foods, deranged criminals on the loose, and newly-discovered incurable diseases. Life in *Scare City* just seems to be getting worse all the time, and sullen minds behind sunken eyes wonder, "What ever happened to the good old days?" There is no respite from the daily grind. Life is a struggle, and then you die. That's just the way it is in *Scare City*.

Sound familiar? The existence you have just read about is the dominant theme for billions of human beings on the planet now and throughout history.

Perhaps you will also recognize this place:

Just down the road (a thought) from *Scare City*, there is a domain entirely unlike it. Those who live in this realm enjoy abiding peace, harmony, and gratitude for the beauty and goodness they find wherever they look. That is why their buns are dancing all the time, and the kingdom is appropriately called *A Bun Dance*.

Relaxed people walk the pathways of *A Bun Dance* at all hours of the day and night, trusting that Spirit walks with them. Bun Dancers live beyond the belief in opposing forces of good and evil that dominates the consciousness of those in *Scare City*. They acknowledge one Force of Love that gently holds the entire universe in its benevolent care.

Those living in *A Bun Dance* enjoy loving relationships. They appreciate the gifts bestowed by their loved ones, rather than criticizing them for what they are not. While the residents of *Scare City* are always seeking, the denizens of *A Bun Dance* are constantly finding. Bun Dancers have discovered that the riches of life are available right where they are.

When a stage of relationship is complete in *A Bun Dance*, both partners acknowledge and celebrate the gifts that each has brought to the union. Each partner knows that only greater good awaits, and there is a sense of yet deeper blessing as each partner takes the next step toward their destiny. When people unite in *A Bun Dance*, their love and friendship last for a lifetime and beyond.

188

The prevalent theme of livelihoods in *A Bun Dance* is creativity. When Bun Dancers awake each morning, their minds and hearts are brimming with creative ideas through which they can bring new expression, art, and color to life. Bun Dancers choose their professions out of passion, not entrapment; they work and play for love, not money.

Money in *A Bun Dance* is equated not with lack, but with the delight of passing along energy to expand freedom and service. Whereas those in *Scare City* have made money into an emotionally charged issue over which to fight, Bun Dancers recognize that all of their supply comes not from people, but from God. Manifestation is not a function of earthly supply, but spiritual consciousness. Money in *A Bun Dance* is an expression of good, and the more it passes along, the more it expands.

Since there is no perception of victimhood in *A Bun Dance*, there are no villains. As a result, public monies are not required for defense, crime protection or punishment, and the repayment of massive loans, as they are in *Scare City*. Instead, community monies are channeled into service, education, health care, and the endowment of the creative arts and sciences. As a result, the quality of life in *A Bun Dance* steadily expands.

Education in *A Bun Dance* is a delight for students and teachers. The goal of the school system is to draw forth the greatness in each child, in honor of their unique gifts. Competition in *A Bun Dance* is unknown; instead, collaboration, mutual support, and win-win models are promoted. Children are taught only those skills and knowledge they express an interest in mastering.

There is no organized religion in *A Bun Dance*. Instead, each individual follows the voice of Spirit within his heart. Somehow everyone is in their right place at the right time, and they work together well. The notions of competition between religions, holy wars, arguments over the correctness of dogma, inquisitions against infidels, and damnation of sinners, is entirely unheard of in *A Bun Dance*. God is a loving reality that is felt in the heart, and drawn into expression by simple caring; peace cannot be organized; it can only be shared.

Social activities in *A Bun Dance* center around the sharing of creative talents. As everyone in the realm is in touch with their unique creative gifts, they enthusiastically participate in the expression of art, music, dance, and unique craftsmanship.

To look down from above, one would be amazed to see that *Scare City* and *A Bun Dance* are not very far from one another. Both have the same resources available, yet each realm uses them in an entirely different way. The distance and difference between hell and heaven is measured not in altitude, but in attitude.

ACTIVATION:

SCARE CITY OR A BUN DANCE?

I

Choose a situation that has occupied a great deal of your thoughts, feelings, and attention. On a separate piece of paper, write down all the thoughts and feelings that have occurred to you in relation to this situation. Record in detail every notion, musing, judgment, feeling, fantasy, deduction, pondering, and conclusion you have about this.

Leave space around each response for you to cut it out of the page with scissors, and when you have completed all of your responses, do so.

Put the pieces aside for now, and wait until the next Activation for further instructions. (No peeking!)

By Grace I Live

While the residents of *Scare City* labor under the law of sin and punishment, the people in *A Bun Dance* enjoy a state of Grace. The acceptance of Grace begins with our recognition that we are worthy of it. By virtue of our birthright as children of God, we deserve everything that is worthy of the Kingdom – *and no less*. God does not worry about paying His rent. God does not struggle with health challenges. All of God's relationships are rewarding. As God's children, neither must we settle for less.

Jesus taught that "It is the Father's good pleasure to give you the Kingdom." God takes no delight in our suffering and finds no necessity in our pain. God rejoices only in our happiness. God has no problems, and if we do not go looking for them, we might find that we have none, either.

The story is told about three men who were sentenced to death by guillotine. One was a doctor, another a lawyer, and the third an engineer. The day of execution arrived, and the three prisoners were lined up on the gallows.

"Do you wish to face the blade, or look away?" the henchman asked the doctor. "I'll face the blade!" the physician courageously replied.

The doctor placed his neck onto the guillotine, and the executioner pulled the rope to release the blade. Then an amazing thing happened – the blade fell to a point just inches above the doctor's neck, and stopped!

The crowd of gathered townspeople was astonished, and tittered with speculation. After a bevy of excited discussions, the executioner told the doctor, "This is obviously a sign from God that you do not deserve to die. Go forth – you are pardoned." Joyfully the doctor arose and went on his way.

The second man to confront death was the lawyer, who also chose to face the blade. The cord was pulled, down fell the blade, and once again it stopped but a few inches from the man's naked throat! Again the crowd buzzed – two miracles in one day! Just as he did minutes earlier, the executioner informed the prisoner that divine intervention had obviously been issued, and he, too, was free. Happily he departed.

The final prisoner was the engineer who, like his predecessors, chose to face the blade. He fitted his neck into the crook of the guillotine and looked up at the apparatus above him. The executioner was about to pull the cord when the engineer pointed to the pulley system and called out, "Wait a minute! – I think I can see the problem!"

Within each of us there resides an overworking engineer who is more concerned with analyzing the problem than accepting the solution. Many of us have become so resigned to receiving the short end of the stick in life, that if we were offered the long end, we would doubt its authenticity and refuse it.

We must be willing to drop the heavy load of guilt, unworthiness, and self-denial we have carried for so long, perhaps lifetimes. We must openly affirm that we are ready to receive all the good that life has to offer us, without argument or wariness. Then we must accept our good – not just in word, but in action. In so doing we claim our right to live in a new world – one which attests that we are deserving not of punishment, but of release, freedom, and celebration.

ACTIVATION:

SCARE CITY TO A BUN DANCE

II

Copy the headings below on a separate piece of large paper. Then take the pieces of paper you cut up for the last Activation and place them in one of the categories, indicating which belief system the thought represents.

| *Scare City* | *A Bun Dance* |
| *Thoughts and Feelings* | *Thoughts and Feelings* |

Use your list to become aware of the ways you are helping or hurting yourself by dwelling on thoughts in each domain. What pattern do you see about the way you are approaching this situation? What can you do to shift your focus and energy from *Scare City* to *A Bun Dance*?

Let the Love In

There are several techniques you can practice to enjoy a deeper, more abiding experience of grace:

1. *Be willing to accept greater good when offered.*

Allow yourself to be loved and supported by family, friends, and the universe-at-large. I meet many people who complain that they do not have enough time, money, or emotional support, and then when these very gifts are offered them, they refuse them. My aunt regularly complained about the condition of her living room carpet; when I offered to buy her a new one, however, she turned me down flat. There are two key elements in the transmission of a gift – the gift must be given, but it must also be received. Consider the possibility that you have been, and are being given many gifts which are simply waiting for you to accept them.

Become a champion for your own deservingness and an authority on your worth. You do not need to go around bragging about how wonderful you are (bragging is just a cover for insecurity) or demanding that people treat you better (demanding is sign that you do not trust the universe to provide for you naturally). Simply know that you deserve to be supported in the finest way ("Surely goodness and mercy shall follow me all the days of my life") and demonstrate that you are worthy by asking for the best and accepting it when it comes.

Receiving a compliment, for example, is a very simple demonstration of self-worth – yet it is extremely difficult for many people to gracefully welcome praise. In some of my seminars I ask a few people to stand before the group to accept compliments. You should see them squirm – you would think they were being asked to face a firing squad! Most people think so little of themselves that, when put in the spotlight, they fear they will be exposed and condemned. Meanwhile the universe is simply seeking to give them the love and acknowledgement they deserve. Their fearful fantasies of failure obscure the gifts that are being offered. The way you receive compliments is symbolic of the extent to which you are willing to let love enter and fill your life.

Try this experiment: for one week or month, imagine that the love you are being offered is real. Do not question or analyze the gifts placed at your doorstep, in word or deed. Assume that if someone says or does something kind to you, it is because they truly mean it, and you deserve the blessings they proffer. Interpret all invitations and opportunities as loving endowments from a benevolent universe extending itself to enfold you with ever more joy. As you let the love in, your life will change in miraculous ways, and you will wonder how you ever could have questioned the intentions of a generous world.

2. *Forgive yourself now.*

Give yourself the release you hope to receive from other people. Do not wait for God or others to pardon you. God has already pardoned you – it is you who need to pardon yourself. (*A Course in Miracles* suggests that "God does not forgive because He never has condemned.") Take back the power you have given human beings to make you or break you. People may or may not forgive you; it does not matter. What matters is that you let yourself off the hook now. When you have forgiven yourself, you will live in a forgiven world.

I notice how hard I have been on myself for making mistakes. I grew up with a high value on being right, looking good, and succeeding. For a long time I regularly whipped myself with a perfectionist attitude. If I made a mistake, I believed there was a moral stigma attached to it; it meant that I was inept, "less-than," or stupid. Even if I performed ninety-nine percent of a task with excellence, I would remember the one percent that in my judgment was not perfect.

One day I had a turning point. As I was feeding the birds in my aviary, I bumped into a water dish and knocked it over, spilling the contents on the ground. As I picked up the bowl I noticed that I did not have a charge on making a blunder. I saw the event in a completely neutral way. It was simply information, an occurrence, a fact of life. There was nothing good or bad about it. It was a scene in a movie, and it had no more or less meaning than I gave it. The act deserved no more attention than a moment's notice. I was not less good or less lovable because I had made an error. If I chose, I could use the information to not repeat it. In any event, the information would be encoded within me, and I would learn from the experience whether I observed it consciously or not.

As I closed the door of the aviary behind me, I experienced a sense of release akin to having a thousand-pound weight lifted off my shoulders. Through this mundane event, I recognized that all of the judgments and attacks I have ever made upon myself were unwarranted. Never again need I hurt myself with harsh thoughts or frighten myself with expectations of punishment. God had no charge on this error, and neither need I. Errors occur only on the most shallow dimension of life; beneath and behind the surface of appearances, love remains in full force, flowing limitlessly like a great artesian well that never runs dry.

A Course in Miracles asks us to affirm, "I will not hurt myself again." The *Course* distinguishes between a sin and an error: a sin calls for punishment, while an error requires but correction. The *Course* explains that in the eyes of God there is no sin; it is only our picture of reality that makes sin appear to be real. So ends sin, not eternally in the pits of hell, but in a gentle moment of liberating awareness.

3. *Extend support and forgiveness to others.*

In demonstrating to others that their mistakes are not sins, we release ourselves from the punishment we expect for our perceived iniquities. It is impossible to give something without receiving it the moment you give it; whatever energy you broadcast to others must flow through you before it gets to them.

Anger, judgment, and resentment take their toll on the giver before they reach the intended recipient; and if the other person refuses to accept the poisoned "gift," the only one who suffers is the sender. By the same principle, love, compassion, and forgiveness will heal you before they are delivered to their recipient. And even if the receiver is unable to accept these gifts, you will enjoy their blessings.

If you want to be forgiven for your own sins, demonstrate to your friends that the sins they believe they have inflicted against you (and others) are not real. To offer pardon and release to those who believe they do not merit them, is to fulfill our highest function as divine beings, created in the image and likeness of a compassionate God.

Recently I received a phone call from a woman who was organizing a program for me. Melissa sheepishly told me that she would be unable to manage the event. I heard great anxiety in her voice as she confessed that she had bitten off more than she could chew, and she needed to attend to her family's needs. Listening to Melissa's trembling apology, I could sense that she was just waiting for the axe to fall.

"That's O.K." I told her, "I understand your situation."

There was a long silence on her end of the line, followed by a deep sigh.

"Those are the two sweetest syllables I have ever heard," Melissa told me. Her anxiety was replaced by a deep relief. "I was being terribly hard on myself for not being able to complete this project. I thought you would really be upset. You don't know how much it means to me that you understand and support me. Thank you with all my heart."

As we hung up, I felt the most rewarding feeling in the depths of my being. Yes, I was disappointed that Melissa was unable to complete the job she took on – but I felt so much better to regard her with appreciation instead of anger. I could (and did) find another person to oversee the program; that was not a big problem. In light of the peace and freedom she and I both felt when I released her, the worldly job meant very little.

Perhaps the entire purpose of our entering into that job together was for us to experience the compelling results of that conversation. Perhaps the destiny of our interaction was not for her to be the organizer, but for me to have a chance to offer grace, and for Melissa to receive it.

I have remained good friends with Melissa, and my being understanding with her has only added to my life and hers. Further, at times when I have been unable to complete a job I have taken on, I have been much more forgiving of myself. I understand that love and compassion far outshine the task at hand. Love and compassion *are* the task at hand.

4. *Celebrate the good that befalls others.*

When we become excited about the good that comes to others, our focus on abundance stimulates the universe to send the same blessings our way. To curse another's fortune is to sabotage your own. ("That which you give shall be meted out to you.") In ignorance, the fearful mind sees another's gain as our loss. The ego, steeped in competition, believes in a limited-supply universe in which those who succeed are taking good from those who do not.   Such an attitude reinforces our self-image as a victim and throws the self into a sense of "less-than."

What the ego fails to recognize is that the universe is infinite in resources and possibilities. Gaze into the heavens on a clear starry night, and behold the vast potential of life. In the same way, each of us has the capacity to manifest full abundance. There is no ceiling on life; any borders we experience are erected by our own minds. As Ernest Holmes declared, "All limitations are self-imposed." There is room at the top for everyone.

Just as we have engineered our own limitations, we can release ourselves from them. A powerful way to reprogram envy is to re-form the word into an acronym. The letters *N.V.* stand for *New Vision.* When you see a colleague receiving something you would like, remind yourself that this person represents a part of your mind; the fact that someone in your immediate world is gaining something you value, means that the success you seek is coming closer to you. You are beholding a demonstration that such an event is possible, available, and that you, too, can and will manifest the same experience for yourself. The recipient is a harbinger of similar good on its way to you. Don't shoot the messenger who bears good tidings. Envy is wasted energy; take the emotion behind envy and let it work on your behalf.

A friend of mine won six millions dollars in a state lottery. There was a time in my life when I would have inwardly whined, "Why can't *I* win six millions dollars? I bought a ticket, and she won – and *I* didn't." Instead, upon hearing the news, I became excited. "Wow!" I thought. "Someone I know became six million dollars wealthier overnight. Here is a clear demonstration that an immediate and unexpected delivery of abundance is possible. Bonnie represents the part of myself that is coming closer to greater abundance." So it is for all the good we observe.

5. *Bless life for the gifts it brings rather than cursing it for what it lacks.*

When someone shows up in your life, choose to celebrate the good they are doing you, and overlook their shortcomings. Everyone we encounter brings us a blessing – but we must be open to receive it. Sometimes the blessing is obvious, in a form you expect or can relate to, and sometimes the gift is wrapped in a cloth that looks like a challenge. No matter what package in which the present arrives, eventually the blessing is all that remains. When we leave this world, and all of our experiences are seen in the highest perspective, it is the love that we will remember and take with us. All of the other drama ends up like edited film on the cutting room floor. It was just the vehicle for healing to occur.

Perhaps you met someone you believed was the long-awaited friend, soulmate, guru, ticket to success, or savior you had been praying for. In this person you found some of the most important qualities you value. Then, to your disappointment, you discovered that this person was a human being, and you felt disillusioned, ripped off, and resentful. You may have been tempted to curse the person for misleading you. You may have even become angry at God for teasing you or letting you down yet another time.

There is, however, another way to regard such an experience – one that will empower you. Consider such a person to be a *representation* of your desired good. The person showed up to demonstrate that the qualities you desire are not a pipe dream. If there is one person who embodies the traits you seek, there is another. Such qualities are real and available. Just because this person didn't turn out to be what you expected, does not mean that this is the end of the story; it may just be the beginning. This person may have come to help you clarify what you are seeking. Through this experience you may have learned what you want and what you don't want. You are closer to your goal than when you began.

There is no need to be hard on yourself, either. Congratulate yourself for attracting someone who nearly matched your vision. You must be a powerful manifestor to draw greater good to you. Remember that whatever you concentrate on, grows; focus on the gifts and more will come to you.

Mastery Through Grace

If we experience lack in an abundant universe, it is not because life is unable to supply what we desire; it is because we have been unready or unwilling to accept it. One immediate step you can take to receive more good is to ask for it. The act of asking for something is an affirmation that you deserve it. Now is the time to make a stand for your worthiness. Asking for what you want is not arrogant; it is a pure and humble declaration that you are the child of a loving God who delights in Her children's well-being. Humility does not mean sitting in a corner meekly waiting for God to drop you some crumbs, if you are lucky. It is the state of being an open and receptive vessel. To ask for what you need is an act of mastery.

Master Key:

Asking for What You Want
Increases Your Chances of Getting it.

You cannot receive what you do not request. Love yourself enough to accept richer blessing, and the universe must supply it. Life will work on your behalf, but you must know your worth for it to bestow all it has to give.

Case Dismissed

Albert Einstein posited that all philosophical and scientific enquiry could be boiled down to one simple question: "Is the universe a friendly place?" The way we answer this question determines whether we will live in *Scare City* or *A Bun Dance.*

A Course in Miracles offers a humorous yet liberating assessment of our fears of crucifixion. "Will God judge you?" the *Course* asks. "Indeed!" the *Course* affirms; "everyone will be judged in the end." Yet here is where the *Course* goes beyond castigation and into grace: "And the final judgment on everyone will be *'Case dismissed.'"*

Many of us have put ourselves through unnecessary trials for years. Even if we never set foot in a courtroom, we mentally and emotionally go over argument after argument for our culpability. We anticipate awful punishments, and then attempt to do good things to offset the guilt we believe will lead to our conviction. Below the table of the obvious, we pay the lawyer for our prosecution, while undermining the counsel for our defense.

The judge, jury, and executioner live in your head alone. Sally Kempton noted, "It's hard to fight an enemy with outposts in your head." Your fears of persecution are unfounded. No one can or will persecute you more than you persecute yourself. We cannot blame others for laying guilt on us; we live with only as much guilt as we accept. We will not gain freedom by casting daggers at shadows, which present themselves only when we stand with our back to the light. Change your outlook, and you will change your world.

The knowledge that you deserve love is your ticket from *Scare City* to *A Bun Dance*. Release yourself and you release the world. You have lived in limits long enough; a new life awaits you as you open to embrace it.

> *By grace I live. By grace I am released.*
> — *A Course in Miracles*

GOOD ENOUGH
TO BE TRUE

*Show me a perfect person and
I'll show you a perfect nuisance.*
– Hilda Charlton

I am a reformed Do-Gooder. I did good for many years before I realized the error of my ways. Now I do not try to do good, and I do a lot of good.

My recovery began when I visited the home of some new friends in Toronto. I admired my hosts Tom (an accomplished author) and Christine (a gifted clairvoyant), and I wanted to impress this couple as being a kind and thoughtful person.

After our dinner the dishes were cleared and dessert was served to the gathered party. Being a card-carrying Do-Gooder, I donned my Samaritan garb and headed for the kitchen to wash the dishes. (To let everyone know what a humble servant I was, I whistled occasionally to let them know I was sacrificing my social time to be helpful.)

After finishing the dishes, I noticed there remained one item to be cleaned – a wok. Since the implement seemed fairly greasy and rusty, I decided I would really do good. I found a large piece of steel wool and scrubbed that baby to the bone!

What I didn't know, in my zeal to display helpfulness, was that woks are *supposed* to be tarnished; the ingrained oils season the metal for superior cooking.

Just as I finished scouring the wok, Christine walked into the kitchen to see what I was doing. Proudly I held up the wok like a child showing his mommy a finger-painting he has made in kindergarten. "Look, Christine," I announced gleefully, "I cleaned your wok!"

Christine's jaw dropped almost to her knees. "It took me three years to season that wok!" she exclaimed.

I am delighted to declare that was the last time I ever did good. If you, too, can identify with terminal helpfulness, you are welcome to join my newly founded chapter of D.G.A. – *Do-Gooders Anonymous.*

Truly Helpful

There is an essential difference between doing good and serving. When one is bent on doing good, she proceeds from a preconceived notion of what good looks like, and superimposes that picture over the situation at hand – usually at the expense of what is actually required for the occasion. The Do-Gooder is more interested in being seen as a helpful or charitable person, than in meeting the need of the recipient. The classic Do-Gooder is the young man who takes a little old lady across the street and then finds out she didn't want to go.

True service, on the other hand, is born of the giver's sincere desire for the recipient to be happy. The donor bases his actions on the receiver's requirements rather than the giver's need to give. The act of service is not a box into which the present situation is stuffed; it is a loving supportive hand, offered to be used as Spirit requires.

A Course in Miracles suggests an affirmation to apply to any situation in which we are unsure of our role:

"I am here only to be truly helpful."[1]

The key word here is *truly.* In rendering real service, we seek to do what will actually serve, rather than what will look good, what societal etiquette would dictate, what will make us feel like a good Samaritan, or what we or others have done in the past that has worked.

In the course of my travels I have stayed with many hosts, most of whom have afforded me caring hospitality. Occasionally I find myself in the home of someone who feels anxious or unsure of herself in my presence, who overreacts with attempts to be helpful. While I always appreciate such a hostess's efforts to make me comfortable, sometimes they are downright annoying! I have had hosts (without asking me) wash my clothes and run cotton garments in the dryer so as to shrink them; lay huge spreads of food before me when I wasn't hungry and insist that I eat; make appointments for me to counsel their friends when I had other plans; and greet me at the airport at nine o'clock in the evening (after a ten-hour plane ride) with the announcement that "everyone is waiting to meet you at the pot luck dinner arranged in your honor."

I remember staying in the home of one woman who couldn't do enough to please me. She was continually asking me if everything was alright. Her most frequent question was, "Did you enjoy the [last activity]?" I actually enjoyed many of the activities, but I felt unnerved by her anxiety in trying to make sure that I was having a good time. More than any of the activities, I would have been most pleased by her peace and trust that all was well.

The Psychology of Doing Good

The Do-Gooder does not recognize his intrinsic worth, and believes he must prove himself to be a valuable person. Feeling unlovable or inadequate, he equates his worth with outer acknowledgements of gratitude, rather than an inner knowledge of his wholeness. From this position, the Do-Gooder will never be able to earn enough love to offset low self-esteem. That is because love is not earnable. Any love you earn is not love; it is an empty substitute for real love. To earn love is to purchase cheap oil to fill a lamp that is already full. Being lovable is not an achievement; it is a condition, a state of grace bestowed upon us as offspring of a loving God.

Master Key:

You Are Lovable Not for What You Do. You Are Lovable for What You Are.

The Do-Gooder needs to realize that she is entirely worthy even if she never does another act of good. Heaven is gained not by deeds, but by awakening to our true identity.

The film *Cool Runnings* portrays the amazing but true story of the Jamaican bobsled team that entered the 1988 Winter Olympics. In a poignant scene, the coach is confronting a team member who is anxious about the possible disappointment of going home without a medal. "Don't equate your worth with a medal," the coach advises him. "If you don't know that you are good enough without the medal, you will not be good enough with it."

When we relinquish the crusade to do good, we start to really do good. We become an expression of fullness rather than a cry of incompletion. The most helpful people I have ever met are those who are content with themselves. They are living affirmations of the fullness of their spirit. Even if they do not say a word, a sense of peace pervades any room they enter. We teach not by our words, but by our being. Emerson declared, "What you are, speaks to me so loudly that I can hardly hear what you are saying."

ACTIVATION:

THE DO-GOOD FAST

For a day or a week, do not do anything in order to be good. Instead, move only with your creative urges and natural inclinations. Act only on the impulses that bring you joy and enthusiasm. When considering action, consult your gut feeling. If your spirit stirs, say "yes." If your heart says "no," decline. Allow your choices to be led by happiness rather than guilt or fear. At the end of your fast, you will be amazed at how happy you feel, how much energy you have, and you have served others.

The End of Sacrifice

There is nothing glamorous about self-mortification. *A Course in Miracles* reminds us that "I am not asked to make a sacrifice to find the mercy and peace of God."[2] Yet many of us who grew up in the Judeo-Christian tradition have carried with us the belief that in order to gain, we must give up something we love. It is human beings, not God, who believe that good is acquired through bargain, trade, or loss.

If your service is costing you your well-being, it is not true service. How do you know if you have gone too far in your attempts to be helpful? Ask yourself, "Am I experiencing a sense of loss?" If your answer is "yes," you must stop and reevaluate what you are doing, and why. *Service with resentment is no service.* If you are giving with anger, bitterness, or a silent protest, your gift is poisoned. Eventually your sense of depletion will catch up with you, and you will have to return to the point at which you resigned yourself to bitterness, and choose instead the path with heart. You may choose not to give what you have been giving, or look deeper into yourself at the fear or upset that accompanies your offering. Perhaps there is a good reason for you not to give, or perhaps you will discover that your feeling of fear or loss is unwarranted. Uncovering the dynamics behind either course of action will move you back into the position of a healthy giver. You may ultimately give more because you want to, not because you have to.

As spiritual beings, the key element of any act is not the deed itself, but the spirit in which it is performed. When we believe that we are material only, we are apt to be seduced by the form of what we are doing, rather than remembering the essence. To give something without love is to give nothing. On the other hand, if you have nothing material to give, but you give love, you make a major contribution.

Sacrifice is not an action; it is an attitude. No outer rules govern what constitutes a sacrifice. There are people who are so busy that to give a friend (or spouse) five minutes of uninterrupted quality attention, would feel like a sacrifice. And there are parents who would willingly donate a kidney to their child and experience no sense of loss whatsoever, only immeasurable gain.

The word "sacrifice" means "to make sacred." Those three words contain no notion of self-annihilation, gnashing of teeth, or loss of any kind. To the contrary, they invite us to lift our acts to a level of joy and celebration. That may mean letting go of things or activities that hurt you, but it never means giving up anything that will help you. If something makes you truly happy, it is helping you, and there is no need to cast it aside.

If you must sacrifice something, renounce fear and dump self-blame and emotional torture. Place into the fire of freedom all the beliefs about yourself that keep you bound in chains of smallness and unworthiness. Give up seeing yourself as a body only, and accept your reality as a living spirit. Then you will have sacrificed all that you are not, in favor of becoming all that you are.

ACTIVATION:

FROM SHOULD TO WOULD

Make a list of the things you think you should do,
and then ask yourself where your heart really lives.

Situation	What I Think I Should Do	What I Would Love to Do

Practice leading with Love rather than Should,
and observe the results.

Beyond the Missionary Position

One of the most seductive and destructive ploys of the ego, in the name of doing good, is the temptation to influence others to believe or act as we do. Such a campaign always springs from insecurity, and should be avoided at all costs. A survey of the world's bloodiest wars, crusades, and inquisitions reveals a long series of missionary attempts to draw converts into the fold – and get rid of anyone who does not parrot the party line. The Spanish Inquisition and Hitler's rampage are classic examples of painfully deluded vendettas in which many millions of people were killed in an effort to scourge the world of infidels.

When we seek to influence someone to join our program, convert to our religion, or purchase our product, we must be extremely careful that we are acting out of a sense of service rather than rote enrollment. No activity is necessarily made better because more people join it; numbers of participants are not a measure of worth. When we set out on a campaign to enroll more devotees, we have confused quantity with quality. The ego takes pride in numbers amassed; the spirit, on the other hand, delights in the quality of the energy of those who participate, regardless of the numbers.

At the completion of my seminars I talk to the graduates about applying the principles of the program back home. I tell them that it is more important to *be* the message than talk about it. I advise them to say as little as possible about the training, while practicing its principles continuously. I suggest that they go home and shine so brightly that others will remark, "Wow, you look great! What have you been doing that has made you shine so bright?"

Given such an invitation, you might share your experience of your seminar, religion, or product. You do not need to brag, influence, or cajole. You just need to *be*. In the atmosphere of your radiant being, those who will be served by knowing more about the program will naturally be attracted to ask.

I have found that this kind of organic growth works deeper,

stronger, and longer than a hyped-up campaign. Hype is the progeny of insecurity. It is only when you do not feel fully confident in yourself or what you are doing that you need other people to do it with you to justify your behavior. When you proceed from inner confidence, you need no outer validation; you may receive agreement, or you may not – it does not matter. You are justified by the quality of conviction that springs from your spirit. Nothing in the world can match the joy of a heart at peace with itself. The results you obtain will be infinitely more powerful than anxious solicitation. Spirit is the greatest salesman.

It is not my job to rescue the world; my role is to be at peace. It is not my function to fix anyone; my purpose is to find the highest good in everyone I see. It is not my responsibility to make everyone happy; trying to make everyone happy is insane, impractical, and impossible. If someone does not wish to be happy, it will do you no good to try to wrest their misery from them. They will not part with it readily, and you will become frustrated. (Country wisdom advises, "Never wrestle with a pig; you will both get dirty, and the pig likes it.") Simply love those who do not recognize their own worth. Your vision of their inner beauty will invite them to discover it themselves.

Before you attempt to help someone, first clarify your own consciousness. Correct your vision so you see them as whole and powerful, along with yourself. Practice empathy with their strength rather than sympathy for their weakness. Feeling sorry for someone only adds more weight to the stone under which they are sinking. In knowing that they have the power to choose love over fear, you behold them with the dignity they deserve as a creative master rather than a helpless victim. Thus you establish the optimal field for their transformation. Everyone you touch will become empowered to be more fully what they are. Then you will have done more good than you ever imagined possible.

Don't Just Do Something – Stand There

If you are not clear about what to do, I suggest you do nothing. If you do not know what is your next step, there may be something you need to see or learn before you can act effectively. In such a situation, step back (for even a moment), and turn inward. Ask the Spirit within you for guidance. Release all preconceived notions of what the situation is and what you are supposed to do, and invite your higher wisdom to enter into the situation and manifest the highest results.

If you act out of panic, or do something just because you are too uncomfortable to sit with confusion or upset, you will probably have to retrace your steps to find the clarity you overlooked because you believed that doing something is always better than doing nothing. If you must do something, do peace, and right action will proceed from that all-important foundation.

My friend Colleen was living in Los Angeles during the turmoil following the Rodney King trial. Feeling concerned about her, I called to send her my love and support.

"I'm just holding the light," Colleen told me. "I'm going about my regular business keeping peace in my heart. This is the role my spirit told me to take."

Thinking about her response, I realized that she was making a paramount contribution to the healing of the disturbance. Those who act out of fear or panic only add to the darkness. One who proceeds from peace, however, brings only more light with every word and deed that stems from calm inner knowing.

There is a significant difference between actions stimulated by peace, and those that proceed from being bullied by one's mind. I have come to recognize a specific voice in my head that rarely brings successful results. The voice lobbies, "A good person would do this in this situation." I have found through experience that every time I act in an effort to do what "a good person" would do, something backfires. The universe is showing me that it is more important to trust my sense of wisdom than fall prey to an intellectual concept of duty. When I follow the lead of joy, I end up serving in ways more powerful than I imagined.

Kindness without consciousness is of little service. Paramahansa Yogananda explained, "Etiquette without sincerity is like a beautiful but dead woman." It is infinitely more important that your service proceed from love than from righteousness. Jesus told the parable of the farmer who asked his two sons to help him do some work. The first son answered, "Yes," and then did nothing. The second son answered "No," but then, after thinking about it, decided to help. "Which son," Jesus asked, "did his father's will?" The answer, obviously, is the second son. Often a sincere "no" leads to a sincere "yes." If, after exercising your right to refuse, you feel moved to act, your service will bear integrity that exceeds half-hearted, perfunctory performance. It is more important to act with a whole heart than to do "the right thing"; sincerity *is* the right thing. A sincere error will lead to genuine wisdom; fake righteousness, on the other hand, will only delay your awakening.

Acts of kindness and selfless service are the gifts that make life worth living; to deny their value would be like removing the colors from the sunset. What we are lobbying for here is *conscious* kindness, in which you are proceeding from conviction, not prescription. When in doubt about what to do, try doing nothing until you are moved by your heart to do something. Then it will really be something.

Right Where You Are

You do not need to prove your worth to anyone – not to others, yourself, or God. You cannot prove your worth; you can only recognize it. Your value is not dependent on outer attainments; it rests on inner vision. Your goodness may be an issue for you, but it has never been a question for God. Acting the nice guy is just as self-demeaning as the guise of the villain. Seeking to measure up to societal standards is a never-ending, impossible task. Even if we do all the right things and receive all the coveted accolades, within us remains a hungry child who is lonely and longing for real fulfillment. We serve best by honoring the truth of our being rather than the laws of goodness we have superimposed over the integrity of our spirit.

As you release any neurotic need to demonstrate your value, your acts will serve in ways far more powerful than anxious attempts to justify your life. If you simply love yourself, just as you are, right where you are, you will become an unstoppable force for healing and transformation.

We are making the all-important shift from reliance on external authority, to internal knowingness. Because we are spiritual beings, nothing in the outer world compels us like the wisdom of our soul. You can bring some truth to life by living good, but you will bring more good to life by living true – true to yourself, to your heart, to your vision, to your destiny.

Holiness can be an insidious form of denial; we are less likely to question our saint-like acts than our iniquities. But there comes a point on the spiritual path where even sainthood is a trap. The only thing more important than being good is to *be*. When we choose to be just what we are, we bring our most precious gift to the planet. It is said that you can distinguish a saint by his utter ordinariness. Very few enlightened masters advertise themselves as such. Beware of those who hang out a shingle as the self-proclaimed avatar of the new age. Neither do you have to broadcast your worth; God takes it for granted, and so can you. Wisdom does not have to lobby for appreciation, and innocence is winning not by its presentation, but by its simplicity. Love is strong enough to fulfill its destiny simply by being itself.

As soon as you trust yourself, you will know how to live.
                                        – Goethe

SHAKE UP, WAKE UP

We turn to God for help when
our foundation is shaking,
only to recognize that
it is God who is shaking it.
— Charles Weston

While strolling through a small town in the mountains of Bali, I came upon a cremation ceremony. Death, like life in this innocent culture, is held in an attitude of reverent celebration. The Balinese would never be able to relate to the Occidental's dark, mournful, heavy aura enshrouding death. In this childlike society, everything points to life, including the passing beyond the body.

I joined the procession from the home of the deceased to the cremation grounds, about a mile outside the village. The body, that of a grandmotherly woman, was placed on a high throne-like wooden tower, called a "horse," ornately decorated in white enamel paint and gold foil. At the foot of the horse lay many offerings to the gods, including food, flowers, incense, photos, and written materials. A marching gamelan (oriental xylophone and bell) band formed itself behind the horse, striking a trance-like rhythm on their rudimentary metal instruments. A group of about sixteen men slipped under the bamboo base of the edifice, lifted it onto their shoulders, and carried it along the main road of the village to the cemetery.

Then I observed a most fascinating practice: every few minutes during the procession, the pallbearers would break into shouts of glee and laughter, and twirl the horse, with the body fastened to its apex, in circles. When I asked a local fellow what this ritual was all about, he explained that the pallbearers spin the bier to confuse the deceased's spirit so it cannot find its way back to the body, and thus hasten the soul on its journey to the next life.

This struck me as a perfect metaphor for the changes we are going through. From time to time life shakes us up, twirling or even destroying the foundation we have built. Such an experience can be quite disorienting – and it is supposed to be. The purpose of change beyond our control is to shake us up so we must hasten in a new direction.

Like the soul that has left the body of the deceased, we may not be able to find our way back to our past base. But the past is dead, and there would be no purpose to return. Our need is to move on to discover a new life in a new world. Upheaval is actually a gift of love; its theme is, "shake up and wake up."

Keep the Change

More people on the planet are going though more changes more quickly than ever. We are living in a time of rapid evolution on earth. When I ask my seminar audiences, "How many of you are going though major life changes?" usually at least fifty to seventy-five percent of the people raise their hands.

The question is not how to avoid change, but how to make it work for us. When a change comes to us, we have two basic choices about how we will deal with it: we can resist it, or we can move with it. Fighting change results in a great deal of pain and struggle. A woman in one of my programs confessed that "everything I let go of, I leave claw marks on." I have also heard the motto, "If it walks out of the refrigerator by itself, let it go." The message is clear: *Trust life.*

To stay on the cutting edge of evolution, we must be like surfers. The wave is moving, and we cannot avoid it. If we try to hold our position, it will drive us anyway. If we try to swim against it, it will bowl us over. The wisest approach is to catch the energy and ride on it. The wave will take us to shore much faster than we could take ourselves, and if we are skillful we may have some fun in the process.

Small Price to Pay

If you are the kind of person who likes to be in control all the time, change can appear to be a threat. You may feel frustrated in your inability to engineer the people or events around you. If you look more honestly at your need to control, however, you will see that it has brought you a great deal of anxiety and pain. To take over God's job is a massive enterprise indeed, and the small self will never be able to do it.

The good news is that there is a great self within you (it *is* you) that knows the right order and timing of all things. This infinite wisdom is available only on a "need-to-know" basis. Eager as you may be to understand how it will all work out, you must have faith that the right players and elements will show up in the right way and time. A trucking company on the east coast boasts its name in huge letters on the side of its trailers: **G.O.D. –** *Guaranteed Overnight Delivery*. The God of the universe is adept at quality delivery of goods, services, experiences, and relationships. They may not always come overnight, but they will arrive just when you need them.

An intrinsic intelligence is guiding your life and all lives. This awareness is the portal to peace. When we release the burden of understanding and control (Werner Erhard noted that "understanding is the booby prize"), we discover that our needs are constantly met by a higher power. Approach Spirit with the innocence of a child, for, as Jesus explained, if you want to get into heaven, you're going to have to get out of your head and into your heart. Children are not busy trying to figure out how to secure their positions and protect the rest of their lives. They show up ready for action and make everything into an adventure.

Momentary disorientation is a small price to pay for lasting joy. If you fear that you have lost something, assume that what was taken away has been removed to make space for something better. Breathe. Trust. Allow. Imagine that there is a higher plan operating, grander than you can perceive in the moment.

The more you fight to hold on, the longer you delay your next good from arriving. It is said that there are only two things to remember in life:

1. **Don't sweat the small stuff.**
2. **It's all small stuff.**

Image or Essence?

One of the enemies of constructive change is the desire to look good. I saw a magazine ad for a woman who promotes herself as an "image consultant." She assists her clients to build and maintain a chosen professional image. While such a practice is helpful in the business world, it can be an awful stifling cross to bear when carried over into one's personal life. If we feel that we must maintain a particular public impression, any change that might upset that presentation is perceived as a threat. Then we lose our peace as we battle feverishly to hold on to the way it looks, at the expense of the way it is. The irony of our struggle is that the more we fight to keep up an image, the worse we look, and the less effective we are. In the long run, the only person we have fooled is ourself.

Real healing comes when knowing and living the truth becomes more important than looking good. I learned this principle when two of my friends were getting divorced. The Martins had enjoyed many years of a happy and creative marriage, and they were honored in the community as a model couple. During the last several years of their relationship, however, the juice ran out. Although they both tried very hard to keep their marriage together, it became clear to each of them that their work as a couple was finished and they needed to move on.

One of the Martins' greatest challenges was confronting the image they had established in the community. Many people revered this couple and drew strength from their relationship. For a long time the Martins tried to live up to their image, even though they were falling apart inside.

Finally the weight of their differences was too great to bear, and they decided to go public with their parting. As soon as news got out, the breakup sent waves of shock and panic through the community. The divorce frightened many people who were insecure in their own relationships. Observers thought, "If the Martins can break up, so can we!" A swell of emotional resistance rippled through the social circle. Many couples' boats were being rocked in the storm.

As I watched the process, I realized that the Martins were actually performing an invaluable service to the community. They were introducing the element of realness into a community that had an investment in fantasy. They reminded people that there are no guarantees in the forms of life or relationship, and that the truth of the moment is always more important than clinging to something that has been outgrown. The Martins' divorce forced many couples to look more honestly at the foundation and issues of their relationships, and deal with them from a more forthright perspective. It was a community test and initiation in integrity.

An unexpected blessing came when the community observed the positive changes in the Martins' lives after they parted. Mrs. Martin went on to blossom as an individual; she dropped a significant number of pounds and developed her own career and interests, which she had put aside in her efforts to support her husband with his work. Mr. Martin, who had buried himself in his office work in an effort to escape the emptiness he was feeling in the marriage, became more fully in his body and began to play a lot more. His friends were delighted and amazed to see him out dating and dancing. Both of the Martins went on to develop relationships with other people who brought out different and colorful aspects of their beings. The separation was not a death, but a rebirth. Thank God that this couple found the courage to go beyond their investment in the image they had built.

The key to the Martins' resurrection was in telling a bigger truth and living it. Telling the truth is always an adventure; you never quite know what form the results will take. Sometimes greater honesty may move bodies apart, but ultimately it moves the relationship to deeper spiritual joining. We cannot afford to harbor an investment in how it will look once we have dared to be what we are; we must simply trust that living from honesty will open doors that hiding kept closed. This is the leap of faith required to really be free. We must honor reality above image; vulnerability above protection; openness to new possibilities above clinging to the past. As *A Course in Miracles* reminds us, "In my defenselessness my safety lies."

Make Way for Love

The most powerful way to capitalize on the changes in your life is to bless them. Remember the *Course in Miracles* principle that "all change is good." If something shifts that is beyond your control, ask to see the gift in it. If you look, you will find one.

If someone leaves your life, let them go. No one has ever improved their relationship by corralling their partner. (It is said that "we do not have relationships; we have hostages.") Domination through emotional manipulation only drives resentment and self-hatred deeper, both of which will surface in a disguised form at a later time. The greatest gift we can offer one another in relationship is the freedom to allow our spirits to breathe. The fearful mind will try to scare you by telling you that if you let the other person be him or herself, they will leave you and you will lose. It is not so; the bestowal of freedom can only bring reward and success. Most likely the person will love and appreciate you more. And if they do not, you don't want them anyway. Do you want a partner, or a hostage?

I used to take it personally when a student cancelled their attendance at one of my programs. I imagined that this person didn't like me, or was making a critical statement about the quality of my offering. When I first experienced such a withdrawal I tried to influence the person to attend anyway – to quell my insecurity. This kind of clinging, of course, didn't work. In my efforts to manipulate others, I was simply affirming that I was not worthy and that the universe was making a mistake.

Then I began to release people to their highest good. I realized that the greatest gift I could give would be to empower people to follow their own heart, even if it was not what my little mind wanted or thought it needed. Instantly I began to see the results. Individuals would thank me profusely for encouraging them to be true to their path, even if it did not match my own. Sometimes they received more from my support in that one interaction than they would have if they attended the entire program!

Perhaps the most poignant demonstration of the wisdom behind change, occurred as I was preparing for one of my small group seminars, an intensive week of transformation for twelve participants. A short time before the program, one of the participants dropped out. I experienced a brief moment of upset, but I quickly reminded myself that divine order was in force. I trusted that there was a reason for this change, and my role was to support what the universe wanted to have happen for the highest good of all concerned. I blessed Theresa and told her that I, too, wanted her to be in her right place.

One person on the waiting list, Nina, was happy to take Theresa's place. Around the third day of the program I noticed that Nina was spending a lot of time with one of the men in the workshop. By the end of the week this couple announced to the group that they had an instant recognition as soulmates. Eight months later Nina and Ron were married. They are a beautiful and dedicated couple, and it was a delight to see them connect!

Looking back on the process, I see how perfect it was that

Theresa dropped out, so Nina could drop in! At the time I had no idea of the purpose behind the switch, but there was a mighty plan indeed! The fascinating postscript to the story is that Theresa attended a subsequent session of the training, and it was perfectly clear why she was supposed to be at that gathering. Theresa's strongest need to was to resolve some father/authority issues, and there was a man in the group who fit the bill perfectly; he simultaneously had some child issues to handle. The two of them served one another powerfully in dumping many old limiting programs, and came to stand side by side in dignity and integrity. The entire process was divinely orchestrated.

Now I see how foolish it would have been for me to act out of disappointment to Theresa's cancellation, or to try to manipulate or hold her to her agreement. The agreements we make on earth pale in comparison to the agreements we make for ourselves in heaven. Don't try to stand in the way of love; if you saw the big picture, you wouldn't want to, anyway.

The Destiny Smoke-Out

I have been experimenting with a prayer that has yielded remarkable results. When I am experiencing frustration or confusion in making a decision (usually about a social or business relationship) I say, "Okay, God, I have no idea how this is supposed to turn out. I am not sure if or how I am to develop this interaction with this person. I ask for the manifestation of the highest results for everyone involved. I do not dictate how it is supposed to look; I seek only a quality of blessing. I am willing to have it turn out any way that will truly serve. Let the highest destiny be manifested now."

I have found this affirmation to be a potent time-saving device. Rather than having to play out situations by trial and error until I recognize their true purpose, with the aid of this prayer I usually get an answer soon after I declare my intention. I call it *"The Destiny Smoke-Out."* The prayer (proceeding from my intention) brings relationships and situations to a head, so the dynamics and next step are clear and unmistakable. Sometimes the Smoke-Out reveals to me precious opportunities and opens doors that it would have taken a long time to discover; and sometimes it shows me that a situation is headed in an unhealthy direction, and I would be wise to head it off before things get worse or someone gets hurt. But the form of the result doesn't matter; what we want is the truth, and the truth always yields empowerment and blessing.

Never be afraid of the truth. The truth will not hurt you; it is your best friend. It is said that "the truth hurts," but the only thing the truth hurts is illusions. In the Catholic religion the Archangel Michael is pictured with sword in hand, poised to sunder the head of a dragon. The sword symbolizes truth, and the dragon represents fear and illusion. The truth is the dispeller of deception; bring any situation into the light, and good must come for everyone concerned.

On a planetary level, we are living during the era of the ending of secrets. One of the prime characteristics of a dysfunctional family is the keeping of secrets. As a civilization, we have kept much hidden for a long time, and it is no wonder that we have lived in a socially dysfunctional world. Now those secrets are being brought into the light for healing. The 1960's were a time of tremendous social awakening, and the natural result of higher consciousness, manifested beginning in the 1970's, was a cultural unwillingness to put up with hiding. From the exposure of the Watergate break-in and President Nixon's subsequent resignation, to the downfall of many televangelists in the wake of sexual and financial scandals, to the revelations that millions of people were sexually abused as children, to the international focus on homosexual identity as a result of AIDS, to the popularity of investigative reporting television shows, we see a deep and common theme for the last decades of the twentieth century: *it is no longer possible to hide who we are and what we do. The time of secrets on the planet is ending. It is now time to live fearlessly in the light.*

While coming out of the closet is frightening to the separated self, it is incredibly liberating. Deep in our hearts we do not want to hide; we want to be free to be all that we are. But cleansing often brings the worst to the surface before it is dismissed. The first stage of a washing machine cycle is called "agitation." The clothing needs to be stirred up to loosen the accumulated dirt. To look into a washing machine while the basket is agitating, you see a fowl mire of grime rise to the surface of the water. If you did not know better, you might think that the clothes were getting dirtier and be tempted to shut off the machine. But that would be foolish; the dirt is not being added, as it might appear – it is being removed. In the presence of flowing water (metaphysically representing Spirit), the dirt is drained away, leaving fresh, clean garments. If you just stay with the process, the cycle will complete itself, and soon the clothes will be much cleaner than when the process began.

This kind of purging is exactly the predicament in which we find ourselves now, as individuals and a culture. Internally and externally, imbedded psychic pollution is being called to the surface. Many people are alarmed, for example, about the explosive increase in reports of child sexual abuse. But most people do not realize that child sexual abuse has been going on for thousands of years; there is nothing at all new about it.

What *is* new is the reporting of abuse, and holding it up to the light. We hear of more and more famous people, such as Roseanne Arnold, and a former Miss America, who are openly sharing their history of abuse, along with their subsequent recovery from their psychic trauma. There has not been an increase in the practice, but rather a tremendous increase in the *consciousness* around it – which *must* result in a change in the practice.

Keeping secrets is the element of dysfunction that ensures its passage to the next generation. Bring a secret to the illumination of higher consciousness, however, and the dark cycle is broken. Transformed through love, compassion, and wisdom, the next generation will not reap the pain of its parents, but the strength of their awakening. *This* is gift we are bequeathing to our children and subsequent generations. We are finding the courage to break the chains of fear and hiding that have kept us, as individuals and a society, locked in the dungeon for millennia. Our time is, in many ways, a difficult and painful one, but when healthier future generations look back on this crucial era, they will regard it as a pivotally important period. We are finally shovelling out from under a heavy cloak of fear, and never again will such terrible unconsciousness rule our lives. We are telling the truth, and in so doing we are taking back the strength of our spirit.

This is why we must honor the changes in our lives, and view them not as curses, but as gifts. (The letters in the word "curses" are the same as those that comprise the word "cures"; we can take what seems to curse us, and through looking at it from a different perspective, transform it into something that cures.) Many say that we are living in the time of the Apocalypse, and we are. But hardly anyone knows the true meaning of the word "Apocalypse," which literally translates from Greek as "the lifting of the curtain." The word says nothing about terror and pain; it is an expression not of punishment, but redemption. We will experience hardship only to the extent that we cling to an old way that is no longer working. There is another way that will work, and that is the path to which we are being directed. The veil is being drawn away from the terribly self-defeating beliefs that were running our lives behind the scenes, and these warped pictures of reality are being called into consciousness so we can release them and make a new choice. Thank God for the Apocalypse. Only one situation could be worse than the changes we are going through, and that would be for things to remain as they were. Living under the thumb of fear is not our destiny; our destiny is to walk tall in the dignity in which we were created.

The move from the dungeon to the royal chamber requires a significant shift in attitude and activity. A prisoner who has lived in a dungeon for a long time may find the sunlight painful when he first beholds it. Some prisoners might even plead to be returned to the darkness to which their vision has become accustomed. It may seem easier to see nothing than to have to adjust to see something. But we have come too far to turn back now. Like the Balinese soul who is being propelled to a higher realm, our "horse" is being spun, and there is no turning back. The old world is dead, and there is no purpose in trying to crawl back into a useless carcass. The chains have been broken, the door is opened, and we have been told that we are free. Now all we have to do is take the next step, and trust. A new world calls to us, and we will live in it. We will be what we came to be, and do what we were born to do.

Running in circles
Desperate we hold to yours and mine. . .
But oh no
Open the door
And let the wind blow
Take my hand and together we stand
In the eye of the hurricane

If you believe in me
I will believe in what will be
We want the world you've only dreamed of. . .

Out of control
Out of my mind at last
Into my dreams
We sail away

– "If You Believe" by Kenny Loggins and Steven Wood

MIND MATTERS

All limitations are self-imposed.
— Ernest Holmes

When he stepped up to the starting line, the crowd laughed. "What's the matter, mate — d'ja take a wrong turn from the outback?" a brash voice chided from the back of the throng.

Cliff Young gave the briefest glance to the area from which the voice issued, and turned his attention back to road ahead of him.

Clad in coveralls and galoshes, the sixty-one-year-old farmer from Australia's bush seemed an anomaly in a grueling race. Most of the other runners, world class athletes in their twenties and thirties, had trained rigorously for many months in preparation for the annual four-hundred-kilometer marathon. Wearing the sleekest aerodynamic running uniforms and buttressed by the latest scientific endurance techniques, the younger men mentally psyched themselves to run for eighteen hours a day and sleep for six hours a night.

The starting gun boomed over the cheering crowd, and as the smoke lingered above the field irreverent teetotalers took bets on whether Cliff Young would last a day or two, or if he would collapse even before then.

But then an amazing thing event occurred. A day and half before the lead runners were expected to finish, a sixty-one-year-old foot in rubber galoshes crossed the finish line. Cliff Young completed the race in record-breaking time, thirty-six hours before men forty years his junior.

No one, you see, had told Cliff that he was supposed to sleep. While the younger men were snoozing, Cliff Young was cruising.

Cliff Young's astounding performance stands as a striking demonstration of the power of our mind to create our reality and subsequent physical experience. We live as large as we think we are.

The next year of the race, an equally amazing event occurred. Several runners broke Cliff's record. They adopted his method of running without sleep, and they exceeded his feat. They gave up their premature cognitive commitment (mind made up about how it is supposed to be) that one had to sleep six hours a night to win the race.

The Incredible Universe

In a museum I saw a display of several sea shells that could conceivably have been the successive homes of the same animal over the course of its life. When these creatures outgrow one shell, they crawl out and spin a new one.

We, too spin shells. Our shells, however, are mental. They are called "belief systems." Instead of moving from body to body, we progress from smaller beliefs to grander ones. When I was ten years old, I believed that the purpose of life was to have a great collection of baseball cards. My bedroom closet was brimming with shoe boxes containing hundreds of cards of all the big league players, including the *piece de resistance*, Mickey Mantle. Within a few years, however, rock 'n' roll had become the purpose of life in the universe. All the Mickey Mantle cards in America seemed trivial when laid next to two tickets to a *Doors* concert; God had slipped out of Yankee pinstripes and into Jim Morrison's leather britches. Years later, when the *Doors* movie came out, I surprised myself by not even going to see it. I had moved into a bigger shell.

No matter how far-reaching your belief system, there is always a larger one than you can think of. Just when you feel you have a handle on life, or think you know it all, something comes along to show you that you actually know very little. (Sir James Jeans noted, "Science should leave off making pronouncements; the river of knowledge has often turned back on itself.") Personally, I find this a great relief! It means that I am not limited to the reality I have accepted.

Consider these facts:

• When Johnny Weismuller won the Olympic gold medal in 1932, he set a new world record for swimming. Now swimmers in that event must surpass that record *simply to qualify.*

• A modern Boeing 747 jumbo jet is longer than the original flight of the first airplane flown by the Wright brothers at Kitty Hawk.

• When Magellan circumnavigated the world in his clipper ship in the sixteenth century, his cruise took him two years. When the steamship came into vogue, such vessels made the same journey in two months. With the advent of jet airplanes, the trip was reduced to two days. Space capsules circled the earth in two hours. Currently, through satellite television, we can see and hear anywhere on the globe within two seconds.

Near Portland, Oregon, there is a huge department store called *The Incredible Universe.* When I am in that area I love to call the store just to hear the operator answer, *"This is the Incredible Universe; how may I serve you?"* Her salutation is symbolic of the way the entire universe operates. It reminds us that we will live as big as we believe. We can and will have whatever we ask for with our thoughts. Now *that's* an incredible universe!

Master Key:

Do Not Limit Life to Your Beliefs.
Expand Your Beliefs to Include
All That Life Has to Offer.

Author James Baldwin declared that "The purpose of life is for the individual to become greater than the definitions he has inherited." To advance in life, we must expand our self-image beyond the identities others have given us. Each generation stands on the shoulders of the one that preceded it. I am amazed by the depth, wisdom, and presence of the children being born today. I regularly meet children who are advanced light years beyond anyone I knew when I grew up. These children are reflecting the higher consciousness that has evolved on the planet since our birth. They symbolize the truth that we have expanded our world view beyond the one that was shown to us. We are pushing beyond the limits of ignorance and paving new highways to greater awareness.

The greatest gift we can give to the planet is to demonstrate the falsity of the illusions to which most people have subscribed. We must be willing to walk beyond fear, even when few others are doing so. Do not wait for outer approval to live your truth; inner approval is all that counts. You may encounter resistance, judgment, or criticism, none of which matter. All that matters is that you are true to your inner calling. Spirit asks no more of you than this – and no less.

Many are Cold; A Few are Frozen

We live in the world we think is real, and our subsequent experiences confirm the picture of reality we have adopted. James Robinson noted, "Most of our so-called reasoning consists in finding arguments for going on believing as we already do."

230

Anyone can prove what he believes, not because it is so, but because he believes it. It is said that "logic is the process by which we arrive at the wrong conclusion with confidence." We do not decide what to believe on the basis of evidence presented to us; we find evidence to prove what we wish to believe.

A trainyard maintenance man went into a freezer car to clean it. When he was ready to leave he discovered, to his dismay, that he had locked himself in the car. When his co-workers opened the car the next day, they found the man's lifeless body. Looking around for clues to his death, they found his handwriting scribbled on the wall: *"Cold. . . Getting Colder. . . Freezing. . ."* This tragic death was all the more poignant in light of the fact that the freezer unit on the car was not working. The man was frozen not by a machine, but by his mind.

A Course in Miracles tells us, "Illusions are as strong in their effects as the truth." The man in the freezer car was just as dead as if he had been physically frozen. This astonishing incident serves as a powerful metaphor for the ways we hurt ourselves by holding false images about ourselves and our environment. In truth, no one or no thing in the outer world has the power to hurt or save you unless you give it power with your beliefs. Thoughts are things; energy goes where attention flows; thoughts held in mind produce after their kind.

Master Key:

You'll See it When You Believe it.[1]

When I practiced hypnosis, I observed astounding demonstrations of the power of the mind to manifest tangible results. I saw hypnotized subjects develop blisters on their hands at the suggestion of a flame touching them; I watched a yogi pierce his arm with a thick needle, with no bleeding or pain; I saw a two-hundred pound hypnotist stand on the stiffened body of a frail elderly woman suspended between two chairs; and I personally walked barefoot over eleven-hundred-degree burning coals.

While such demonstrations belong to the world of show business, they lead us to a crucially important truth: *the world we live in is created by the thoughts we think.* If a man's mind is powerful enough to kill his body, *it is powerful enough to heal it.* If you have struggled with a physical pain or illness, *the key to your freedom is within you now.* Begin to think new thoughts, and you will build the foundation for a new life.

I Fought the Law, and the Law is One

To enjoy true freedom, we must re-examine the "laws" to which we believe we are subject. Have you ever questioned or tested the limits beyond which you have been told you cannot pass? They are not true, unless you believe they are. *A Course in Miracles* reminds us, "I am under no laws but God's." George Burns corroborated, "My doctor gave me six months to live – but when I couldn't pay, he gave me another six months."

Many people have experienced physical healings that have defied, denied, or reversed the "laws" of medicine. I know a man who, after accidentally cutting off a section of his finger with a power saw, grew a new thumb. An Italian woman, after receiving the prayer of saintly priest Padre Pio, found her eyesight restored although *she had no cornea.* A woman in my class reported that after having a lung removed, she grew a new one. If such healings seem implausible, consider the starfish, which has the capacity to grow a new limb if one is severed; or the worm and lizard, which regenerate tails if these are lost. It seems quite reasonable that we, advanced beyond such creatures by millions of years of evolution, should be able to heal at least as well as worm!

If we do not, it is not because we cannot; it is because we have allowed our potential to lay fallow through ignorance and disuse. We have believed it is the world that makes us what we are, rather than we who create our world. We have lived within the borders prescribed by *Scare City,* and lost sight of *A Bun Dance.* To come home, we must give up our quest to import good from a foreign source, and use what we already have.

When the medical profession is unable to explain a healing, it is categorized as a "spontaneous remission." The medical model has not, until recently, been big enough to incorporate spiritual causation, the power of prayer, the strength of sheer will, and the healing energy of love. But any system of healing that does not honor the power of Spirit is limited indeed! There are no accidents in the universe, and we, as divine beings, are stronger than viruses. *A Course in Miracles* reminds us that "chance plays no part in God's plan." Eventually the laws of medicine, though valid within the belief system that subscribes to them, must be incorporated into a higher way of seeing.

There are now support groups for "former terminal cancer patients." I love that phrase – "former terminal." It bears the ring of grace. It means that nothing is necessarily terminal. Many years ago I saw a magazine ad stating that more people have been healed of cancer than the entire population of Los Angeles. I am certain that number has increased significantly by now. Just because someone in a position of authority says you are going to die as a result of a particular condition, does not mean you will. Your life and death are not subject to any external force; you choose when you will come and when you will go. It is time for us to take the power of life and death back from outside authorities. *There is no outside authority.* There is only inner authority – the authority of God within you, through you, *as you.*

I know a man of great faith who has facilitated the healing of thousands of people through prayer, affirmation, and touch. He teaches that *"we walk in the atmosphere of our own believing."* We are subject only to the laws we accept as real. While the mind of man has invented thousands and millions of laws, God has only one: *love is real.* Use this law as your guide, and all else will fall into place.

Send Back the Rag

In my seminars I lead participants through the "snotty rag" exercise, which I invoke if someone is struggling with a burden of guilt laid upon her by another. I take out a handkerchief and ask the participant to imagine that someone has just blown his nose in it, leaving it quite dirty. Then, without warning, I throw the handkerchief at her. Some recipients automatically raise their hand, catch the hanky, and hold it. Others just let the rag fly past them, or bounce off their body onto the floor.

"This process symbolizes the way we deal with guilt or limits when they are offered to us," I explain to the students. "When someone attacks you, calls you guilty, or attempts to dump on you in any way, they are offering you their snotty handkerchief. You have a choice as to whether or not you will accept their 'gift.' If you take it and wear it like a coat, it is yours. If you do not accept the package, it must pass by you or return to its giver, leaving them to deal with it."

We strengthen ourselves and others by refusing to accept the limits they would lay upon us. We must be vigilant to remember our wholeness in the face of the many ways we are invited to live puny. Discussions of "the flu that is going around," "the state of the economy," or "what happens to you when you hit a certain age" are all snotty handkerchiefs passed around *en masse*. If you agreed and aligned with all the news, gossip, and predictions you heard, you would be a sorry mess indeed, and many people do function at this abysmal level of existence. At the same time many individuals are not thwarted by the flu, the economy, or the age, and they even gain strength and aliveness while others are giving away their life force to popular fears. Such individuals demonstrate that these conditions are not related to universal laws – they are belief systems, reinforced by those who subscribe to them. You have most likely had a salesperson telephone you to ask if you wanted to subscribe to a particular magazine. If you did not find value in their offer, you probably told them, "Thank you, but I am not interested." Similarly, when someone invites you to buy their drama or vendetta, they are asking you to subscribe to their dark publication. You are free to dive into the inferno with them, or lovingly decline their offer. You will help them more by honoring your commitment to peace than by jumping into the pit with them. It is not unkind or uncompassionate to refuse the snotty handkerchief; to the contrary, it is the greatest gift you can bestow. By standing on higher ground you are able to offer a helping hand that may assist your friend to find his way out.

Helled Over

Do you know the origin of the word, "hell"? There is nothing blasphemous or even religious about the word. It is a real estate term. (If you have made real estate deals, you may be nodding your head in agreement.) "Hell" is a perfectly valid old English word meaning "fence" or "pen." If you wanted to keep a cow or pig in captivity, you would "hell" the critter in by erecting a stockade. Then the animal is "helled," or in its derivative form, "held" in.

Hell is nothing more than a sense of limitation. As divine beings we are, by nature, unlimited. There is nothing that we cannot do or be. To say "I can do this, but not this," or "my power to create my life stops here," is to draw a border of hell. The Chinese patriarch Hsin Hsin Ming taught, "The great way is not difficult for those who have no preferences; make the slightest distinction, however, and heaven and earth are set infinitely apart."

I invite you now to get out of hell. Walk out of your self-created prison and fly. Just because you have bought limits from your parents, teachers, or religion does not mean that you have to keep them. As a child you were too small to reason otherwise. Authority figures told you that something was true, and so you believed it. But you are bigger than that now. You are spiritually mature enough to choose what world you will live in.

Whose Side are You On?

Maintaining smallness is not a passive condition; we must work hard to stay weak! Victimhood requires vigilant effort. Even concrete must be maintained to keep grass from growing through the cracks; nature is always seeking to restore itself to life and balance. No one stays sick or stuck without (unconsciously) choosing so. To remain in darkness, we must buttress our body against the door of healing and keep it shut, at great cost to our joy and aliveness.

Many of us have become adept at arguing for our limits. A friend tells us that we are wonderful, and we tell them why we are not. A suitor compliments us as being attractive, and we think that they must be blind, lying, or want something from us. A teacher tells us that we are free, and we present all kinds of evidence for our bondage. In *Illusions*, Richard Bach notes, "Argue for your limitations, and sure enough they are yours." Some of us have become lawyers for our own prosecution! We argue to the death for everything we cannot do, and then we wonder why we feel limited.

Imagine how powerful our lives would be if we brought the same commitment to living our magnificence! At any given moment – even this one – we can become lawyers for our release. We can begin to make a case for what is right with us, our life, our relationships, and our universe. We can stand for our possibilities rather than our limits. We can release ourselves from hell.

Imagine That

How, then, do we extricate ourselves from beliefs systems that do not work? By replacing them with higher beliefs that do work. It will do you no good to fight your desires, your mind, or yourself, for such an abusive vendetta will only strengthen what you are trying to get rid of. Instead, turn the other cheek and look in a new direction. Align your energy with your vision and proceed as if your goal is already real.

Albert Einstein proclaimed that "imagination is more important than knowledge." Imagination is the power of creation, yet we have often used it against ourselves. Worry is simply vision used destructively; we manufacture what we do not want instead of what we do. Imagination is the God-given faculty with which we can breathe life into what our heart desires. The generative power of our mind is so vast that Niagara Falls is small in comparison. We are all geniuses; the only difference between famous creators and struggling artists is that the creators believe in their visions and have the faith to move with their impulses.

The imaginative faculty is the force that lifts us beyond mental constraints. To simply think about something is not enough – you must *feel* it to draw it into manifestation. Smell the fragrance of the night-blooming jasmine that will adorn your dream home; hear the sound of the excited applause of those who attend your recital at Carnegie Hall; see the caring and compassion in the eyes of your ideal mate. Turn yourself on with every possible detail of your dream come true, and live as if it has already come to pass. Emotion contains *motion*. To fantasize, imagine, and dream with a stirred heart, generates the psychic electricity to draw vision into manifestation. We have made ourselves small with our imagination, and we can use the same faculty to restore life to the grandeur for which we were born.

It is of the utmost importance to *keep yourself inspired*. Inspiration is our daily bread, and if you are not feeding your soul, your chances of advancement are slim. Do whatever you need to do to keep your heart alive and your thoughts high. Your foremost responsibility is to keep your joy light burning. If you do not, all else will be of little value to you or others.

Happiness is the corridor that leads to all other rooms of success. Delight is the atmosphere in which we thrive. Cultivate delight, and you will magnetize the greatest events possible, often by miraculous means.

The Power to Change the World

The most direct way to change your world is to change your mind. It will do you no good to try to chisel your world in vain, frustrating attempts to manipulate events and people to meet your expectations. Instead, we do far better to dismantle our notions of victimhood, powerlessness, and loss. None of these thoughts reflect truth, and they will only hurt you to invest energy in them. When you adopt the self-image of a victim, you operate at a zero degree of effectiveness to create constructive change. People who define themselves as victims perpetuate situations in which they play out a victim role; self-actualized people, on the other hand, continually create situations manifesting what they want. It is not events that make victims; it is what we do with them. Many people take experiences that would seem to victimize them, and use them as a fulcrum to empower themselves. These people are called masters.

Such mastery is available to you and me, but we must first reconstruct our images of who we are and what we can do. While our nature is unalterably divine, our experience will bear out what we think we are. The game of life consists of shifting our vision to align with the light that we are.

We are not who we thought we were, and thank God for that. The world plays on lack, and we must be vigilant to send back the snotty rags it offers us. Instead we must walk tall in the knowledge of our worth. The Bible tells us that "the sons of God married the daughters of men," symbolically indicating that our divine nature became interwoven with material identity. We have spent lifetimes exploring our limits, and now it is time to own our divinity. It is time to recapture the golden essence which runs like a healing river at the center of our being. It is time to honor the inward journey, the adventure of the soul.

> *Living out your dreams can be more*
> *therapeutic than analyzing them.*
> — Hawaiian hotel advertisement

LOOKING IN FOR
NUMBER ONE

How many more idols must you find
before you realize that you are the one
you have been searching for?
– Dan Fogelberg

The Captain Cook Syndrome

On a sunny morning in January 1779, Captain James Cook piloted his stately clipper ships *Discovery* and *Resolution* into the idyllic Kealakekua Bay on the verdant western shore of the Big Island of Hawaii. Cook and his crew came in search of treasure and knowledge to return to the Crown of England, under whose charter the adventurers had set sail.

What Captain Cook did not know was that the natives were awaiting the return of the great god Lono, whom ancestral visionaries had prophesied would descend from the west on a "moving island with trees." The light-skinned Lono, the seers foretold, would then restore peace and harmony to the Hawaiian people.

The Hawaiians on the beach that day looked up to behold the high-masted vessels taking shape on the horizon. Quickly they ran to gather the other natives. Soon the king, queen, and warriors excitedly paddled their outriggers to greet the revered Lono and celebrate his long-awaited return.

The Hawaiians gave "Lono" and his entourage all the honor

and amenities befitting gods. Feasts were prepared, processions and ceremonies ensued, and the Hawaiian women made themselves available to the "gods." The ruddy crew, at sea for months, took full advantage of all the amenities.

Too full, however. Disrespectful of the honors accorded them, the sailors drank, brawled, desecrated the sacred gifts, and abused the sexual favors afforded them.

Before long the islanders began to wonder if these were gods after all. The sailors were not behaving like any gods the natives had ever heard of! When some Hawaiians happened upon the burial a seaman, they were hard pressed to understand how an immortal god could have fallen prey to death. The natives, as they say, became restless. The Hawaiians waxed resentful of the deities and grew angry at their all-too-human nature.

The disillusionment peaked when Captain Cook took a *kahuna* priest hostage in retaliation for a rowboat that had been stolen. This was the last straw for the Hawaiians. In a spontaneous riot, an angry mob stoned and drowned Captain Cook on the beach just paces from where he had landed in glory. So much for the "god."

Sticks and Thrones Can Break Your Bones

The demise of Captain Cook is a spectacular metaphor for the trouble we invite when we make a god out of a human being, or allow ourself to sit on a pedestal built by another. If we do not fully recognize or accept our own power, we will forge gods or devils of entities outside ourself. We will erect thrones to worship those whom we believe are better than us, along with crosses to crucify "evil" people whom we believe can take away our good. Neither of these situations represents the truth. *You alone are responsible for the manufacture of the gods and devils around you, and only you have the authority to release them – and yourself –* from your projections. Then and only then will you take your power back, where it belongs.

240

Master Key:

Idols Always Fall on Those Who Worship Them.

When you view someone else as greater than yourself, you belittle yourself. No guru, teacher, therapist, parent, spouse, or friend is closer to truth or God than you are. If you see them as such, you have hurt yourself in the most unkind way. When you deify another, it is at your own expense.

Neither can you afford to allow yourself to sit on a pedestal erected by another. In so doing you diminish yourself as well as your fan ("fan" is short for "fanatic"). The relationship between a worshipper and a god is not a real relationship. Plato noted that "friendship can occur only among equals."

Wrath After the Fall

Worshippers of false gods always become angry with the deities who inevitably disappoint them. Such anger is a projection of the self-hatred we incur when we give our power away. Idol worship is a no-win situation. To sit willingly on someone else's throne is to perpetuate an addictive illusion that will end in pain. I have learned firsthand that "a halo has to fall only a few inches to be a noose."[1] When my books became popular I began to receive letters of adoration from readers who put me on a pedestal. Inspired by my writing or seminars, some students made me into a god and saw me as capable of no wrong. Sometimes they developed the thought that I was their soulmate.

While all of this was very flattering, I quickly learned that it was a mistake to indulge it in any way. At first I enjoyed the adoration and played on it in subtle ways. But then I began to see a pattern. After receiving several letters of lavish compliments, I would get an angry letter chastising me for not being the person my admirer thought I was. They would tell me that I was not living up to my teachings, and I had misled them. But it was my admirers who had misled themselves by making me into a god at the denial of my human qualities. Some of them carried on an entire fantasy relationship without ever meeting me!

Later I discovered a final element of the syndrome. With stunning predictability, a month or a year later I would receive another letter in which the writer apologized for her upset. The writer would own the fact that she had given her power away to me, discovering that the purpose of the experience was for her to reclaim the greatness she had projected outside of herself.

After going through this process several times, I became sensitive to signs of the pattern in the early stages. I learned not to give any fuel to fantasy relationships. I also introspected deeply to ferret out any vestiges in my subconscious that sought to encourage adoration around me. I had my share of being stoned and drowned. Now the moment I get off the ship I announce that I am a sailor, not a savior. This approach builds a much stronger foundation for real friendship over a longer time.

Declaration of Inner Dependence

With stunning regularity we observe the fall of the gods we have fabricated. The last three decades have constituted an era of unprecedented disillusionment. Television evangelists, gurus, political icons, business moguls, sports giants, media celebrities, and historical heroes have been exposed to be human beings, just like the masses they seemed to outshine. While seeing our idols tumble before our eyes is at first disappointing, such a radical education is ultimately empowering. The word "disillusioned" is a positive one – it means that an illusion has been exposed, and the truth behind it has come to the fore. We are moved to withdraw the reverence we bestowed upon false gods, and restore it to the self we abandoned in favor of graven images. To renew the quality of life on the planet, we are learning to look *within* to find wisdom, strength, and heart.

In my workshops I am hearing more and more people state that they are taking back their power. We are detaching ourselves from addictive, debilitating patterns with parents, spouses, children, employers, religions, work, money, substances, and sex. No longer are we willing to give control over our happiness to entities outside ourselves. We are growing beyond the idols we have forged, and finding the God within.

As we rethink the power we have attributed to those in authority, we are expanding the notion of being a minister, priest, or prophet, to include every soul that lives. Jesus was not the only son of God, Buddha was not the only enlightened being, and Mohammed was not the only holy one with the capacity to move mountains. These luminaries simply discovered their identity in divinity, and now they beckon to all of us to join them.

In the wake of our fallen heroes, a new kind of teacher is emerging – one who empowers students rather than diminishes them. The leaders of the new era seek not to foster their students' dependence, but their *inner dependence.* True guides refuse adoration, identifying themselves not as messiahs, but mirrors. The teacher of integrity continually redirects the student to find divinity within himself. One master told an audience, "It's going to be a little tricky for you to fall in love with yourself if you are fascinated with me." Such a mentor finds no merit in icon worship, and all merit in self-appreciation. The word "guru" is spelled "G. . .U. . .R. . .U" – *"Gee, you are you."* The best gurus affirm to their disciples, "I am an aspect your own true self."

The greatest service a guru can perform is to get rid of his disciples. Herein lies the paradox of true instruction; a teacher's job is to make himself unnecessary. When students come to my workshops I tell them, "This is the 'Un-training.' If you get the message of this course, you will recognize that you didn't need to come." I am not concerned about losing disciples; I am concerned with making masters. My real reward is to see seminar participants awaken to their own magnificence. As Benjamin Disraeli explained, "The greatest good you can do for another is not just to share your riches, but to reveal to him his own."

ACTIVATION:

TAKE YOUR POWER BACK

Which of the following authority figures do you believe has more power than you, or power over you?

☐ God
☐ Jesus
☐ the Bible
☐ angels
☐ father
☐ mother
☐ spouse
☐ sibling
☐ child
☐ President of the U.S.
☐ court judge
☐ attorney
☐ policeman
☐ doctor
☐ nurse
☐ landlord
☐ employer

☐ men
☐ women
☐ attractive man/woman
☐ psychologist
☐ psychic
☐ astrologer
☐ guru
☐ clergy
☐ neighbor
☐ genius
☐ wealthy person
☐ business mogul
☐ accountant
☐ sports hero
☐ media celebrity
☐ others:

_____
_____
_____
_____
_____

_____
_____
_____
_____
_____

Coming Home to Number One

One area in which we have given away a great deal of our power is relationships. Many of us have invested vast amounts of energy, time, and effort to find "the one" – that single special person who will embody all the qualities we desire, and make us happy. We dream of the day when our eyes will meet theirs across a crowded room; instantly we will recognize that this is the one we have waited for, we will fall into their arms without a word, and live happily ever after.

Well, I have good news and I have bad news. (Actually, it's all good news.) There is no one out there who has the power to remove your loneliness, give you everything you have longed for, reward you for the pain and sacrifice you endured in your last relationship(s), and fix what is not working in your life. If that is what you are seeking, I suggest you give up your search right now. The desire to have someone give you what you have not given yourself, is probably what has kept you from manifesting the relationship you seek.

There is, however, one who has the power to manifest the visions you hold so dear. The one you have been searching for is not out there, but in here. Instead of looking out for Number One (and repeatedly stepping in number two), the next step is to look in for Number One.

Our search for the ideal mate has been confusing and bewildering because we have been looking for the right thing in the wrong place. The vision of joy, happiness, and fulfillment in relationship is a noble, worthy, and true one. It is the fuel that fires us to be fully in life, write poetry, act silly, toss convention to the wind, risk telling more truth about who we are, heal our body and spirit, and unlock the creativity that reflects the greatest in us. Many of us have searched long and hard, yet something in us urges us to keep on keeping on. We must honor that something. We must love ourselves immensely to keep stretching to achieve a loving relationship.

Never give up your quest for the ideal mate, for through it

you will find yourself. Through the process of seeking someone to make you happy, you will learn how to make yourself happy. You will unearth your own magnificence and awaken your ability to channel love – beginning with loving yourself. You will learn how to take any relationship and turn it into a blessing. Those in rewarding relationships report that their partner is not magically perfect; they just decide to see them as precious. Finding the goodness and godness in your partner, yourself, and your relationship is not a boon that mystically drops into your lap out of heaven – it is a choice you make. You will get more of whatever you concentrate on; you can focus on your partner's faults or divinity, and he or she will become more of whatever you energize with your thoughts. In learning how to see the good, you will master a principle with universal application and infinite worth.

Before you find the person you seek, you must find yourself; before you can know your soulmate you must know your soul. When we set out to find someone who will make us complete, we deny that we are already whole. When we forget who we are, we are drawn to people who embody character traits we believe we are lacking. We feel as if we are half, and they are half, and together we will become a whole.

Relationships, however, are multiplicative, not additive. When you multiply one-half times one-half, you get one-fourth – even less than you started with! Two people trying to complete themselves through one another end up feeling even smaller than when they began, for they have approached their togetherness with a sense of "less-than." The voice that tells you that you are "less-than" will never be satisfied, and it cannot be offset by borrowing the strengths of another. If you are to be whole – which you are – you must listen to the voice of self-appreciation, not self-effacement, and proceed from strength rather than weakness.

When you multiply one times one, you still have one. When two people who know their wholeness join in a relationship, the result is more oneness. The most powerful approach to relationship is to proceed from wholeness, rather than toward it.

Comedienne Elaine Bousler warns, "Beware of anyone who tells you, 'I have so much love to give, and no one to give it to!' Immediately translate that statement into, 'I am the emotional black hole of the universe, and I will suck every ounce of life force from you if you let me.'"

No relationship can make you more than you are, because you are already everything. Every strength and beauty you perceive outside yourself already exists within you. If you did not already have it, you would not be aware of it. A good relationship can draw forth your divine qualities and assist you to recognize your own majesty. But it cannot fill you in, because you are not empty.

Birthpangs of Inner Power

Taking our power back may at first be difficult, as there speaks a voice in our mind that insists that we are nothing and everything we need is out there. The truth, however, is the reverse: we are everything and there is nothing out there.

The world we live in has been founded on seeking power outside ourselves. Herein lies the cause of misery. Throughout history, human beings have struggled, killed, and died in attempting to import the power they did not know they already owned.

To truly reclaim the power you have given away, you must reverse the laws of living you have been taught. Observe those who are striving to amass more power, and see if they are happy. They cannot be, and neither will you be if you follow their course. There is a course for you to follow, and it leads not out, but in.

You and I are part of a phenomenal upheaval of values now transpiring on the planet. We are giving up the notion that someone or something else can fill our empty cup. That concept does not work because we are by nature a full cup; to try to add

247

to it will only make a mess. This planetary transformation is being stirred by many individuals (like you) reclaiming sovereignty over their lives. The cultural upsets we are undergoing are akin to the ancient Hawaiians revolting in anger when they realized they had mistaken Captain Cook and his crew for gods. The real problem, however, was that the Hawaiians mistook themselves for not-gods. If they had realized who they were, they wouldn't have put the sailors on a pedestal which was destined to crash.

The Road Now Taken

I sat on the beach at Kealakekua Bay at the foot of the monument to Captain Cook's landing, ironically the same site of his demise. I watched the azure waves gently lapping upon the shore with a steady, almost hypnotic rhythm. It was hard to believe that two hundred years ago on this very strip of sand, a man who played God was stoned and drowned by an angry mob. I looked out at the majesty of the amber sun dropping behind the curtain of the western sea, somewhere lighting a new day as the old one fell away. Was it symbolic, I wondered, that in the wake of the violence we inflict upon ourselves by casting our greatness like a net onto others, that tranquility should come and wipe clean the sands we bloodied with our self-diminution? Might we actually be awakening to the realization that the only being worthy of adoration is the Spirit that lives within us? On the heels of my questioning came a soothing awareness that we are living at a most auspicious time on the planet – the very era in which idolatry gives way to divinity. Ah, discovery. Ah, resolution.

> Now the Egyptians are men, and not God;
> and their horses flesh, and not spirit.
> – Isaiah 31:3

CREATE OR DIE

You've got to sing like you don't need the money
Love like you'll never get hurt
Dance like there's nobody watching
It's got to come from the heart if you want it to work
                           – Susanna Clark and Richard Leigh

One afternoon I sat on a park bench in Tiburon, California and watched commuters walk off the ferry from San Francisco. Nearly all of these people looked tired, haggard, and frustrated. Their skin was sallow and none of them were smiling. Without a word they were making a strong clear statement about the low level of joy and satisfaction in their livelihoods.

When I ask my seminar audiences, "How many of you are living some kind of lie in your work?" usually sixty to seventy-five percent of the participants raise their hands. What a sad statement about the way we spend half or more of our waking time! No wonder so many people suffer from heart disease, respiratory problems, and psychological distress. It's hard to be happy when you spend so much time doing what you dislike.

Can you guess what time and day of the week most people die? More people expire on Monday morning at nine o'clock than at any other time. The implications of this phenomenon are staggering: most people would rather drop dead than go to work.

Something is radically wrong with the way we approach our livelihood. Too many of us have made self-defeating compromises for too long. We are sick and tired of jobs that make us sick and tired. There must be a better way.

Honest Living

You don't have to work for a living. You can create for a life. We have gotten our notion of livelihood terribly crosswired. Many of us believe that an honest living is one in which we struggle and toil at something we hate, and the reward for our hardship is money. *This is not so.* It is but a sick belief system that we have reinforced by agreement. There is another way.

Buckminster Fuller noted that "human beings are the only creatures on the planet who tell time and believe they have to earn a living." Jesus taught the same truth in a metaphor: "Behold the lilies of the field. They do not toil and neither do they sow. Yet I tell you that Solomon in all his glory was not arrayed like one of these." The master went on, "Will your Heavenly Father not take even better care of you, who are His Children?"

Master Key:

Don't Work for a Living. Create for a Life.

What is your secret dream? What would you really love to be doing with your life? When you close your eyes and fantasize about how great your life could be if you had unlimited love, abundance, and support, what comes to mind?

I often pose these questions to waitresses, taxi drivers, and passengers I sit next to on airplanes. Usually those I ask are startled at first by the intimacy of the question; then they smile. No matter how frazzled, tired, or impatient they seemed before I inquired, they light up and become very present. The lines in the hotel clerk's face begin to soften as he loosens his tense grip on his pen. The dental hygienist's shoulders drop as she lets her head fall back in a moment of welcome laughter. The pizza delivery man takes a deep breath, stepping back for a moment from the rush of his deliveries. If you ever want to see someone transform before your eyes, ask them what is their heart's desire.

Why would considering such a question make a difference in someone's day? Most people are dying, rather than living in their work. They do not realize that *livelihood* begins with *live*. They wake up in the morning, groan at the prospect of another exhausting day, force themselves out of bed, and drag their reluctant minds and bodies to jobs that are boring at least, and abhorrent at worst. They do not realize how profoundly they are dishonoring themselves and their talents by tolerating careers in which their life force is diminished to the tiniest trickle of creativity and self-expression.

Don't Ration Your Passion

How would you be approaching your livelihood differently if you knew that it is possible to do what you love most, receive abundant material support for it, and enrich the lives of many people in the process?

This is not a pipe dream. To the contrary, it is the way the universe is set up to work. You came to earth with a talent which, if shared, will bring you great joy, draw to you plentiful money or substance, and offer blessings to those you serve. The reason most people do not enjoy abundance through their livelihood is not because they do not have gifts to share; it is because they do not believe in themselves enough to share those gifts with confidence. A great teacher once told me, "No one comes to earth unarmed." She was explaining that every soul is born with a particular gift which, if offered to others, will draw to them the substance they need to lead a creative, healthy, and prosperous life. Even a little experimentation with offering your true talents will demonstrate that the world needs what you have to offer, and is willing and able to reward you for it.

ACTIVATION:

RIGHT LIVELIHOOD INVENTORY

Check the boxes that apply to your experience in your work:

☐ My livelihood brings me more joy than most other activities.

☐ I feel creative and alive as I engage in my work.

☐ When I am done I feel more energized than when I began.

☐ I often lose track of time when I am working.

☐ I am delighted with the results of my work.

☐ I deliver a real service for which recipients acknowledge me gratefully.

☐ I would do this even if I weren't getting paid.

☐ I sometimes feel that I should be paying people to let me perform my service.

☐ The universe rewards me with money and/or other forms of material support.

☐ I sleep well at night.

☐ My health is robust.

☐ I am becoming more creative.

☐ I have more inspiring ideas than I can keep up with.

☐ I attract and associate with others who are fulfilled, creative, and prosperous in their livelihood.

☐ I feel that the work is being done through me by a higher power.

☐ I feel a sense of loving detachment; I enjoy the results as if I were looking upon the good work of another.

☐ I act on my intuition, which bears successful results.

☐ I enjoy a sense of ease and flow in the process.

☐ Synchronistic or miraculous events occur which demonstrate that I am part of a greater plan.

☐ I would want my child to approach his/her work with the same attitude as I approach mine.

☐ If everyone enjoyed their work as much as I do, the world would be a happier place.

Scoring:
15-21 *Yes*: You are in your right livelihood, enjoying following your spirit, and serving others in the process.

8-14 *Yes*: You are honoring some of your heart's desires, but still compromising. There is more you can do to enjoy your current work, or you have another dream you are not acknowledging. Go over your list of "no" and consider what you can do to shift them to "yes."

1-7 *Yes*: You still equate work with suffering and sacrifice, and do not believe in yourself enough to let your creativity be your livelihood. Stop what you are doing, tell your truth, and take steps to live it. Do not waste any more time in dissatisfaction.

The Key is at your Fingertips

Dr. Bruce Logan, a renowned psychotherapist who earned a huge income, was in many ways the picture of success. He had a comfortable house in the country, a loving wife, and vacations in the Hamptons. All of this was wonderful, except for one glitch – he was bored. One day as Dr. Logan was listening to a patient talk about her life, he noticed he had been doodling. Looking over his note pad, he found on the margins of his note pad rough drawings of sculptures he was envisioning. Sculpting, Dr. Logan had to admit, was much more interesting to him than psychotherapy. So he quit his practice and devoted his creative energies to sculpture. Now Bruce is a well-respected sculptor, making vast amounts of money for his artistic talents. And he is not bored.

Dr. Logan was sensitive to the signals within him, and he had the courage to follow them. A similar voice of inner wisdom speaks to all of us, nudging us along our personal path to fulfillment. If we act on its guidance, we will move gracefully to our next level of good. If we do not pay attention to the inner signals, life will move us to our next adventure – whether or not we realize (or like) it at the time.

I met an attorney whose firm had gone bankrupt. Andrew did not enjoy the practice of law, and it was no surprise that he went out of business. Andrew's real interest was in computers.

During his bankruptcy process, Andrew researched bankruptcy laws and recorded his notes on his computer. After several months he realized he had arranged a wealth of information in a way that no one else had. Andrew took his notes and program to some executives at Macintosh Computers, who were so impressed by what he had done that they offered him a handsome sum of money to develop the program. Now he works with enthusiasm as a legal program consultant for Macintosh.

We can consciously move toward our dream, or *In-Your-Face-Productions* will advance us. The current of evolution is always moving us ahead. Our job is to listen as keenly as we can, act on our instincts, and trust that the universe is supporting us.

The Path with Heart

Many of us are familiar with the maxim, "Do what you love and the money will follow." Yet many people do not know what they would love to do. It is hard to follow your bliss if you do not know what it is. The following exercise will light your path:

ACTIVATION:

BLISS POINTERS

1) What do you love to do the most?

2) What do you do the best?

3) What does the universe support you for doing? For what do thanks and money come to you most readily?

4) If you had money, time, and support to meet your needs, what creative activities would you pursue?

5) What action step(s) could you take now to express more of what makes you happy?

Life is moving to support you to do what makes you happy. Your role is to move with the energy you feel. That is where a leap of faith comes in. You must act as if you are worthy of reward before the universe can demonstrate that your faith is justified.

In my work I have heard the testimonies of thousands of people who have found the courage to take the next step toward living their dreams. Without exception, the sense of joy and exhilaration in these people is entirely compelling. I have no doubt that the secret of happy living is to follow your spirit without hesitation.

A Fine Mess

As you set out on the adventure of creative self-expression, your world may turn inside out or upside down. That is the best thing that could happen, for a life out of harmony with your destiny will only hurt you if you keep living it.

I would be suspicious of any creative process that did not make a mess. To step into a sculptor's studio, a building construction zone, or a quality psychotherapy session, it would be rare to not walk through some kind of chaos.

You cannot change the world and keep it the same. You cannot cling to the old and usher in the new. You cannot simultaneously create and control. You must take a risk to explore the unknown, no matter how scary it seems on the edge. There must be an undoing – sometimes a radical one – before things can come together in a new and better way.

Messes are not bad; used creatively, they are the birthing pools of new life. In a seminar in Hawaii, a participant was undergoing tremendous emotional upheaval as she confronted the issues of her life and began to see how much she had been compromising herself in her marriage and career. As Lonnie spoke from the depths of her spirit, I felt as if I was witnessing the rebirth of a soul. After this courageous woman went through an intense period of emotional labor, she tearfully asked, "But why does the process have to be so messy?"

I asked Lonnie, "Do you think this is a beautiful island?"

"Of course," she answered. "It's one of the most exquisite places I've ever seen."

"Do you know how it got that way?"

"What do you mean?"

"A long time ago, there was only water here," I explained. "It was just like the Bible described, 'without form and void.'

"Then one day a tremendous explosion shot millions of tons of molten lava up from the depths of the sea. Huge rocks and rivers of fire spewed forth, making tumult of the waters for hundreds of miles in all directions. Awful-smelling sulfuric gasses issued into the atmosphere and filled it with volcanic ash thicker than the heaviest smog in our modern cities.

"Over centuries the molten material spilled chaotically over itself as the jagged, rocky, uninhabitable island took shape. The formation was unpredictable and repulsive to human senses.

"After thousands of more years, some seeds were dropped onto the craggy island by winds or birds blown off course by tropical storms. The tiny kernels took root, and rudimentary mosses painted the faintest green on a bleak terrain. Later simple ferns raised themselves toward the sun, and trees attracted clouds to pour life-giving rains on the parched hardened lava. Over a long painstaking evolution, this lush island paradise was formed. Today we delight in crystal streams pouring themselves in ribbons of waterfalls from towering peaks to the welcoming ocean. Millions of people come to bask in its splendor, yet but a few consider that this place was born from chaos.

"The upheaval you are undergoing is the birth of something so magnificent that you cannot begin to understand its power and potential. The form of your life will change so radically that it will bear little resemblance to the desolate psychic island on which you've been living. The momentary disorientation and confusion you are experiencing is but a transitional movement in a grander symphony that will lead you from hell to heaven."

Tears welled up again in Lonnie's eyes, and began flowing down her cheeks like the gentle waterfalls I had just described. This time her tears were born of joy, and she was smiling.

I picked up *A Course in Miracles* and read this passage:

Every leaf that falls is given life in you. . .Every bird that ever sang will sing again in you. And every flower that ever bloomed has saved its perfume and its loveliness for you. . .How better could your own mistakes be brought to truth than by your willingness to bring the light of Heaven with you as you walk beyond the world of darkness into light?[1]

YOU CAN'T STEAL HOME
WITH YOUR FOOT ON THIRD

To see what few have seen,
you must go where few have gone.
– Buddha

"I went to the woods because I wanted to live deliberately. I wanted to love deep and suck out all the marrow of life," Thoreau affirmed. Very few people on this planet live deliberately. Instead of sucking all the marrow out of life, the life they reluctantly lead sucks the marrow out of their souls. Many waitresses, cab drivers, and bank tellers look tired, angry, and balled up with frustration. Such *angst* is so prevalent not because joy is unavailable, but because they do not know that their heart's desires are available for the asking.

Are you living *deliberately*? Are you at choice about your relationships and activities, or do you play it safe, being sure that you have the approval of friends or authority figures before you act? Are you subject to the laws of social expectations, or do you know that you are free to be yourself? You can play it safe or play it real. The only true security abides in living from your heart. Leading with your truth will take care of you in miraculous ways that feverish manipulation could never accomplish. No person, thing, or institution in the outer world can guarantee you more than you will receive by trusting and following your inner guidance. A group of five millionaires was asked what advice they would give to a young person seeking to carve a successful career. Every one of these magnates agreed, "Be true to your unique gifts, hunches, and dreams."

The key to successful risking is to look ahead, not behind. If you try to keep one foot in the old world while attempting to plant your other foot in your new life, you will be pulled apart like a wishbone. Instead of trying to straddle the widening gap between worlds, you would do better to stay fully where you are or jump boldly into the new. Many skeletons lie at the bottom of the chasm between the past and the possible. They tried to join two worlds that cannot be joined, and gained neither.

When Your Heart is Strong

A mugwump is someone who sits with his mug on one side of the fence and his wump on the other. I laughed as I read a newspaper classified advertisement that typified mugwump consciousness. It said, *"Car for sale. . . $500 firm or best offer."* Obviously the seller did not have a strong sense of "firm." He couldn't make up his mind if he would hold his ground or dicker.

This ad symbolizes the way some of us have lived our lives. We say we want one thing, but act as if we will accept another. Then the universe gives us ambivalent results, and we wonder why our affairs are confused. Our affairs are confused because our minds and intentions have been confused. Here we may apply the immortal wisdom of Yogi Berra, who advised, "If you come to a fork in the road, take it."

Sometimes you have to make a stand for your vision and trust that you will somehow be taken care of. Do not expect the universe to give you what you want before you set out to claim it; your actions are the magnets that will draw your good to you. To step out on faith and live the life you envision is a bold statement of intention. Act as if your vision is real and important. Thumb your nose at fear and follow your gut instinct. Helen Keller declared, "life is a daring adventure – or nothing."

On the threshold of recording her blockbuster album *Unforgettable*, Natalie Cole wrestled with her soul. The notion of electronically marrying segments of her dad's famous 1950's song with her voice in response, was a bold and unprecedented experiment in the music industry. But in spite of potential criticism, there was something inside Natalie that kept pushing her to produce the song. Subsequently the recording became a top-selling album and Natalie won numerous Grammy awards for it. Natalie looked back and summarized the process: "When your heart is really strong about something, there comes a point at which you just close your eyes and go for it."

Master Key:

To Get Something New, Do Something New. No Guts, No Glory.

Swimming Naked

One of my favorite pastimes is swimming *au naturel*. The mountains near my home are filled with countless magical hidden waterfalls, where I delight to hike and swim bottomless in the chilled pools.

One morning a friend and I set out for a day of play in the waters. Soon after we arrived, a few more people showed up. "I should probably put on my bathing suit," I thought. "These people may find my nudity offensive."

The thought was followed by a staunch, "But I was here first. Besides, most people are used to skinny-dipping here. I'll just carry on as I am, and trust that everyone will be fine."

A little while later a family arrived. "Now I should really put my suit on," I thought. "The family may be uncomfortable with me and my friend being naked."

"But we were here first," I thought. "And kids usually   go

naked anyway. I'll just go on as if all is in order."

Then a tour group arrived. Off the mini-van the Japanese marched, camcorders rolling. "Now I really better get dressed," I figured.

By this time, however, I was enjoying myself immensely. "If they don't like it, that's their problem," I reasoned. "Besides, I was here first."

So went the day. No one else removed their suits, but everyone seemed fine with us being naked, and we all enjoyed ourselves. The visitors came and went, and the sun began to dip behind the mountains. My friend and I calmly got dressed and made our way back down the path.

As I left, a deep sense of peace pervaded my being, along with a magnificent awakening. The key question of life, I recognized, is this: Do you have the courage to swim naked even when others are wearing their suits?

The idea is, of course, a metaphor. I am not referring simply to physical nudity. It is infinitely more important to be spiritually naked; to be who you are, whatever you are, where you are, and act from a sense of inner honesty rather than social accommodation.

Life on the Edge

Across the bay from the picturesque Alaskan fishing town of Homer, sits an idyllic little island that refreshes my heart just to think of it. Halibut Island can be reached only by a ferry greeted by orange-beaked puffins soaring along its windy route. The island sports a famous seafood restaurant connected by a winding wooden sidewalk to a potpourri of offbeat art galleries.

The resident sage of Halibut Island is an old-timer named Will Tillion. This amiable patriarch is often found sitting against his rough-hewn fence just down the lawn from his house on a hill overlooking the windswept bay. On the day the tides of destiny drew me to Halibut Island, Will happened to be at his picket office. Not wanting to miss this juicy opportunity to pick his seasoned brain, I decided to toss my hat into the philosopher's ring.

I approached Will as nonchalantly as I could (feeling terribly clumsy as an obvious city slicker), made some small talk, and asked Will if he could tell me in a nugget the most important thing he's learned over his many colorful years.

"I'd say, just go out and do what you want, and if you don't get killed, you'll have some fun."

There was a time in my life when I would not act on anything I could not understand or control. Now I am becoming more and more comfortable living with uncertainty. After experiencing tremendous awakening as a result of venturing into unexplored territory, I recognize that life's most exciting discoveries await just over the horizon of uncharted seas.

We cannot know what we will find until we hoist our sails and move out of the harbor. My friend Salvator is one of the most dynamic and enlightening lecturers I have ever heard. When he speaks, noble and inspiring words of poetic wisdom issue from his lips as if uttered by the gods. He is a living channel for illuminated truth. During one of his discourses, Salvator described his process: "Often when I begin a sentence, I do not know how it will end."

We, too, are asked to live on the edge of life. Often we must play it by ear, trusting that if we start a sentence (or any path) on faith, Spirit will assist us to finish it. We may enter into relationships, careers, and spiritual paths, feeling that what we are doing is right for us, but not understanding why. Sometimes all we can do is take the step immediately before us. We just have to be true to this moment. This moment, well lived, will lead to the next, and the next, as we weave the tapestry of our lives thread by thread – all the while directed by the Great Artist who holds the master blueprint. From the standpoint of the little ego, the process is a mystery. From the overview of the Great Mind that orchestrates the great symphony, it is mastery.

ACTIVATION:

THE FEARLESS VISION

*Complete the following sentence with
as many answers as come to mind.*

If I were not afraid, I would _____.

If I were not afraid, I would_____.

If I were not afraid, I would_____.

If I were not afraid, I would_____.

If I were not afraid, I would_____.

If I were not afraid, I would_____.

If I were not afraid, I would_____.

If I were not afraid, I would_____.

If I were not afraid, I would_____.

If I were not afraid, I would_____.

If I were not afraid, I would_____.

If I were not afraid, I would_____.

If I were not afraid, I would_____.

If I were not afraid, I would_____.

Continue on a separate sheet of paper if necessary.

To Gain it All

All healing occurs outside the safe zone. It's okay to feel afraid, but do not allow fear to keep you from moving ahead. Psychologist Alfred Adler noted that "The chief danger in life is that you may take too many precautions." The fear-based world we see is the result of a mass hypnosis that there lies a greater power outside us than there is inside us. If everyone woke up tomorrow morning and recognized that what lies within is infinite, and what lies without is impotent, the world would quickly move toward reflecting the heaven on earth it could be.

When tomorrow morning comes, perhaps not everyone in the world will wake up with the knowledge of the power within them – but you and I can. Nor do we need to wait until tomorrow; we can live our greatness today. We can change our world by changing our minds about what the world is, who we are, and what we are here to do. We are spiritual beings, the world is a projection of our thoughts and beliefs, and we are here to remember that we are the light, and live it. This is all you need to know to restore the presence of love to a world that has lost it. This is all you need to know to restore the magnificence you were born to express. This is all you need to know to be happy.

All risk is illusion. As a spiritual being, you cannot lose. Danger seems real only in dreams. Wake up and realize that you have cast, directed, and salaried the characters you ran from in your nightmare. You do not need to vanquish your enemies; you need to wake up to the fact that you have no enemies.

To gain it all, you must risk it all. Whether you win all or lose all, you will ultimately recognize that you have it all, just as you have had it all the time.

> *"Come to the edge," he said.*
> *"We are afraid," they answered.*
> *"Come to the edge," he said.*
> *They came.*
> *He pushed them, and they flew.*[1]

265

FIRST CLASS FLYING

I dreamed I had a child, and even in the dream I saw that it was my life, and it was an idiot, and I ran away. But it always crept into my lap again, clutched at my clothes. Until I thought, if I could kiss it, whatever in it was my own, perhaps I could sleep. And I bent over the broken face, and it was horrible. . .but I kissed it. I think that one must finally take one's life into one's arms.
— Arthur Miller, *After the Fall*

Defending Your Life is a film playfully advertised as "the first true story of what happens after you die" — and it is closer to the truth than the horror stories we were told as children. Albert Brooks portrays a man who, after suddenly leaving this world, finds himself in a heavenly realm before a panel of judges. Daniel is told that the purpose of the hearing is to review crucial scenes from his life in which he had to choose between courage and cowardice. The purpose of his life, Daniel discovers, was to learn to love and honor himself.

Daniel meets a guide, Bob, who has been assigned to present his case. "You were a fairly generous person, weren't you?" Bob asks.

"I think so."

"But there was one person with whom you were consistently stingy."

Daniel's mind begins to churn. He remembers favors, forgiveness, and gifts to his friends. He was a kind and thoughtful man. "Who are you talking about?" Daniel asks, puzzled.

267

"*Yourself.* You were good at making sure that everyone around you was happy – but when it came to giving to yourself, you hardly ever did it."

Daniel is stunned. He had thought that taking care of himself was selfish. Now he is being told that believing in himself was one of the most important elements of living.

When Daniel's case comes up, there is not much evidence on his behalf. He made most of his choices from a feeble position of low self-appreciation. Time and again he retreated from asking for what he really wanted. Daniel does not stand much chance of convincing the tribunal that he learned to care for himself.

There is, however, one scene which moves the panel in Daniel's favor. After a devastating divorce, Daniel was left with nine thousand dollars (a small portion of his assets before the split), plus an airline ticket for an Oriental vacation. As the life-review movie rolls, we see Daniel standing at the Japan Airline check-in counter, ready to take off on his first pleasure outing since his divorce. The agent tells Daniel, "You have seat 38B."

Daniel's face blanches with disappointment. "Does that mean I will be sitting in the back of the plane between two other people for ten hours?"

"I'm sorry, sir," the agent answers. "There are no other seats available."

"How about in first class?"

The agent's fingers dance over the computer keyboard, her eyes intent on the monitor. "There is one first class seat left; to upgrade will cost an additional three thousand dollars."

Daniel deliberates for a moment; then a smile lights up his face. "I'll take it!"

Master Key:

Taking Care of Yourself Is the Greatest Service You Can Offer to Others

It is not selfish to be happy. It is your highest purpose. Your joy is the greatest contribution you can make to life on the planet. A heart at peace with its owner blesses everyone it touches.

The energy you broadcast is more important than the activities you undertake. Remember that it is the *spirit in which we act* that nourishes or starves us. You may perform many saintly deeds, but if your heart is sullied with resentment, self-criticism, or fatigue, you are not truly serving. By the same token, you could sit in a cave and meditate, and if your soul was emanating tranquility, you would be serving life on the planet in a most effective way. Your thoughts, attitude, and energies radiate like ripples in a pond, and have a profound impact on the psychic environment we all share. To make yourself happy will only enhance the quality of life on earth.

Let it Out and Let it In

Many people are prolific givers, but resistant receivers. Often those who are constantly giving to others, are reluctant to accept love themselves. It is as important to be able to wholeheartedly receive compliments, gifts, services, and forgiveness as it is to bestow kind acts upon others. Strangely, some who have the hardest time accepting nurturing are those in the service professions. Mothers, nurses, doctors, psychologists, and ministers are often the most in need of soul nourishment – and the most deft at deflecting it when it is offered. In the name of service or business they care for others at the expense of their own health, happiness, and relationships. They do not recognize that the best gift they could give their families and patients would be to take better care of themselves.

You can squeeze a sponge until it is dry, and then you must refill it. You can keep squeezing, but nothing will come out. In the helping professions this is called "burnout." If a lake has an outlet but no inlet, it soon becomes arid and devoid of life. A heart must be replenished with life-sustaining blood, or else it has no energy to pump to the rest of the body.

Playing in the Majors

You are no good to anyone if you are burnt out. The moment you begin to feel that you are depleted, stop what you are doing, or make a plan to stop at the next possible opportunity, and feed your spirit. Your soul nourishment may require as little as stepping out of doors into the sunlight for a few deep breaths, or as much as a radical transformation of the way you are living. Whatever you do for the sake of spirit renewal will be well worth it. It is your life in which you are investing – and perhaps saving.

I remember intensive lecture tours during which I felt so exhausted that I functioned like a walking robot. I would speak the words, smile warmly, counsel and hug people – but I was not there. Nothing new or creative was proceeding from my heart or consciousness. My body was showing up, but my spirit was depleted and aching.

Old faithful *In-Your-Face-Productions* helped me recognize that, feeling so spent, I was not truly serving. Subsequently I began to build rest periods into my travels. Instead of speaking four or five nights a week, I scheduled no more than three events, leaving days in between for soul replenishment. If an organization requested a program on one of my days off, I would tell the sponsor, "That is a renewal day for me; let us consider another date when I will present a much better program because I will come to you rested."

When one sponsor insisted that I speak to her group close on the heels of another presentation, I told her, "In major league baseball there is a rule that a pitcher must rest for at least three days between games. That is because managers would abuse their good pitchers by scheduling them too often. As a result, the players would be ineffective and hurt themselves, ultimately shortening their pitching careers." I explained to her, "I would be happy to speak to your group another time, but first I need to replenish myself – I am playing in the big leagues."

It is said that the surest sign that you are on your way to a nervous breakdown is the belief that your work is extremely important. Fatigue, irritability, poor results, ill health, interpersonal conflict, and a sense of never being caught up with your work, are signs that you are trying to save the world before taking care of yourself. If you exhibit any of these symptoms, STOP what you are doing and build regular self-nurturing activities into your lifestyle.

The first responsibility of any giver is to have an ample supply to give. The gift we came to share is spirit. If we lose our spirit, we have lost everything. If our spirit is alive, we have everything for ourself and everything to give. Before you enter your day, work, or relationships, fill yourself from your inner well. Linking with your higher power gives you the optimum strength and perspective to handle any situation. Through prayer, meditation, artistic creation, music, dance, physical exercise, or spending time in nature, find your center and then act from the strength it imbues. Then you will be giving from a sense of overflow, and you will enjoy giving as much as your receivers appreciate your gifts.

ACTIVATION:

FIRST CLASS FLYING TICKETS

1. Cut down on scheduling
2. Learn to say "no"
3. Ask for what you really want
4. Take mini-retreats and vacations
5. Stop when you feel tired
6. Honor your home as your personal renewal space
7. Receive massages
8. Soak in a hot tub
9. Release the person whose life you are trying to run or save
10. Play more with your family and friends
11. Tell a deeper truth in your significant relationships
12. Spend more time in nature
13. Listen to your favorite music
14. Make love in the middle of the afternoon
15. Make time with your children and don't change your plans
16. Dance 'til you're giddy
17. Take a friend to dinner at your favorite restaurant
18. Call an old friend and talk at length about your lives
19. Take a class in something you've never done before
20. Write a love letter to your favorite relative
21. Write a love letter to your least favorite relative
22. Meditate
23. Consider making your hobby your career
24. Write a letter of appreciation to someone who inspires you
25. Spend time in your garden
26. Buy your sweetie her/his favorite gift
27. Buy yourself your favorite gift
28. Turn off your answering machine and telephone for a day
29. Go out to a movie
30. Rent a video, make popcorn, and invite friends over

Add to your list on a separate sheet of paper.

These are just a few of the many ways you might raise the mercury level on your joy barometer. Begin to pay attention to what turns you on, and you will add many more of your own. Do WHATEVER YOU NEED TO DO to renew the breath of life in your body and activities. There is no greater investment you could make in your own life and the lives of those you touch and serve. You will be amazed at how much more effective you will be as a result of feeding your spirit.

Fully Human, Fully Divine

Humility can be a fool's cloak for suicide; you may not destroy yourself physically, but you can deplete your life force to the point where you are not there. There is nothing spiritual, glamorous, or helpful about self-abrogation. To put yourself down will not bring you closer to heaven. When we impugn our spirit we dampen the light God has given us to shine into the world. Certain religious sects have played upon masochism and called it devotion. But pain is not love, and torture is not healing. You would not delight in your child's agony, and neither does your Creator.

As a young man, my friend Larry lived as an ascetic in a monastery. "While I enjoyed many inspiring moments as a monastic," Larry told me, "in the cloister there occurred practices that were just plain sick. Some of the monks regularly flagellated their bodies with hooks on straps, to the point of drawing blood. Once a week we brothers were given twenty-five cents and allowed to walk into town to buy an ice cream cone. We were instructed to shower with our underwear, so as to avoid stimulating our animal passions. Meanwhile, in spite of the fact that we had avowed chastity, many of the monks were carrying on homosexual relationships. The practice of self-denial was not working." Eventually Larry saw the hypocrisy of his presence in that monastery and left to live a more creative and rewarding life. He raised three beautiful children and became a legendary teacher in a public high school (very much like Mr. Keating in *Dead Poets Society*). Larry instituted revolutionary courses in self-esteem and was consistently voted "Best Teacher of the Year" by the student body. Through his own painful odyssey, Larry discovered that gentleness with one's journey is a far more powerful ally than self-torture.

Religious zealots have long decried the pleasures of the flesh as evil. But evil exists not in acts; it lives in minds only. As Shakespeare elucidated, "nothing is good or bad unless we make it so with our thoughts." Everything in life has the potential to be used for divine upliftment, including food and sex. *Babette's Feast* is a delightful film in which a young French woman wins the national lottery and transforms an entire village of crabby old cynics by making them a feast that delights their hearts as well as their senses. What a marvelous example of nature in service of spirit! J.D. Salinger's fine short story *Teddy* shows us life in our times through the eyes of a wise soul who is born into a middle-American family. As a child, Teddy describes his mother nursing his little sister as "God pouring God into God."

Conscious sexuality is also God pouring God into God. When two people join in loving intimacy, sexuality becomes a powerful vehicle to express our highest spiritual nature. The term "making love" describes the highest potential of our sexual being. In truth, we cannot "make love," for love is already fully present in every atom of the universe. What we can do is to join in the celebration of love and glorify its presence as the divine gift it is. The sacred is fully available to be touched through the forms and experiences of this world. St. Ignatius declared, "To become fully divine, we must first become fully human."

274

Are You Worth It?

As my friends Marc and Anastasia were planning their wedding, they learned an important lesson in first class flying. "When we considered the cost of flowers, our initial reaction was, 'That's beyond our budget,'" they told me. "Then we looked at each other and said, 'We and our wedding are worth the flowers!' The floral arrays turned out to be one of the most meaningful aspects of our celebration."

Master Key:

Your Life is a Reflection of
What You Believe You are Worth

A Course in Miracles tells us, *"Every decision you make stems from what you think you are, and represents the value that you put upon yourself."* When we are disappointed, we are prone to blame others for not valuing us, but it is we who have failed to value ourselves. It is no accident, then, when others give us less than we deserve; behind the obvious story line it is we who have underestimated our deservingness.

The secret to first class flying is not to go around battling others to give you your due; those who undermine you are simply actors in a play of your own production. The key is to *change your mind about who you are and what you are worth.* On the heels of such a fundamental shift in self-appreciation, the universe, represented by all of its players, will have no choice but to mirror your enriched self-image.

James Allen posited,

> *We think in secret and it comes to pass;*
> *Environment is our looking glass.*

Master Key:

To Receive More,
Upgrade Your Sense of What You Deserve.

In my early years of public speaking I asked a relatively low fee for my programs. My business partner kept telling me that my fee was small in relation to the quality of the service I was offering and the results my work was manifesting. My friends continually urged me to increase my fee. When I did, my sponsors and clients balked, and I ended up receiving the same amount of money I had been getting. Then I entered a relationship that did wonders for my self-esteem. I spent several years with a loving, communicative woman who saw the greatness in me, and fanned the flame of self-appreciation within me. She knew that I and my work are worth a great deal, and her vision stimulated me to know the same.

As our relationship progressed and my sense of self-worth expanded, I began to ask for a higher fee, and I received it without argument. Within two years I was receiving eight times the original amount I had settled for! Last year I was offered twenty-five times my original fee – for a one hour lecture.

I see these increments in material support not as a function of the economy (about which many people complain) or my increased presentation skills (which, although somewhat improved, remain the same at their core). Rather, I see the increase as a direct result of my deepened appreciation of my worth. As I more fully recognize my value, the universe has to mirror it.

When you know that you are worth first class flying, life will automatically advance you to the forward compartment. There is room in first class for everyone, but the passengers seated there are those who request it by right of their consciousness of deservingness. All manifestations of success begin with self-appreciation.

The Gulp Factor

I once asked a successful businessman how much of a fee I should request for a particular job I was offered. "I suggest you use the *gulp factor* as a guideline," he told me.

"What's the 'gulp factor'?"

"You ask for as much as you can without gulping audibly."

This entrepreneur was encouraging me to play the cutting edge of my sense of self-worth. What we ask for is an indication of what we believe we deserve. If we ask for a little, we demonstrate that we think little of ourself. If we ask for a lot, we make a clear statement that we are worth a great deal. When you practice a high estimation of your worth – by declaring it in the form of your request – you might be pleasantly surprised that others are willing to agree with you.

It is not simply your words that magnetize success, but your *beliefs*. All the self-affirming words in the dictionary will do you no good if you are not convinced they apply to you. You can ask for fifty thousand dollars, but if you believe that you or your product is worth only thirty thousand, the transaction is not likely to yield more than what you expect. You can polish your negotiation skills to the hilt, but if you don't change your mind about your merit, you might as well not waste your time trying to deal. Ultimately the person with whom you must negotiate is yourself. Your adversary is not your customer, but the part of your mind that questions your worth. Your employer or client will then play out your beliefs.

Before going into your negotiating session, talk yourself into your good. Remind yourself of your valuable qualities, and find reasons why you should receive what you are asking for. Think of others who command what you are requesting, and know that you are as good as they are, if not better. Prime yourself with *belief*, and you will be amazed at how readily others respond.

Prosperous people know that they are worth it. You cannot know your worth, and have the universe give you less; and it is just as unrealistic to deny your worth, and have the universe manifest more. I know people who are extremely gifted, but they do not recognize their talents, and so they are struggling to make ends meet. Ironically, everyone around them sees their beauty and talents, but they have a blind spot for their own preciousness. All the pieces are in place for them to manifest success and service; their only need is to awaken to the splendor within them.

Money is just one metaphor. You may wish your partner would respect you more and speak to you with greater kindness. It is the same issue. He or she is reflecting your level of perceived deservingness. Instead of arguing, have a talk with yourself. *You* are the one who needs to be convinced that you deserve better. When you know your value, your partner will have to change, because you won't settle for less than love. Don't stop until you know that you deserve it all, and manifest the same.

No More Paper Clip Calls

Life is too precious to waste time. Jules Renard noted, "I am never bored anywhere; being bored is an insult to oneself." We dishonor ourself and others to participate in lifeless activities.

I used to engage in what I call "Paper Clip Calls." Several individuals regularly called my office and rambled on about matters in which I had little interest. I felt too guilty to put them off, so while they were going on I dusted my desk top, wrote notes to my secretary, and reorganized paper clips into their slots. Every now and then I would say, "uh-huh," but I was not really listening to what they were saying.

Afterward I realized I was not serving the caller or myself by making believe I was listening while I actually found more value in sorting paper clips. So I made an inner commitment to be fully with whatever I was doing. I would give them my full attention or engage wholeheartedly in my cleaning project. In being half present with them and half present elsewhere, I was wasting their time and mine. Both of us could be doing more rewarding things.

Now (depending on what is appropriate) I invite such callers to a level of communication that I find rewarding or, failing that, let them know that I have to go. Perhaps there is someone else they could talk to who will be more interested in the subject matter they are sharing. I would not want someone to humor me by making believe they are present when they aren't, and it is unkind for me to do the same. Now when I say goodbye I send them off with a blessing rather then hanging on with resentment.

Select, Don't Settle

I spoke with a woman who had enthusiastically signed up for one of my seminars, and was thinking about cancelling. "I'm not sure if my boss will let me off work," Lisa told me.

I asked Lisa, "What would *you* like to do?"

"I would love to come; I have been looking forward to this for a long time, and I would be disappointed if I didn't attend."

"Then why not be at choice about your life?"

"What do you mean?"

"Instead of rearranging your life around the choices others make for you, decide what you want to do, and then invite the universe to rearrange itself around your vision."

"That sounds a lot more exciting to me!" Lisa exclaimed.

"It *is* more exciting, and it is how we were meant to live," I told her. "Most people do not recognize that they have options and the power to choose the option in line with their highest good. If this workshop is your highest choice, then make a clear statement that it is, and ask the universe to support you in it."

"Thank you," Lisa sighed. "That's just what I needed to hear."

The next day I received a phone call from Lisa. "I just talked to my boss," she excitedly reported. "When I told her how important it was for me to attend this workshop, she told me that she wanted to support me. We worked out a way in which I could go, and not lose any of my vacation days. The universe *did* rearrange itself to support my highest choice!"

ACTIVATION:

MY HIGHEST CHOICE

List seven important decisions you are now living with, or that you need to make. Note what you would really love to be doing in each situation, regardless of what you have been doing, what others want you to do, or what you have said you will do. What does your heart say?

My Decision   *My True Choice*

1.

2.

3.

4.

5.

6.

7

As a teenager I regularly heard a jingle on the radio: "Select, don't settle at Barney's" (a men's clothing store). We can and must apply the same motto to our lives: *Select, don't settle.* As W. Somerset Maugham astutely declared, "It's a funny thing about life; if you accept anything but the very best, you will get it."

If you are not using your mind, who is? There is a strong competition in the world for the use of your mind. Commercial advertisers would like it to buy their product. Politicians would like it to get your vote. Your kids would like it to give them an extra ice cream for dessert. You could literally allow your mind to be used by every outside influence for every moment of your life – and some people do! Many people are walking automatons, programmed by the media, religions, jobs, families, and friends. It is the exceptional person who makes her own choices from an internal guide rather than external influence. "Few are those who think with their own minds and feel with their own hearts."

You and I must be one of those few. As we proceed from strength rather than fear, we inspire others to do the same. *You serve life immeasurably when you live at choice, not default.* Computer programs use default settings, which means that if you come to a choice point and you do not tell the computer that you want to do something different, it will automatically make the choice for you that most people would make. Default settings may be appropriate for computer work, but they do not work for life. To live at default is to sell your birthright of free will. There are choices available to you that you are not aware of. If you feel trapped or stuck in any way, look again – *you have another choice.* Take every choice laid before you, and try it on for size. If it resonates with your internal guidance, go ahead and dive in. If you cannot wholeheartedly take this path, you must not walk it. Commit yourself to acting only from your heart, and deny all calls to follow any other voice.

You can live the life your heart desires. You may have given up on such a grand vision long ago, but if these words resonate even faintly in a remote and long untouched chamber of your heart, the door is still open. Don't give up. You have come too far to turn back now. All the seats in coach may be filled, but perhaps that is a blessing. Perhaps there awaits a better place in first class with your name on it.

> *I have an everyday religion that works for me. Love yourself first and everything else falls into line. You really have to love yourself to get anything done in this world.*
>
> – Lucille Ball

THE FUTURE ISN'T WHAT IT USED TO BE

Never make forecasts, especially about the future.
— Samuel Goldwyn

While sitting down for a late afternoon snack in a San Francisco hotel dining room, I noticed a couple at the next table enjoying what looked like some very tasty garlic toast. When I asked the waitress for a side order of the same, she furrowed her brow and answered, "I'm sorry sir; the garlic toast comes only with the dinner."

"Would it be possible for me to order some as a side order?" I persisted; "I'll be glad to pay for it."

She looked even more puzzled. "I don't know if that's ever been done, sir."

My ears perked up; now she was stepping into my domain. I suggested, "Perhaps this is our opportunity to change history and create a new destiny."

She smiled, went into the kitchen, and soon returned with a dish of piping hot garlic toast – an historic day for the Grosvenor Hotel restaurant!

Simple as this interaction was, it stands as a powerful metaphor for how we can transform our lives by changing the way we think about possibilities. We are prone to picture our future as an extension of our past. But we have no guarantee at all that our future will be anything like our past. As I look back upon the important transformations in my life, I recognize that the nature of a consciousness shift is the release of an old belief system, and its replacement with a new and grander one. Just when you think you know it all, life comes along and says, "Here, let me show you a bigger universe!' Thank God we do not know it all; if we did, we would be in big trouble, for most of what we know has made us small. Be grateful that the universe is willing to take away your impotence and replace it with magnitude.

There is a marvelous scene in the film *The Princess Bride* in which the hero Wesley takes his beloved Buttercup's hand and encourages her to follow him through the perilous Fireswamp. "But Wesley," the fair lady protests, "we'll never make it through the Fireswamp!"

"Nonsense!" replies our hero. "You're just saying that because no one has ever done it before!"

Possibility thinkers love to tread where others have not ventured. *Scare City* thinkers, on the other hand, stay within the prescribed boundaries of what has been done. Their world is limited to the known. Hypnotized by the past, they equate familiarity with safety, at the expense of growing beyond imaginary boundaries into limitless freedom.

Master Key:

Your History Is Not Your Destiny.

A Little Concerned About the Future

The endearing film *The Graduate* bestowed a classic ad depicting young Dustin Hoffman standing open-jawed before the sultry Anne Bancroft, poised open-legged in a terribly seductive posture. Mrs. Robinson, mother of Ben's girlfriend, was inviting Ben to play at a level he never expected. The caption noted, "Benjamin is a little concerned about his future."

284

You, too, may be a little concerned about your future. Like many people, your future may be coming at you more quickly than you feel you can field it. Life on the planet is evolving so rapidly that it is increasingly difficult to look to our old models as guides. The world shown to us by our parents is not the one we are living in, and neither will we pass it on to our children. We will take our forbears' legacy and forge a grander destiny. The future is not cast in bronze by a mysterious whimsical God who sits haughtily on a distant cloud and throws gum drops to a lucky few and casts lightning bolts at others. The future is clay in our hands; we are free to mold it as we intend. The future *is* uncertain, and that is a wondrous gift. We have the power to choose what the future will be.

Yet even as we build tomorrow's events with the thoughts we think today, we want someone else to tell us what our future holds. We are quick to turn to psychics and channelers, open *Elle* to the astrology column, pull out the Ouija board, pick fortune-telling cards, pay large sums for subscriptions to economic forecasts, and ask our friends what they think are our chances of marrying the person we're dating. We look for answers everywhere but within our own self, where they live.

In graduate school I took a course in consulting. On the first day of class the professor walked into the room and wrote this definition on the blackboard: *A consultant is someone who borrows your watch to tell you what time it is.* Humorous, but true! If you don't have a watch or don't know how to tell time, a consultant is a worthwhile investment. If you know that you already have what you need, and you have some tools to tap your resources, you will find the best consultant in the inner office.

The journey to wholeness is symbolized by the fable of the musk deer. This fleet-footed animal searches the highest mountains and deepest valleys to find the source of an enchanting aroma that seems to always be coming from around the next bend. Eventually the deer discovers that this entrancing scent is emanating from its own body. The delight the creature sought lay within it all the time.

The future we wonder about is sprouting now. Ponder this magnificent principle! The scientist who will discover the cure for AIDS is now in her laboratory. The next great social leader, in the lineage of Christ, Lincoln, Gandhi, and King, sits at a desk in an inner city elementary schoolroom at this very moment, stirring with visions that will change life on the planet forever. The solutions to our environmental issues are knocking at the doors of young inquisitive minds playing in their garages with rudimentary chemistry sets. And there are many more fantastic discoveries we haven't even dreamed of. The world to come is on its way, and it is coming through us.

Free Will-y

I saw a newspaper article about a psychic convention in Kansas City that had been cancelled – due to unforeseen circumstances! While it may seem unnerving that people who are supposed to know the future couldn't predict their own, I find it liberating to consider that the future is not a fact; it is an adventure. Nothing is certain to happen, unless we choose it.

A Chinese sage advised, "If you keep going in the direction you are walking, you will end up where you headed." The basis of any forecaster's accuracy is an awareness of trends – economic indicators, psychic propensities, astrological cycles, medical models, social leanings, ecological likelihoods. The best any predictor can say is, "According to the course that events are now taking, this result will follow."

When Bill Clinton built his presidential campaign on the theme of positive change, he defined insanity as "doing the same thing in the same way and expecting a different result." If you always do what you've always done, you'll always get what you've always gotten. Because most people go on doing the same things in the same way, it is fairly easy to predict that they will keep getting the same result.

Enter now, *free will.*

Because our world is evolving at lightning speed, it is becoming more and more difficult to make predictions according to the old models. (Remember the shift in physics which threw out the Newtonian model and replaced it with quantum physics; all of a sudden the "laws" of the universe changed.) As a result, we are approaching the point where *all bets are off*. Our future will arrive not as a result of a predictable linear progression stemming from history; it will be the result of the choices we make based on the level of consciousness we have attained. The new world will be quite unlike anything we've experienced. Sound uncertain? You got it. Frightening? Perhaps. Unlimited possibilities? Most assuredly.

Let's consider a practical example of free will in action. Going into the 1990 World Series, the World Champion Oakland A's were heavily favored to trounce the underdog Cincinnati Reds. The A's were riding high on a long string of post-season victories, including several world championships, and the Reds had not seen World Series action since they faced the Yankees in 1976. When one Cincinnati fan asked for the odds of the Reds winning the series in four games, he was given thirty-to-one. He believed in the Reds, and bet fifty thousand dollars on a sweep.

To nearly everyone's astonishment, the Reds went on to win the series in four games. On paper, the victory made no sense. Every statistic was dead against Cincinnati. But destiny is not etched on paper – it is spawned in the heart. The Reds were highly motivated to triumph, and rather than lying down to accept the fate offered them, they created their own. Sports experts consider the Reds' victory to be one of the most dramatic upsets in baseball history. And the Reds fan who made the big bet? He collected winnings of one and a half million dollars.

A few years ago I experienced my own lesson about free will in action. As I was planning a lecture tour, a well-respected astrologer looked at my horoscope, furrowed his brow, and told me, "That time of year will not be a good one for you to travel; the planets are aspected for some possible problems en route. I would advise you to go at another time if you can."

Immediately all manner of catastrophic images came to mind. I took a little trip to *Scare City* and began to think of everything that could go wrong. Prompted by fear, I started to consider ways I could rearrange my travel schedule to avoid a collision course with unfavorable planets. The more I thought about it, the more confused and upset I became.

Soon thereafter I was speaking to my spiritual advisor, who has a knack of calling forth my strength. She sees me as unlimited, and assists me to remember my power and live it. When I told her about my fears of disaster as a result of bucking an adverse planetary configuration, she laughed and told me, "You outgrew your chart a long time ago!" She reminded me that I have spent a long time cultivating my identity as a spiritual being, beyond limiting external factors. Deep in my heart I know my destiny is what I make it. I cannot be ruled by planets, bacteria, or economics. And neither can any of us be injured by anything outside our own mind – unless we agree it is so.

My advisor further told me, "If you go with a sense of fear, trepidation, or worry, you may very likely attract harmful events; not because they are pre-ordained, but because you draw them to you with your consciousness." She went on, "If you can go with joy, confidence, and celebration, you will find only success."

After meditating on her insights, I decided I would go forth in the name of love. I would not give my power away to planets or any other perceived sources outside my own mind and choice. I was going to share the gifts I have been given to give, and I would not stop now. I went ahead with the tour, which turned out to be a great success without mishap of any kind. Over the course of a month I presented a series of dynamic seminars, during which many lives were changed, as well as my own. I was very glad that I did not stop with the astrologer's predictions.

At another time I received a telephone call from my friend Sharon, who sadly informed me that her husband Gary was dying in the hospital. "His liver has failed, along with his kidneys, and a host of other complications have set in," Sharon tearfully explained. "The doctors have told me that Gary has but hours to live. Can you come and conduct his memorial service?"

While I wanted to accommodate Sharon, I explained to her that I was on a lecture tour and I would not be able to come. "I will, of course, join you in prayer," I told Sharon. "Please call me when you have more news."

I sent Gary love to bless his passing. When I completed my tour, I called Sharon to find out how she was doing. You can imagine my surprise when Gary answered the telephone.

"Gary!" I exclaimed. "I sure am glad to hear your voice!"

"Same here," he replied; "I decided to stay for a while."

Gary had miraculously turned from death's door. To the consternation of his doctors, Gary had recovered and left the hospital within a short time of when he was supposed to be dead. No one could explain his recovery, except as a miracle. Gary went on to live for a considerable length of time, during which he said all of his goodbyes, provided for Sharon's future, and then went on to gracefully make his transition.

Gary demonstrated that free will transcends medical prognosis. The laws of medicine, like astrology and other physical and occult sciences, are valid on the plane at which they operate. But that plane is not the only one, and that is where spirituality and metaphysics come into play. The laws of Spirit are unlimited, founded not in cause and effect, but in Grace. Grace means that any situation can be transformed through love. No matter how long a room has been in darkness, it takes but a flick of the light switch to illuminate it. How quickly a life can be made new! St. Paul, after being tossed from his horse in an electric moment, declared, "change can come in the twinkling of an eye."

There is one factor that no forecaster can predict or control: *a change in consciousness.* If you change your mind, you will change your future. I asked an internationally acclaimed psychic how she could have made an error about a relationship I had asked her about. "Prophecy is our weakness," she told me. "All we can tell you is what will happen based on the configuration of events at this moment. If we see someone walking toward a door, and the door is open, and their intention is to go through it, then we say that the person will walk through the door. But if they are distracted, or become afraid, or make another choice for any reason, that is not something we can know beforehand." Be glad the future is not set in stone; we set it in the heart, *now*.

The Beginning is Near

There has been a lot of talk about the world coming to an end. Our age has so many problems that it certainly seems this could really be the end. Newspaper headlines would have us believe that we are already over the brink, and it is just a matter of time until the last blast or whimper. Survivalists are holed up in camouflaged bunkers in sequestered mountains, stockpiling caches of food and weapons in preparation to fend off roving hordes. These fearful people represent the part of all of us that believes the end is near, and we must arm ourselves to survive it.

There is, however, another way of looking at our world predicament, one that brings hope rather than terror; compassion, not divisiveness. Seen through the eyes of love, we are on the brink not of extinction, but transformation.

I remember growing up during the cold war, when a nervous world seemed continually perched on the precipice of the final conflict. At the shriek of air raid sirens, my elementary school classmates and I were regularly drilled into dark hallways where we were instructed to crouch against the walls with our heads between our knees. (How that position would save us from a nuclear blast, remains a mystery to me.) I watched President Kennedy warn the Russians that we would go to war against them if they delivered any more missiles to Cuba. Soon afterward officials marched into my junior high school and posted yellow and black Fallout Shelter signs in the gym; when I walked into town the next day, the signs were everywhere. At the tender age of ten I surveyed my postage stamp-sized back yard to see if it was big enough to build a bomb shelter for me and my family. I remember waking up with a jolt in the shattering echo of a booming blast, thinking the dreaded bomb had fallen; it was a clap of thunder. Growing up under the ominous shadow of the mushroom cloud was an awful introduction to life.

Yet somehow the wave of hysteria blew over and we are still here. (If you want to see an astounding documentary on the insanity that fear bred, watch the video *Nuclear Cafe*.) Perhaps, in retrospect, the paranoia ultimately contributed to healing. The nuclear armament buildup frightened me so much that when I became an adult I went to Russia to personally make peace between our nations. I organized three citizen diplomacy missions which brought large groups of U.S. citizens to the heart of "the evil empire"' to build bridges of trust and love between American and Soviet people. When we forayed into the streets and subways of Moscow and Leningrad we found, to our utter amazement, that the empire was not Godless at all; to the contrary, the Soviet people were intrinsically spiritual, deeply sensitive, and copiously generous. We enjoyed lavish dinners in Russian homes (with otherwise little means), exchanged gifts with laborers we met on trains, prayed in the churches, encountered gifted healers, sunbathed on crowded beaches, danced in nightclubs, studied underwater birthing assisted by wild dolphins, and traded photos of our children and pets. We felt that the people we met were our relatives, not enemies, and we were transformed by joining. We came home with a stunning discovery: *the cold war was a hype.* The people on the other side of the iron curtain were just like us. They valued their lives, loved their kids, and yearned to live in a world free of war. The Russian propaganda we had long been warned about was equalled by our own. Pogo's aphorism became brilliantly yet painfully clear: *"I have met the enemy, and he is us."*

Within a few short years after many groups of our kind made heart-to-heart connections with the Russians, the Berlin wall fell, Communism unraveled before our eyes, and the Soviet Union, that sprawling vicious bear that once threatened to devour us, dissolved, whimpering into a host of smaller nations, each seeking democratic self-determination.

The world as we knew it did come to an end – and blessedly so. The fear, the hiding, the lies, the threats, the trillions of dollars of crazed defensiveness, disappeared like a dark dream. Even as I write, I am stunned to realize that the terror under which I lived as a child has been undone – and I was a part of the undoing. Tears are welling up in my throat as I consider the miracle wrought in our lifetime. If, twenty-five years ago, someone would have predicted these events would come to pass, they would have been scoffed at: "Dreamer!" "Fool!" "Naive idealist!" Such a visionary would have been pummeled by "realists." But history now demonstrates that reality is not a fixed commodity; it is pliable; it is what we make it. Events are not determined by external forces; they spring from our belief in possibilities. Healing begins with vision. If there is anything worth bequeathing to our children, it is the knowledge that they will live in a world as big as their vision. Let us bestow magnificent visions for them to spin into reality.

Before we leave this planet, we will behold sweeping changes that will make the ones we have already seen seem small by comparison. I believe that within the next fifty to one hundred years we will reverse the notions that war and starvation are facts of life, and end their manifestation on the planet. The key to their undoing is to withdraw our belief that these conditions are necessary, or must persist. Our planet will manifest abundance to the extent that we can imagine it; now we must think bigger, aim higher, know more fully. When we refuse to accept human-inflicted sorrow as a given reality, it will be no more.

Not much more than a hundred years ago, slavery was a commonly accepted practice on the planet. Millions of human beings were bullied into subservience, sold to the highest bidder, and treated more cruelly than animals. Few questioned the practice; slavery was simply a fact of life. But then a great shift in consciousness occurred; a handful of compassionate leaders began to challenge the legitimacy of indentured bondage. As the issue was brought to a head and our country fought a great war over it, all who looked upon slavery had to face their conscience about it. Once ignorance is brought to the light, the truth must be known and manifested. Now slavery is unthinkable; it has practically disappeared from the earth. If a hundred and fifty years ago an African slave sweating in a sweltering Caribbean cane-burning factory on a humid summer day, was told that it would not be very long before slavery was eliminated from the earth, he would have perhaps become angry and called such a prophet cruel or insane. But appearances at hand are a poor index of destiny. That is why you must pray sincerely that the end *is* near, for the nearer the end, the nearer the beginning.

A Course in Miracles reminds us that there is no order of difficulty in miracles. The limited mind sees dead ends and believes dire prophecies. The divine mind remembers that *anything is possible*, no prognosis is set in stone, and the power to create our lives rests not in the hands of doctors, politicians, theologians, parents, or prophets, but in our own. If within a few short years Russia can become democratic, Nelson Mandela can be elected President of South Africa, and the leaders of the P.L.O. and Israel can jointly receive the Nobel Prize for Peace, *anything can happen*, sometimes *quickly*.

You and I have come to this planet at this time because we have the consciousness, willingness, and tools to release the earth and its people from the pain under which we have so long labored. The issues that confront and alarm us are in our field of consciousness because we are in a position to transform them. Just as an individual is not given any challenges greater than she is capable of handling, so is our civilization capable of turning crisis into creation. Child abuse, AIDS, and gang crime are in our face not to overwhelm us, but to stir us. They are not the end of a sad story, but the beginning of a better one. They are calls for truth, compassion, and the remembrance of the sacredness of life. They will not go away through medication or legislation; they will be transformed only through *awakening*.

Every generation has suspected it would be the last one – always with good reason. Horrific plagues, massive starvation, and heinous wars have beset humanity with sorrowful regularity.

From the viewpoint of the fearful mind, there has always been more evidence for annihilation than redemption. But we are still here. The sun continues to rise each morning, and with our every heartbeat Spirit votes that life is good and we are worthy to live it. We deserve a better world than we found, and we are here to live the vision that will manifest it.

The world is always coming to an end. In each of our lives, the worlds we once knew have come to an end many times. Look back upon the world in which you grew up; it is not here anymore. Consider your old friends, relationships, activities, and belief systems; they are gone, as well. Observe your body; do you know that not one cell in your body is more than seven years old? While your cells have formed themselves into long-standing patterns, your physical body is not more than seven years of age. As you read these words, cells in your body are dying and new ones are being born to take their place. Death is not a bad thing; it exists only on the most superficial level. Behind the appearance of death is transformation. Death is the opposite of birth, not life. What is born, dies, but what lives in spirit is eternal. Identify and align yourself with what is changeless, and you cannot be ravaged by transience.

Rather than worrying about doomsday, focus on today. If you are not living with a whole heart now, the end of the world poses no threat; your life is already gone. Life is only as valuable as our presence to enjoy it. To miss the beauty of the moment because you are preparing to protect yourself from the next one, is to trade a precious gem for a cheap trinket. *A Course in Miracles* reminds us that it is not what we are being saved *from* that is important; it is what we are being saved *for*.

Doomsday predictions play on fear and insecurity. Do not contribute to the pool of terror generated by mass hysteria. Refuse to indulge in media exploitations of havoc and destruction. We vote for a particular destiny with the thoughts we invest in it. When you go into alignment with soothsayers of disaster, you invest in its manifestation. Consciously hold your thoughts on your most cherished visions, and they will come alive. If humanity realized that we create our destiny with our thoughts, we could transform this planet in a short time. Begin that process now, with your own life. Let the old world come to an end, so we can get on with the new one.

Earth Changes Within

Earth changes have long been a popular topic in new age and metaphysical circles. Much fearful attention has been invested in distressing prophecies by John in the Book of Revelations, Nostradamus, Hopi elders, Edgar Cayce, and other visionaries. Dates have been set by which southern Californians should leave Los Angeles to escape "the Big One," maps of the new western coastline of Arizona are circulating with beachfront real estate offerings in Phoenix, and morbid soothsayers cry, "I told you so," as newspapers splash sensational headlines of natural disaster. Inordinate thought and energy have been focused on the earth exacting vengeance for the iniquities we have laid upon it.

If equal energy had been invested in healing our world through love, we would be living in paradise by now. When fear kidnaps any idea, no matter how noble its original intent, adherents become entrenched in illusions. Beware of any teacher or philosophy that calls for revenge or karmic retribution. God is not a vengeful God, and life does not punish. We punish ourselves with thoughts of iniquities and unworthiness. There is only one antidote for sin, and that is love. Notions of castigation and the scourging of infidels lead not to purification, but insanity. Child of God, remember that you deserve only love, and the world you live in will reflect your worthiness.

To come to terms with earth changes, we must approach them metaphysically rather than emotionally. The foundation of metaphysics is, "as above, so below." As we entertain pictures of reality, our inner beliefs magnetize events. It may be said that life is one big self-fulfilling prophecy. There was a *Star Trek* episode in which the crew of the *Enterprise* found themselves on a planet where their thoughts were instantly manifested. Captain Kirk had been thinking about one of his classmates at the academy, only to find the fellow sitting on a rock minutes later. A female lieutenant had long fantasized about being swept away by a knight in shining armor riding a white horse; *voilà*, he appeared. The fly in the ointment came to the fore, however, when the crew realized that not only were their dreams coming true, but so were their nightmares. Neither were thrust upon them by an external agent; they were generated by their subconscious beliefs. Eventually the crew discovered that the planet was a kind of galactic amusement park, where people could experience their hidden thoughts coming to pass instantaneously. This episode was more science than fiction; our world is not much different than that one. There is no one "way that it is"; the meaning of life is what we bring to it. The events we attract reflect the images we nurture. The future in which we will dwell tomorrow is being constructed with the thoughts on which we dwell today.

The outer changes we are experiencing mirror the restructuring of our inner life. Earthquakes represent the shaking of our foundation, underscoring the flimsiness of the world we have superimposed over the nature we were given. Tumultuous storms outpicture the inner turmoil we must weather as winds of change move us from an old life to a new one. Famine and drought symbolize the ways we do not feed ourselves or reach out to nurture one another; we are confronted with the spiritual thirst we long to quench. AIDS is not a cosmic indictment or a scourge upon humanity by an angry God; it is a call for self-love, compassion, and the awareness that we are all connected. None of us can afford to sit righteously on a pedestal of judgment; we must open our hearts and seek ways to undo fear, the root epidemic behind all others. Environmental pollution is not simply the result of overpopulation and lack of technological foresight; the smog enshrouding our cities but magnifies the self-suffocating thoughts we generate with stifling beliefs; a polluted physical atmosphere reflects unprocessed psychic debris. When we love ourselves enough to be inspired (inhalation) and to express our creativity (exhalation), we will discover ways to clean up our physical environment. "We think in secret, and it comes to pass, environment is our looking glass."

So our external problems in the form of earth changes are not what we thought they were. They are not ontological whippings, but invitations to look deeper and live higher. If we get the message at a subtle level, we will not need to play out a major drama. It is only when we fail to hear the whisper of truth that we must face crisis. Living in Hawaii, I beheld the destruction of Hurricane Iniki, which wrought massive destruction on the island of Kauai. Friends on that island told me that along with the ruin came great purification. "After the leveling, it was as if life was starting all over on the island," many reported. Communities had to pull together to support one another. Those who had become numbed to the beauty of their lives began to re-value their families and livelihoods. In many ways the hurricane pointed people back to their true purpose. The hurricane wrought great devastation, but it also brought blessings.

The way to avoid painful earth changes, personally and collectively, is to change our consciousness. Instead of plotting escape routes from the L.A. basin, make your escape from fear; you can map all kinds of alternate routes to avoid the freeway, but if you have not freed yourself from the tyranny of limited thinking, you might as well stay home. We take our consciousness with us wherever we go. If the purpose of earth changes is awakening, you can beat the rush by waking up now. Then you can enjoy a future founded in Spirit rather than terror.

How the World Will End

While mindreaders, mediums, and maniacs have tendered all manner of prognostications about how the world will end, *A Course in Miracles* offers a perspective refreshing as it is illuminating:

The world will end in joy,
    because it is a place of sorrow ...
The world will end in peace,
    because it is a place of war ...
The world will end in laughter,
    because it is a place of tears ...[1]

The world will end when we realize that the frightening world that intimidated us was but a bad dream. *Only love is real.* If something comes from love, trust and act on it; you are making an investment in a bank that will never fail. When led by fear, you will reap nothing you truly want. The soil of consciousness is now being turned over to plant anew; the world of darkness is coming to an end, to make way for greater light.

We will live in a better world because we will recognize ourselves to be worthy of it. There is no turning back now. While Nelson Mandela was in jail for many years he proclaimed, "The march to freedom is irreversible." Now he is president of the country that incarcerated him. We, too, have been imprisoned, but not by a country. We have oppressed ourselves with self-defeating thinking and subservience to fear. That tyranny is now ending. You and I have come to alter the course of destiny. Look neither to history nor appearances as a guide; history is a fool's guide to destiny; it repeats itself only when we are too fearful or unconscious to try something different. All of the events on the planet are rushing toward wiping the old slate clean.

Will you be present for the grand finale? You will *produce* the grand finale. The closing act will have no meaning unless you are there to enjoy it. The grand finale consists of the recognition that you have produced the entire movie. When our personal movie is over, the universal show begins; it is much grander than we imagined. It reveals that the light we sought is what we are.

The future belongs to those who believe
in the beauty of their dreams.
                                        – Eleanor Roosevelt

BURN THIS BOOK

Do not mistake the finger pointing at the moon,
for the moon.

– Zen proverb

I n the film *The Razor's Edge*, Bill Murray portrays a spiritual seeker on the journey to enlightenment. Larry is a voracious reader who is pulled away from his studies to weather the horrors of World War I. In the aftermath of his painful experience he makes a pilgrimage to India to find answers to his burning questions.

Larry makes his way to a temple near the top of the Himalayas, where he meets a wise guru. "I want to know the secret of life," he tells the master.

"Do you see that hut at the top of the mountain?" asks the sage. Larry's eyes scan the snow-covered peak, where he spies a tiny lean-to near the summit.

"Take your books up there and stay until you find your answer."

Excitedly Larry gathers his volumes and hikes up to the flimsy shelter, where he builds a campfire. Eagerly he opens his books to find the answer he fervently seeks. This is the moment he has been waiting for!

Larry reads for days, then weeks. In each succeeding scene he looks colder and more frustrated; the stubble on his cheeks grows into a beard. Despite his intense efforts, Larry is no closer to enlightenment; to the contrary, he looks more dispirited than ever.

Larry is freezing. Snow is falling, bone-chilling winds howl, and tiny icicles cling to his moustache. If he doesn't do something soon, his quest for enlightenment will be carried over to another life.

The fire dwindles and there is no more wood. Then Larry's eyes wander from the book in his hands to the fire, and back. Suddenly his face glows with a spark of real understanding. Larry tears a few pages out of the book and tosses them into the campfire. As the flame rises, Larry delights in the warmth, and an impish smile spreads over his face. Boldly he stands, rips out more leaves, and flings them into the inferno. His smile grows to a giggle and then howling laughter. Victoriously he takes the entire volume and hurls it into the fire. Larry gathers the rest of his books and transforms them into fuel for warmth. From a distance we see the silhouette of Larry standing at the top of the darkened mountain, enfolded by a bright orange glow.

The next morning Larry marches triumphantly down the mountain to the base camp. He is happy. Larry has found his answer, and it was not in a book. His answer was to live; to do whatever was required to make life fulfilling and joyful in the moment. Enlightenment was not found by escaping into words or suffering in the cold. The answer was not somewhere out there. It was right where he was. He had it all the time.

The Journey Without Distance

The greatest gift you could receive from this book is the awareness that you didn't need to read it. A true teacher reminds the student that the jewel she seeks is already set within her heart. There is nothing to learn, but much to remember. The path to enlightenment is a refresher course.

Beware of teachers, methods, trainings, or spiritual paths that tell you that you need more and more of what they have to offer. A good teacher reminds the students that they need less and less, and the best teachers tell the students that they need nothing. All

300

need is illusion. As spiritual beings, we need nothing because we are everything. Our only need (if we had one) would be to share and express who we are. This is not done by becoming increasingly dependent on an outside agent; it is accomplished by being sovereign.

The mind unwilling to claim its own riches is prone to seek validation outside itself. It does not realize that by claiming strength from a foreign source, it disavows its own magnitude. Find your source within, and no entity outside yourself will ever be able to usurp your power.

We reach a point on the spiritual path where our focus shifts from gathering more and more, to feeling satisfied with fewer and fewer accoutrements. Simplicity becomes more attractive than complexity. Long lists of things to do to purchase enlightenment give way to a few simple goals: *remember who you are, rejoice in the beauty of the moment, and love.* All other practices pale in the effulgence of self-appreciation. The last steps on the path are the lightest.

The time has come for us to let go of the substitutes for our own power that we have fashioned of external objects and persons. Even as we have gone about our mad search for people and methods to save us, the God within sits on the altar of our heart, patiently waiting for us to realize that we are already home. *A Course in Miracles* describes our quest as "a journey without distance to a goal that has no end."

Kill the Buddha

The great Zen Master Kuei-shan asked his student Yang-shan (who was to become an equally great teacher), "In the forty volumes of the Nirvana Sutra, how many words come from the Buddha and how many from demons?"'

Yang-shan said, "They are *all* demons' words."

Kuei-shan said, "From now on, no one will be able to pull the wool over your eyes!"[1]

The Buddhists advise, "If you meet the Buddha on the road, kill him." In this strange admonition lies great wisdom. If you find a god who seems to be outside yourself, you must destroy it. Have no patience for projecting your own divinity onto another form and worshiping it. The true Buddha lives within you, as you. All else is illusion and impostor.

In Herman Hesse's classic novel *Steppenwolf*, spiritual seeker Harry Steppenwolf meets a ravishing enlightened woman who offers to teach him freedom. The condition of her tutelage, she informs Harry, is that "you must do everything I tell you." Harry goes on to a rewarding relationship with this masterful mentor.

Later the teacher hands Harry a knife and instructs him, "Kill me." Harry is struck with fear and apprehension. "You promised to do whatever I told you to do," she reminds him. Harry kills her, but then he is overcome with grief and remorse.

When Steppenwolf later leaves this world, he goes before a heavenly tribunal. Their verdict: Harry wasted much of his life in guilt over "the illusion of killing the reflection of a woman with the reflection of a knife." He is found lacking a sense of humor and sentenced to life on earth – to learn to laugh.

You are not asked to go out and kill anyone; the story is a metaphor. We must annihilate any attachment that keeps us bound. A true teacher does not foster dependency; she leads you to greater freedom in the light of your own divinity. Why become enamored with the mirror when you are the source?

The best teaching methods are those that train the student to go beyond them. *A Course in Miracles* offers a masterful lesson:

> *Simply do this: be still, and lay aside all thoughts of what you are and what God is; all concepts you have learned about the world; all images you hold about yourself. . .Hold onto nothing. Do not bring with you one thought the past has taught, nor one belief you ever learned before anything. Forget this world, forget this course, and come with wholly empty hands unto your God.*[2]

A Good Day to Save the World

In his brilliant book *One*, Richard Bach and his wife Leslie undertake a metaphoric odyssey through various possible realities. The couple meets a monk in France who has just written an extraordinary manuscript containing "the key to truth for any who will read, life to those who will listen. . .a scripture written for the loving inner being. . ."

Astonished by the wisdom he reads, Richard urges the monk, Le Clerc, to publish the manuscript. The sage answers, "Only hearts hold light. Pages cannot."

When Richard presses him, Le Clerc leads Richard and Leslie through a frightening projection of what will happen if this work is disseminated. The book will need a name (*"The Pages"*), someone to protect *The Pages* from being misused (*"The Keeper of The Pages"*) and there will develop a religion (*"The Pageites"*) to defend *The Pages*, for they will "challenge the rules of every nation that keeps its power through fear and darkness."

Eventually, Le Clerc predicts, the Sign of the Flame (the symbol of *The Pages*) will meet the Sign of the Cross on battlefields, cities will be leveled in the name of God, and many will be killed in wars to uphold "Truth." Then *Pageism* will rule the world, and "those reaching for growth and understanding will find themselves burdened with new superstitions, limits, rules, chants, ceremonies, and vestments. . .The heart of *Pageism* will turn from love to gold. . .gold to build greater temples and buy swords to convert the non-believers and save their souls."

Le Clerc picks up a brand from his fire and ignites the pages.

"Burn the truth?" Richard exclaims.

"The Truth doesn't burn. The truth waits for anyone who wishes to find it."

Richard and Leslie recoil in horror as the manuscript crumbles to ashes.

"What a blessed evening!" Le Clerc notes. "How rarely are we given a chance to save the world from a new religion!"[3]

Ice Follies

Around the turn of the century, a man from a small town in the mountains of Tennessee travelled to the big city of Nashville, where he saw for the first time an electric ice-making machine – a revolutionary invention at that time.

Upon returning home, the man glowingly reported his discovery to his church peers. Some listeners, however, did not believe his story. A controversy grew over the verity of the ice-maker, and escalated into an out-and-out feud. A group of people who believed the man left the church and formed their own church, commonly called the "Ice Baptist Church." To this day, somewhere in the hills of Tennessee, reverent devotees show up every Sunday morning to worship at the Ice Baptist Church.

God is love, and splintering cannot be the will of God. Religions have served and glorified the name of God, but misguided adherents have often abused it. God is not the source of animosity. God is the peace that remains when separation and suffering cease.

A black man tried unsuccessfully to gain admission to a white church. Every year the man applied for acceptance, and every year he was turned down for a different reason. Finally the fellow got down on his knees and prayed, "Dear Jesus, I have tried so hard to get into this church for so long, and they won't accept me. Can you help me?"

"Don't feel bad, George," the voice of Jesus returned; "I have been trying to get into that church for a lot longer than you, and they won't let me in either!"

Every great religion was founded in purity. Every holy prophet had a visionary mountaintop experience, and returned to the world to share his or her illumination. As soon as the master departed, however, disciples began to institutionalize, organize, ritualize, and bureaucratize the insights the sage revealed. But truth is not subject to xeroxing; the more you copy it, the darker and more smudged the page becomes, until you can't read what was written in the first place; all you see is a splotchy page of sooty toner. You can play the "telephone" game for just so many generations before the message becomes abysmally distorted.

We have become followers not of truth, but of people – a mistake we must rectify if we wish to regain our own brilliance. The Monty Python film *Life of Brian* offers a hilarious parody of the saga of Jesus (and most other luminaries). Brian is a young man who literally falls into public favor while escaping from Roman guards (for a graffiti infraction). Brian slips off a roof and lands in a public square where a bevy of local pundits stand on soap boxes, hawking their philosophies. To elude the sentries, he delivers a makeshift rap. Soon a group of disciples forms to follow Brian as a new messiah.

To Brian's chagrin, when he leaves the square, his followers will not let him alone. He tells them that he is no prophet, and goes off to the desert to escape their grabby neurotic sucking. But the hordes, ravenous for a savior, follow him beyond thicket and dune. Finally Brian becomes fed up and chides them, "Just *go away!*" In no uncertain terms he informs the fold, "I am *not* your master!"

"But, master," pleads the needy throng in unison, "tell us *how* to go away!"

Here we behold a deliciously striking model of how masters become idolized, and how followers become rutted with self-diminishing dependency. The masses need a master; sometimes anyone will do!

This is precisely the kind of groupie religion we must drop if we are to reclaim our worth and power as equally masterful spiritual beings. I believe we will look back in fifty or a hundred years, and either shudder or laugh at the way we have regularly betrayed our wholeness in the name of worship. The moment we turn to others to tell us the truth, we deny the fact that we already know it. Rather than praying to God, we need to pray *from* God.

Write Your Own Bible

In his delightful compendium of mystical stories, *Tales of a Magic Monastery*, Brother Theophane describes this experience:

> The first time I went [to the Magic Monastery] I forgot to bring my Bible. When I asked the guestmaster if I could borrow a Bible, he said, "Wouldn't you care to write your own?" "What do you mean?" "Well, write your own Bible. . .Ought to be much more interesting than just reading someone else's Bible. And you might learn more."
>
> Well, I set to work. It took me a month. I never learned so much about the official Bible. When I was finished, he recommended I take it home and try to live according to it for a year. . .
>
> It was quite a year. An eye opener. Most certainly I had never put so much energy and alertness into living my official Bible as I was putting into living this one. And my daily meditations had never been so concentrated.
>
> When I arrived back for my next retreat he greeted me very warmly, took into his hands my Bible and my journal, kissed them with the greatest reverence, and told me I could spend a couple of days and nights in the Hall of the Great Fire. On the last night of the year, I should consign my two books to the flames. That's what I did. A whole year's wisdom and labor – into the Great Fire. Afterwards he set me to writing another Bible.
>
> And so it went, these past forty years each year a new Bible, a new journal, and then at the end of the year – into the flames.[4]

ACTIVATION:

WRITE YOUR OWN BIBLE

God has asked you to write a book that will bring inspiration and illumination to spiritual seekers for generations to come.

Record a guidebook for the soul. Impart the most important truths you have learned. Include your deepest intuitive knowing. The only criteria for the material is, "What in my heart do I know to be true?"

Your Bible may be of any length from one word to a thousand pages. It can be in the form of essay, story, poetry, picture, or parable. Be sure it is something you can live with and stand behind.

A Bigger World

The time has come for each of us to claim mastery for ourselves. That is why you must burn this book (and any book) and live your own book. That is why you must take the guru off the throne, and Christ off the crucifix. That is why you must kill the Buddha if you meet him on the road. Be not distracted by the beliefs and opinions of others, unless they show you a bigger world than the one you are living in. Then walk through the door to the brightest light you can see, and claim a larger universe. Do not stop until you come all the way home.

All the teachers under which you have studied, were following the curriculum you set. The books you read were ghost-written under your own authorship. The relationships you fathomed were scripted by your own beliefs. Even as you may have walked unconsciously, each experience polished another facet of the jewel that you are. All the while you have known your own needs, and gone about the business of marching toward your own destiny. Even your sleep was a part of the curriculum to resurrect your innate wisdom. Mastery lies before you. The book of truth lives within you, as you. Open your pages and live.

From the mountain he could watch it all burn
Welcome, friend, to the point of no return
And then the mountain disappeared without a trace
And all it took was a sudden leap of faith

– "Leap of Faith" by Kenny Loggins and Guy Thomas

I'M OFF TO
BE THE WIZARD

If you do not get it from yourself,
where will you go for it?
– Buddha

The film *The Holy Mountain* depicts the journey of a man obsessed with finding the enlightened masters. His lifelong quest is to behold the illumined sages who sit in council atop the remote Holy Mountain, reachable to only those of pure heart and earnest intent.

Over many years this fervent seeker endures all manner of hardships in his venture to bask in the masters' presence. He is sidetracked and delayed by an agonizing series of distractions and illusions, battling fear at every turn; one scene actually shows him stewing in his own feces (a literal portrayal of a familiar metaphoric experience!). Yet no matter how many times this aspirant falls, he picks himself up and continues on his way, gathering strength and determination with each hurdle he overcomes.

After a long and arduous journey this aspirant, along with a band of fellow seekers, arrives at the peak of the Holy Mountain. As the group approaches the summit, their weary eyes behold the legendary round table of the masters. A dozen white-robed hooded figures sit meditatively against the mystical amber glow of the setting sun.

New strength surges through the pilgrims as they draw nigh unto the sacred gathering. When they arrive, however, a stunning surprise greets them: *the robes and hoods are empty.* There were no masters awaiting them. Suddenly they realize what they came to do – they don the robes and hoods themselves, and sit down at the round table for council. *They are the masters they came to find.*

The striking scene atop the Holy Mountain is a perfect metaphor for our own spiritual journey. We spend years, perhaps lifetimes searching, striving, and struggling to find those who will guide and illuminate us, only to discover that the wisdom and majesty we sought were within us even as we searched.

The quest for mastery begins and ends within. No outer master will save you, give you anything that you do not already have, or make you anything that you are not already. The true master stirs within you the awareness of your own divinity. This awakening marks the end of the searching game and the beginning of sacred expression in your life and on the planet.

For thousands of years the prevalent theme of human life on the planet has been seeking – always looking outside ourselves for fulfillment. Now we are entering the era of finding. Can you imagine how powerful and wonderful life would – and will – be as each of us reclaims our own power? Life on the planet will be entirely different than we have known it. We will not be entangled with questions, but celebrating answers. We will not put selected individuals on pedestals at the expense of everyone who worships them. We will not waste energy in competition, for we will realize that there is room at the top for everyone.

You and I have been climbing the holy mountain for longer than we realize. Now it is time for us to approach the summit and don our own robes. There is no more time or need to play the game of smallness. The new game is one of splendor and magnanimity. The rules under which we play are not man's, but God's. We are ready to sit at the Round Table of the Masters, and fulfill the function for which we came.

The Search Ends Here

The search for enlightenment is a distraction from the truth that we are already enlightened. Anything you do to get enlightened is a denial of the fact that you already have – and are – what you seek. Whole beings do not seek outside themselves for completion. The notion that we must become perfect is an illusion. All that needs to be healed is the belief that we are broken. Perfection is not attained; it is realized.

The wholeness of you can never be broken, and the part of you that is broken can never become whole. The world of illusion has little in common with the world of truth, save for the final illusion that we are becoming whole. In truth we do not become whole; we simply recognize we have always been whole.

We are already masters. The power to which we aspire, has been seeded within us as offspring of an omnipotent God. As unconscious masters, we have applied the power of our mind to all manner of thoughts and perceptions that have kept us small. Many of us have mastered drama, emergency, addiction, and manipulation. (If you have ever seen an addict lie and manipulate to protect his supply, you have seen mastery honed to a science.) In spite of the fact that we live in an abundant universe, we have mastered finding lack wherever we go. We have mastered replicating vicious patterns in relationships; we can take any relationship and make it into what we expect it to be, at the expense of what it is. Is this not mastery?

Now we must take our skills as masters and apply them to what brings us joy rather than indulging what removes it from us. We are moving from the mastery of limited living to the mastery of divine expression. Our goal is not to leave the world, but to bring more beauty to it; not to abandon the planet in search of a celestial refuge, but to bring heaven closer to earth. Anything short of total delight will not satisfy us. We know too much to turn back now. The past is behind us; destiny awaits!

The way to bring heaven to earth is to constantly hold heaven in your mind and heart. Do you know anyone who brings love and beauty wherever they go? My housekeeper, Lea, turns everything she touches to splendor. When I come home after she cleans my house, the whole place is sparkling, in order, and there is a touch of peace that seemed absent before. Lea also does landscaping for me, and my gardens look like paradise. At her home Lea sews for a hobby, and her creations are all magnificent. She holds the beauty of heaven in her mind and heart, and so everything she touches reflects it. Lea's life is a cogent demonstration that the world we live in is not the one that is cast upon us; it is the one we create. Bring love to what you do, and everything you touch will sparkle with divinity.

The Touch of the Master's Hand

In high school I played saxophone in a rock band. Reluctant as I was to admit it, my skills were wobbly; I did not know how to produce a vibrant tone with the horn. At the time I believed that the problem was in my saxophone. I knew that if I could just get a better instrument, I could get the kind of tone I desired.

One night when our group was playing for a dance, a man approached the bandstand and asked if he could sit in and play sax on the next song. The fellow picked up my horn, and to my astonishment, he *wailed*! I could hardly believe the vitality he was getting out of the instrument I thought was faulty. When he finished, he handed me the saxophone, and I just held it in my hand and looked at it. Was it the same instrument?

Yes, it was the same instrument – but it was being used by a different player. It is said that "it is the poor craftsman who blames his tools," and it may also be said that it is an unconscious master who blames his situation. That experience made an indelible impression on my mind. I realized that it is not life that makes us or breaks us. It is what we make of life that determines our destiny. Life is like a musical instrument or a blank artist's canvas before us. We have all the raw materials we need. Our role is to take what we have and make what we want.

The Touch of the Master's Hand

It was battered, scarred, and the auctioneer
Thought it scarcely worth his while
To waste his time on the old violin
But he held it up with a smile.

What am I bid, good people, he cried.
Who starts the bidding for me?
One dollar, one dollar - do I hear two?
Two dollars, who makes it three?
Three dollars once, three dollars twice,
Going for three...but no!

From the room far back a gray-bearded man
Came forward and picked up the bow.
Wiping the dust from the old violin,
And tightening up the strings,
He played a melody, pure and sweet,
As sweet as the angel sings.

The music ceased, and the auctioneer
With a voice that was quiet and low said
What now am I bid for this old violin?
As he held it aloft with its bow.
One thousand? One thousand, do I hear two?
Two thousand, who makes it three?
Three thousand once, three thousand twice,
Going, and gone, said he.

The audience cheered, but some of them cried,
We don't quite understand.
What changed its worth? Swift came the reply.
The touch of the master's hand.

And many a man with life out of tune
All battered with bourbon and gin
Is auctioned cheap to the thoughtless crowd
Much like that old violin.
A mess of pottage, a glass of wine, a game,
And he travels on.
He is going once, he is going twice,
He is going and almost gone.

But the master comes, and the foolish crowd
Never can quite understand
The worth of a soul, or the change that's been wrought
By the touch of the master's hand.
                                    – Myra Brook Welch

When Masters Meet

We are entering the time on the planet when all of us will meet as equal and honorable masters. Mastery does not imply dominion over another; it is the acknowledgement of our identity as expressions of a masterful God. Each of us is different while each of us is whole. There is no comparison, competition, or judgment in mastery; only the joy of celebrating the myriad of wondrous ways that Spirit has come into form to play out a great adventure.

Recently I spent time with Swami Satchidananda, a revered sage who has brought many profound yogic teachings to the western culture. Gurudev, as he is affectionately called, is the spiritual leader of many thousands of aspirants around the world. When I first met Gurudev years ago, I was in awe of his wisdom and peace. I regarded him as a high and lofty master, above me in many ways.

As I have travelled my own path since that time, I have come to know the master within me. I recognize that the same God that shines through Gurudev's eyes, lives in my own heart. I remembered the maxim, "You spot it, you got it," and realized that the holiness I perceive in this gentle teacher is a reflection of my own. Since that time I have come to regard him as a friend and peer. He is not a master over me, but a brother with me.

When I last saw Gurudev, I shared a private audience with him at his Virginia center. If this meeting had occurred when I perceived myself as a student, I would have seized the opportunity to ask the guru questions about the meaning of life and seek his counsel on my personal problems. I would have sized the situation up as "student meets master to gain knowledge and blessing."

This time, however, all I could feel was love for this beautiful man, respect for his work, and great delight in being with him. I did not want any knowledge, fixing, or magical salvation. We laughed, told stories, shared insights, and loved one another with profoundly innocent hearts. Gurudev was no longer a god over me, but a child of God with me.

I saw this very rewarding meeting as a model of the way that masters meet. In such blessed interactions there is not a feeling of "I have to get something from this person," or "I have to give something." There is rather a sense of homecoming and celebration. Yes, illumination arises. Yes, blessings happen. Yes, healing occurs. But all of these gifts befall us as natural by-products of our shared awareness of internal divinity.

What do masters do when we meet? Whatever our hearts call us to do. We may speak of God, pray, or meditate. We may share dinner, walk in the park, or go to a movie. We may joke, show each other our creative renderings, or roll down a hill in a refrigerator box. We may weep or comfort one another in a moment of pain. We may go out to dance, show pictures of our kids, get very silly, or make love. We may do anything that life invites us to do. There is nothing outside the realm of love.

Rather than bowing down to persons, we must bow to the divinity within them. Simultaneously we must acknowledge the divinity within us; it is all one. If you bow to the holiness within another, but deny it in yourself, you have missed the point – and the point is everywhere.

This morning I had a vision of what a world of masters might be like. While driving to my office, I stopped at an intersection opposite another car with a personalized license plate. My license plate says, "1 I AM," and the other car's plate said, "NAMASTE" (a Sanskrit word meaning, "I honor the light within you"). How poignant, I thought, that our cars would be meeting and greeting with reminders of the light. I began to fantasize about a world in which everyone sported a license plate offering an affirmation of truth. Wouldn't it be a hoot to drive around and be greeted by blessing after blessing in the form of auto tags?

This vision is symbolic of a way that we can live. We don't need to all get personalized plates, but we do need to deliver a message with our being. When we meet at the supermarket checkout counter, for example, our eyes might connect for a moment, and without a word we might say, "Hello, I am in here, and I see you in there." We might smile for a moment and move on. And that interaction would have been the perfect blessing for the perfect moment with the perfect person. There are no accidents, only opportunities to share love. Don't miss such an opportunity – it is *everything* that life is about.

All of our activities are doors to enlightenment; stages on which we may practice the presence of God. We do not need to travel to distant ashrams in the Himalayas or prostrate ourselves at the feet of a bearded guru in a loincloth. We may just need to hold a sense of gentleness in a business transaction, not give in to fear when we feel tempted, or breathe just a little deeper as our teenager is learning to drive with a clutch. That is what enlightenment is all about – making a game of your kid's shifting.

One day – perhaps today – we will stand at the peak of the Holy Mountain and see that the path of mastery leads to the discovery of our own divinity. If you remember that you are an expression of a perfect God, and so is everyone else, all else will follow. So ends the spiritual path in the knowledge that we are already home.

Master Key:

You Had it All the Time

A scene in the life of Jesus bears tremendous metaphoric import. One of the disciples asked Jesus if they should fast. Jesus replied, "When I am not with you, then you will fast. I am with you now, and so you have no such need."

When we forget that God is with us, we turn to methods and practices to regain our awareness of the Presence. If we recognize that Spirit is present, we do not need to do anything to remind us. If the light is already on, you will only turn it off by flicking the switch. The light is on; let it shine.

Jesus was teaching that grace is an abiding reality. To step onto any path is to leave our source. Thus the world of charms, amulets, practices, and consultations, dissolves into the light of higher knowing. We can leave the raft on the river as we establish camp on the higher side of the mountain.

Eventually all who walk the road to higher knowing come to one realization: *I had it all the time.* Some arrive sooner, and some arrive later; some arrive by the path of pain, and others by way of joy; some come alone and some come together. In the end, the method is not as important as the goal.

A Course In Miracles offers a poignant lesson:

> *You **are** prepared. Now you need but to remember that you need do nothing. It would be far more profitable now merely to concentrate on this than to consider what you should do. When peace comes at last to those who wrestle with temptation and fight against the giving in to sin; when the light comes at last into the mind given to contemplation; or when the goal is finally achieved by anyone, it always comes with just one happy realization;* **"I need do nothing."**[1]

Blessings, beloved brother or sister, upon the completion of your journey. You have not walked alone, nor will you. Your old world has come to an end, but a new and infinitely brighter one stands in its stead. Your place at the Round Table of the Masters has been held in trust for you. The One who created you remembered your destiny even while you forgot it. Now that you know it, you will live in this world not as a prisoner, but as an artist. The canvas is before you, and by the hand of grace, it is made new and clean. Paint upon it the true colors of your heart.

This is what you shall do: love the earth, and sun, and animals. . .stand up for the stupid and crazy. . .argue not concerning God. . .take off your hat to nothing known or unknown, or to any man or number of men; go freely with powerful, uneducated persons, and with the young, and mothers of families; read these leaves in the open air every season of every year of your life; re-examine all you have been told at school or church, or in any books, and dismiss whatever insults your own soul.

– Walt Whitman

REFERENCES

INTRODUCTION
1. Bill Watterson, Calvin & Hobbs, Universal Press Syndicate, 1993

ALWAYS HAD IT, ALWAYS WILL
1. White Eagle, *The Quiet Mind*, The White Eagle Publishing Trust, Liss, Hampshire, England, 1983

ORIGINAL INNOCENCE
1. John Calvin, *Institutes of the Christian Religion*
2. Alan Watts, *The Book on the Taboo Against Knowing Who You Really Are*, Vintage, 1989

YOU CAN'T PREPARE TO BE YOURSELF
1. Thadeus Golas, *The Lazy Man's Guide to Enlightenment*, Bantam, 1981
2. *Inc.* Magazine, September 1993
3. Peter Bowler, *The Superior Person's Book of Words*, David Godine, 1985

LET IT BE EASY
1. Arnold Patent, *You Can Have It All*, Celebration, 1991
2. Jerry Gillies, *MoneyLove*, Warner Communications, 1978
3. Ken Blanchard & Spencer Johnson, *One Minute Manager*, Berkley, 1987
4. Ashleigh Brilliant, Woodbridge Press, P.O. Box 6189, Santa Barbara, California 93160
5. Gary Larson, *The Far Side Gallery 2*, Chronicle, 1986.
6. Rev. Anne Gillis, The Connection Church, 1500 Cherry Road, Memphis, Tennessee 38117

FOLLOW YOUR SPIRIT
1. East Maui Animal Refuge, 25 Maluaina Road, Haiku, Hawaii, 96708
2. SCOTTSONGS, 243 Whitman Drive, Brooklyn, N. Y. 11234
3. Jack Canfield and Mark Victor Hansen, *Chicken Soup for the Soul*, Health Communications, 1993

CARPE DIEM!
1. For the teachings of Hilda Charlton, contact Golden Quest, P.O. Box 190, Lakehill, New York 12448

IF YOU CAN'T FIX IT, FEATURE IT
1. *Chicken Soup for the Soul*

THE ATTITUDE OF GRATITUDE
1. *Lightspeed Newsletter,* Earth Mission, P.O. Box 959, Ste. 432, Kihei, Hawaii. 96753, 1993
2. Stephen Mitchell, *The Gospel According to Jesus*, Harper Collins, 1991. Adapted from Zenkei Shibayama, *A Flower Does Not Talk*, Charles E. Tuttle Co., 1979
3. Eric Allenbaugh, *Wake-Up Calls,* Discovery, 1992
4. John Robbins, *Diet for a New America*, Stillpoint, 1987
5. Harville Hendricks, *Getting the Love You Want,* Harper Collins, 1990
6. Richard Bach, *Jonathan Livingston Seagull,* Avon, 1973

GOOD ENOUGH TO BE TRUE
1. *A Course in Miracles,* Foundation for Inner Peace, P.O. Box 1104, Glen Ellen, California 95442, Text, p. 24
2. *A Course in Miracles,* Workbook, p. 465

MIND MATTERS
1. Dr.Wayne Dyer has masterfully developed this principle in his book, *You'll See It When You Believe It,* Avon, 1981

LOOKING IN FOR NUMER ONE
1. Quote attributed to Dan McKinnon

CREATE OR DIE
1. *A Course in Miracles*, Text, p. 490

YOU CAN'T STEAL HOME WITH YOUR FOOT ON THIRD
1. Stuart Wilde, *The Quickening*, White Dove, 1988

THE FUTURE ISN'T WHAT IT USED TO BE
1. *A Course in Miracles*, Manual for Teachers, p. 35

BURN THIS BOOK
1. Stephen Mitchell, *The Gospel According to Jesus*, HarperCollins, 1991
2. *A Course in Miracles*, Workbook, p. 350
3. Richard Bach, *One*, Dell, 1988
4. Theophane the Monk, *Tales of a Magic Monastery*, Crossroad, 1992

I'M OFF TO BE THE WIZARD
1. *A Course in Miracles*, Text, p. 490

Alan Cohen offers inspiring seminars
which bring to life the principles of *I Had It
All the Time*, and have assisted thousands
of appreciative readers to make their
dreams come true. If you have been
touched by the ideas in this book, consider
attending one or more of Alan Cohen's
programs:

- An evening or afternoon seminar at a center in
  your area

- A weekend or week-long retreat at a fine holistic
  health learning center in a natural setting

- A lecture at an expo, professional conference, or
  convention

*For a free packet of information about
Alan Cohen's programs and a current schedule
of his upcoming events, contact:*

Hay House
PO Box 5100, Carlsbad, CA 92018-5100
1-800-462-3013